CAD

Principles

for

Architectural Design

Analytical Approaches to Computational Representation of Architectural Form

Peter Szalapaj

Architectural Press

OXFORD AUCKLAND BOSTON JOHANNESBURG MELBOURNE NEW DELHI

Architectural Press
An imprint of Butterworth-Heinemann
Linacre House, Jordan Hill, Oxford OX2 8DP
225 Wildwood Avenue, Woburn, MA 01801-2041
A division of Reed Educational and Professional Publishing Ltd

 A member of the Reed Elsevier plc group

First published 2001
Reprinted 2001
© Peter Szalapaj

British Library Cataloguing in Publication Data
Szalapaj, Peter
    CAD principles for architectural design : analytical
    approaches to computational representation of architectural form
    1. Architectural design - Data processing 2. Computer-aided design
    I. Title
    720.2'85

    ISBN 0 7506 4436 2

Library of Congress Cataloguing in Publication Data
Szalapaj, Peter
    CAD principles for architectural design : analytical approaches to computational
    representation of architectural form / Peter Szalapaj.
    p. cm.
    Includes bibliographical references and index.
    ISBN 0-7506-4436-2
    1. Architectural design-Data processing. 2. Computer-aided design. I. Title.

    NA2728.S97
    720'.28'40285--dc21   00-056930

For more information on all Butterworth-Heinemann publications
please visit our website at www.bh.com
Printed and bound in Great Britain

CAD

Principles

for

Architectural Design

'Generalized omni-intertransformable modelability now faithfully permits popular human comprehension of all experimentally derived scientific knowledge regarding physical phenomena heretofore translated only into exclusively abstract mathematical schemes of notationally formalized and formulated treatment, study, discovery.'

(Buckminster Fuller, *Synergetics*, 1975)

To Mum and Dad

Contents

Contents

Foreword

Developments of CAD in architecture have a somewhat back-to-front history. Early developments during the 1960s and 1970s included computer modelling of architectural forms, which supported a range of analyses to do with building performance and buildability. Those developments were undertaken with user involvement, they were ambitious and costly, and outcomes served just the sponsoring practices (which happened to be active in the fields of housing and hospital buildings). The problem identified at that time was that architectural practices varied in unpredictable ways, and the modelling systems could not be generalised to serve more practices.

Later, during the 1980s and 1990s, as computers became smaller and less costly, so new developments had to be targeted at whole markets, such as the market consisting of all architects. Market economics also resulted in computer programmers becoming very distant from end users. Consequently developments became less ambitious, offering drawing and rendering systems which carried no data about what was being depicted. It has taken a long time to get back to design modelling and analysis.

It is against this background that Peter Szalapaj, in this book, has something important to say. He is identifying a set of CAD principles which see designers determining particular modelling strategies, to ensure that their models carry data and support analyses that are relevant to their own interests, to architects and their clients. Moreover, he is saying computer modelling can be available to architects for use during the course of designing, so as to inform themselves about possible design outcomes. Computers then are useful during exploratory stages of sketch design, as well as for drawing and rendering eventual design outcomes.

To illustrate the plausibility of these CAD principles, Szalapaj includes in this book many case studies in which architects are seen to exploit computer modelling. His focus is on user experience, and the ways CAD objects and operations are used in the course of modelling architectural forms. These studies draw on prominent and highly regarded design projects undertaken by well established practices. For some there may be a lingering doubt. Can the cost of introducing CAD modelling and analysis be born by smaller practices engaged in less prominent projects? That question deserves an answer.

CAD objects and operations of the kind described in this book tend to be known by those already familiar with the technology of computers. It is just such knowledge which needs to be available and responsive to people engaged in design practices. That means a technically competent person must be included in, or be available to, a practice. Here we are returning to the earlier position in history when programmers and users worked together on new developments, but now the programmer is replaced by a procurer and manipulator of already prepared programs.

The answer to the earlier question then is that these general developments are making it possible to tune the technology to the demands of designers, at a cost which is becoming affordable even to modest practices.

This difference between now and what was possible in the 60s has further implications. Now there is no need to devise a single modelling strategy which can serve many different architectural practices, and there is no need to look for common working procedures in all practices. Instead, as indicated in this book, the low cost of powerful computers and the availability of software needed for modelling is now opening up the prospect of particular models for particular purposes, to suit individual practices. Supporting the individuality of practices, linked to unforeseen demands of other people, is crucially important in the case of architects who have to be creative, or be innovative.

A move in this direction becomes part of the much more general move towards so called new technology. Those of us who have been engaged in its development have watched this technology move from the rarefied environments of academia and the electronics industry, out into the wider world of industry in general, commerce, and entertainment. Computing now is vociferously advocated from above, by politicians who believe this technology is crucial to our survival in the new global economy.

Over the past decades we have observed the specialised and sometimes evocative language of computing enter into ordinary everyday language. So it is that notions of 'information' and 'knowledge' being held within computers is becoming part of our present day shared common sense. These concepts, and others, are acquiring exclusive and simplified meanings that fit known possibilities in the technology. The trend towards simplification, obscured by the razzmatazz of machines, is worrying to normal intelligent and literate people.

There is an important sense in which this book is disassociated from these wilder leaps of faith. In Szalapaj's terms, the CAD objects and operations, used as the raw material for computer modelling, leave traditional notions of information and knowledge intact, as concepts referring to states of being within people. This is how these concepts have always been understood, and well understood, even if not fully explained. Szalapaj's objects and operations then are an external manifestation of knowledge to be used intelligently, and are presented so as to inform readers.

This is not a trivial qualification. We need to hold on to a clear distinction between what can happen in people and in computers, in order to be clear about the possibilities of innovation and apportionment of responsibility. We need to do so in most fields of human endeavour, and especially so in the case of architecture. It then is reassuring to find that this book's advocacy of computers in no way presupposes they can know what architects know, yet they can be used by architects to expand their own abilities to express themselves.

Aart Bijl

Preface

The aim of this book is to help students in architectural schools, as well as designers in architectural practice, to understand some of the basic principles in the use of CAD in architectural design. It is particularly aimed at undergraduate students taking RIBA Part 1, but sufficient issues of a research nature should have been raised to make it of interest to students studying for the RIBA Part 2 diploma course, masters and other postgraduate students. It may also be of interest to engineering students seeking to gain more of an insight into CAD in architectural design.

I have intentionally tried to present basic principles and ideas without referring to any specific CAD software system. Once the reader has grasped basic principles, in both the possibilities of CAD, and in the application of CAD to real architectural design projects, it should then be easier for them to use CAD manuals to find commands relevant to their own design intentions using particular systems. From my own personal experience of teaching CAD, students often find CAD manuals to be obscure and uninformative. This is partly because many assumptions are made within them about computer operations that design students are not necessarily familiar with; but primarily, it is because software developers themselves have very little design experience that can provide a context for demonstrating CAD functionalities.

Another objective was to avoid immersing students in the mathematical equations behind many CAD functionalities. There are a number of CAD textbooks that describe the mathematical representations of curves and surfaces. Although interesting for those who are mathematically inclined, this seems inappropriate for architecture students, for whom this type of description would be confusing, and a distraction from their main focus, which is to use CAD systems for design work. Regarding the research content of this book, for the more advanced students who might be interested in exploring some of the issues further, my contention is that there has been a real sea-change in the use of CAD in practice, as evidenced by some of the case studies. At the time of writing, the simplest label that I can place upon this new phenomenon is *integrated CAD*.

An integrated approach to CAD in architectural practice is not such a new concept, and was originally proposed in the 1970s, at a time when computing power was so much less than it is today. The motivation for this worthy ambition of integrated CAD systems came from the design community which perceived CAD to be useful in the design process, only if it could accommodate all the information necessary for any design project. In practice, because of the preciousness of computing resources at that time, combined with the fact that software developments were dependent upon specialist programmers who interpreted designers' descriptions into computer operations, the systems developed into dinosaurs that were not capable of evolving to meet new and changing demands from design practice. The vision nevertheless was a worthy one.

The failure of integrated CAD all those years ago was followed by a retreat into functionalism. Many and varied systems were developed to tackle specific design areas such as energy, lighting, and ventilation, for example. Building scientists could produce costed calculations for the internal control of building comfort, involving new materials, central heating and artificial ventilation. The downside of this approach was the fragmentation and compartmentalisation of design that it led to, since buildings have to respond to many criteria other than environmental behaviour.

Subsequently, an even bigger evolutionary battle commenced. On the one hand, a zealous group of researchers fervently promoted the *information processing model of design* in which they claimed knowledge bases (not mere information bases) could be processed intelligently using techniques from disciplines such as artificial intelligence (AI) to develop automated design software such as expert systems and intelligent knowledge-based systems (IKBS). They believed that in developing such systems, they could bypass those awkward beings known as people, designers in particular, who have caused so many problems for computer systems in the past. Where are these applications in architecture now?

At the same time, somewhere out on the fringes of the CAD landscape were the formalists, seeking to overcome the restrictions of computing environments in order that designers could express themselves more freely. They developed powerful but intentionally useless software. They were effectively working as computer system developers, building computing environments such as graphics systems and programming environments, or combinations thereof. The onus was still on designers to make use of such environments by fleshing them out to make them applicable to actual design tasks.

Meanwhile, while these philosophical battles were raging, architectural designers were continually trying to make the technology work for them, to fit technological developments to their own design practices, to make connections between disparate software developments in specialist areas. The experience gained by designers in the application of computing technology to real design projects has now reached a position in which it is entirely feasible for an architectural practice to control projects involving complex architectural form, requiring difficult and varied cycles of analysis and testing, right through to the construction stage. This control cycle involves knowing not simply how to apply CAD techniques, but when to apply them, in a design process that is responsive to the constantly changing demands and idiosyncrasies of individual designers and design practices. I believe that it is now possible for diverse design practices to configure their own integrated CAD environments in response to the kind of architecture they want to produce, and the analytical procedures they need to make it happen.

In re-examining the distinction between the expression of design ideas and the representation of an end result, the importance of *analysis* became apparent. I have tried to portray to the reader, both in the context of the introductory case studies in Part 2, and in the more developed ones in Parts 6 and 7, that the use of analytical CAD modelling techniques allows designers to focus on the most relevant aspects of a design problem. This is achieved through the development of CAD models omitting irrelevant detail. Many different types of analytical model are possible depending upon how a design problem is viewed. The same problem will of course be perceived in different ways by different designers and design practices.

In all of these examples, whichever design stage or medium is used, it is the efficacy of the expression that enables both a comprehension and therefore a development of those ideas. This expression or externalisation of ideas is a constant phenomenon which occurs throughout design formulation, up until the point at which no further development is achievable (due to constraints), at which point both design and expressions cease.

This book has been written from a standpoint of trying to teach basic CAD principles to architectural design students, at a time when the students in question are surrounded by so much commercial hype, and a plethora of abstruse computer training manuals. The trepidation generated in them as a consequence of having to gain architectural qualifications, whilst at the same time having to demonstrate their CAD literacy, has led to the development of training courses that are often far removed from the rest of their design education. It is the hope of the author that this book might go at least a little way towards putting CAD into the perspective of contemporary architectural practice, and hence towards reconciling what are often diverse and fragmented aspects of architectural education. In the words of E.F. Schumacher:

'When a thing is intelligible you have a sense of participation;
when a thing is unintelligible you have a sense of estrangement.'
(Schumacher, *Small is Beautiful*, 1973)

Acknowledgements

I have tried to bring together in this book a range of case studies in the use of CAD in practice that I have been familiar with, interested in, or inspired by, for a number of years now, believing that there are valuable lessons to be learned from each of them about the changing nature of CAD in contemporary architectural practice. As is often the case, the greatest help and support comes from where one would least expect it. I would first of all like to thank the many students that I have had the pleasure of teaching and working with. Some of these have contributed material in the form of CAD models. These include Fazidah Abdullah who modelled the Floating Pavilion by Fumihiko Maki; Mohammed Asri for the computer model of his scheme for Yorkshire Artspace; Stuart Craigen for his work on the same project; David Chang who modelled Merchants Bridge at Castlefields by Whitby Bird & Partners; Victor Hidayat for the model of Foster Associates' Hong-Kong Shanghai Bank; Brian George, a student and architect, for his plan drawings of a school extension; Yoshitaka Mishima for CAD models of Fallingwater and the Villa Savoye. Alexander Jatho translated parts of an article in German by Peter Szammer on the CAD modelling work for Klaus Kada's Opera House in St. Polten, Austria.

I am also grateful to fellow researchers in this field, and design practitioners with whom I have had the pleasure of working. These include Mark Burry and Greg More, both currently at Deakin University, Australia, who provided information on the computer modelling of the columns of the Sagrada Familia church; Josep Gomez-Serrano for information on the computer modelling of the horizontal elements of the Sagrada Familia, as well as being so generous with his time on visits to the site in Barcelona; Klaus Schwagerl of Behnisch, Behnisch & Partner, who provided information on the Harbourside Concert Hall project; Colin Darlington and Nick Cramp, both of Max Fordham & Partners, for information on the computer modelling of the Sardis Roman Baths; Andrew Kane of FaulknerBrowns Architects, for the computer model of the Snowdome in Milton Keynes, his continuing friendship, and for all the work we have collaborated on in the past.

Next is a substantial group of people from design practice, including Michael Moore, IT Manager at Watson Steel, who provided CAD images of the Kansai Airport project; Keith Temple, Technical Manager at Westbury Tubular Structures Ltd., for his carefully preserved drawings of the Waterloo International Rail Terminal; Romain Govett, the slide librarian at Nicholas Grimshaws & Partners, for slides of 3-D CAD-generated models of the Waterloo project; Mark Whitby for his helpful comments; Ian Godwin, the IT Manager at Foster Associates, for providing information on several recent projects of Sir Norman Foster & Partners; Keith Mendenhall of Frank O. Gehry Associates for slides of CAD-generated images of the Guggenheim museum in Bilbao; Steve Bedford of Virtual Artworks for the model of the Welsh Assembly by Richard MacCormac, and Richard MacCormac for his permission to use it; Peter Szammer from Klaus Kada's office for the images of the Opera House in St. Polten, and for his hospitality in Graz in 1995; Professor Ken Yeang for providing me with a state-of-the-art project on the equatorial belt.

Finally, I would like to thank an equally important but motley bunch of people including the following: Jim Hall for his humour, encouragement, enthusiasm for the project, pertinent references, and for sharing his vast knowledge of architecture; our fellow Earnshavian Professor Tony Heathcote for his translation from the Spanish of text on the Sagrada Familia church; Aart Bijl for his support and encouragement over many years – his research as Reader at EdCAAD in the School of Architecture at Edinburgh University, which I was privileged to be involved in, was way ahead of its time, and still has much to offer to those who care to look into it; Peter Lathey for slide scanning; Lois Burt, the architectural librarian for finding things for me when there were hundreds of students in the queue. Finally, to the people at the Architectural Press including Mike Cash and Marie Millmore who encouraged me to put this together, and to Katherine McInnes, Sian Cryer and Pauline Sones for being patient with me regarding lapsed deadlines. I humbly apologise to anyone whose name I may have omitted.

I have tried to avoid any specific references in the text to particular CAD systems, as the intention was to make the book accessible to students and designers, and to avoid the jargon and the technicalities of software use. This book may be used as a coursebook for students of CAD in general, even though the many examples and illustrations are predominantly architectural. Some basic design skills are assumed, as well as some basic computing concepts, but no previous experience of the use of particular CAD software is required. However, I would like to acknowledge at this point the fact that many different CAD systems were used in the generation of CAD models, either by myself, or by those contributing model data. These included the following: Autocad, Catia, CAD-S5, FormZ, Microstation, Minicad Vectorworks, 3D Studio Max and Rhinoceros.

Part 1: Introduction

Chapter 1: Scope and Purpose

Most researchers in the field of CAD look upon the work that emerged from MIT as long ago as the early 1960s (Coons, 1963; Sutherland, 1963) as being the start of computer aided design (CAD) applications related to architectural design. The increasing frequency of releases of new CAD software since then, however, seems to be inversely proportional to the number of new technical developments in this field. Although there have been many new technological advances, these have largely come from other areas of computing, and the principles associated with the functionalities of CAD software systems have stayed fundamentally the same. What appears to be of greater significance, however, are the changes in the ways in which CAD is used in architectural practice. CAD in architectural education, therefore, should recognise and reflect these changes, and offer more to students than mere training or rote-learning of particular technical CAD system facts. By placing CAD in the context of contemporary architectural environments, and looking at case studies of the use of CAD in practice, I hope that students can glean not only technical, but also CAD principles of a more strategic nature.

This book is concerned with the use of CAD in design contexts, and its central premise is that it is the design intention that drives the ways in which architectural form is modelled within CAD environments. It is becoming increasingly both necessary and feasible for architectural designers to express their design intentions as directly as possible, in order to show their clients and fellow design specialists the salient features of a design scheme. With recent improvements in both computer hardware and software technology, CAD is no longer just a drafting tool used in the post-design phases of a project. On the contrary, it is a medium which is increasingly used throughout all phases of the design process.

Even though CAD software (e.g. for rendering) has improved dramatically in both speed and quality in recent years, many respected architectural practices still consider it to be of more importance to be able to communicate the essential architectonic design ideas, rather than to generate seemingly sophisticated renderings that often obscure rather than illuminate the design concept. This should be a warning to students in schools of architecture who, once they become seduced by the deceptive possibilities offered by rendered models, find it more difficult to pare down the presentation of their schemes to the key concepts within them.

A conscious effort has been made in the text to approach CAD from a design perspective rather than from a technological one. The focus in a technological perspective is on the medium or on the technology. A design perspective, on the other hand, focuses on the possibilities offered by the technology for supporting expression in design. The development of computer applications in design has often been seriously hindered by technological approaches (Bijl, 1993). Very often, so-called 'CAD experts' and CAD tutors in schools of architecture work outwards from the technology asking 'what might the user be able to do with this new technology?' rather than 'what might the user want to do with this new technology?'. It is the latter that is the concern of this book.

A designer's architectonic ideas, therefore, should be central to the organisation and generation of CAD models. The expression of ideas, rather than the representation of end form, has two primary objectives. Firstly, it enables the designer's realisation and clarification of a design concept, and secondly, but most importantly, it enables the designer to critically assess these ideas in relation to the contextual situation and brief. From my own experience of teaching CAD to architecture students over recent years, the greatest fear that students have of CAD is the fear of obsolescence. They worry about whether they will be prepared for the marketplace unless they are intimately familiar with the latest version of a particular piece of software. I hope that by attempting to place CAD within the context of design, certain CAD principles can be derived from this process which ease these worries and encourage them to exploit their strengths as designers, irrespective of all the commercial hype.

The traditional view of CAD in architectural practice has been that CAD systems should be used to communicate already completed design schemes. Commercial CAD systems have focused predominantly on mechanising the end process of architectural production, i.e. on the graphical communication of design descriptions to fabricators, estimators, approval bodies, etc. They have facilitated limited analysis of established design proposals according to pre-set criteria such as lighting levels or energy loss. Evidence from the case studies presented later in the book, however, will show that there is now substantial impetus in architectural practice to interface CAD systems with analytical tools as much as possible in early design stages. In other words, CAD in practice is moving towards *assisting design* itself, rather than being a mere production tool.

If it is indeed the case that there is a trend towards the increasing use of CAD in earlier design stages, then we should expect that computational expressions in the form of CAD models should be structured in ways which support designers' intuitive critical assessments of them. This structuring of models will then support the modification and development of the initial design ideas. The repeated transformation of ideas, CAD expressions, and intuitive analysis, can then develop in a cyclical manner until an end proposal is reached. Intuitive analysis which mediates between a design idea and its representation, can itself be computationally supported by a range of complementary methodologies that relate to well-understood analytical frameworks (e.g. energy calculations, lighting, structural analysis, design theoretic analyses, etc.).

Whereas scientists use technical and rationalistic problem solving methods embodied in an *information processing model* to solve problems, architects conversely propose initial solutions (without being fully convinced of their suitability) as a method of more completely understanding and pre-structuring the complexities of an architectural brief. Only by proposing an initial solution and then making a critical assessment of it, can architectural designers fully understand the complexities of the brief in a manner which could not be adequately achieved by rational analysis alone.

In a study of the design methods used by a selection of London housing architects, Darke recognised their intuitive selection of what she described as *primary generators* in the preparation of initial proposals or conjectures:

> '*The term primary generator does not refer to that image* [i.e. conjecture], *but to the ideas that generated it.*'
> (Darke, 1979)

In Darke's study, she discovered that the initial solutions which produced better projects were designed by architects who had realised strong conceptual ideas in the initial proposal stages, and that these architects had maintained the generative and directive force of those initial ideas throughout the extent of proposing and refining a solution.

Darke's study highlighted the dualistic relationship between concept and parti (schematic drawings, often abstract plan drawings, but sometimes sections), which is managed intuitively by the architectural designer. The ability to intuitively select conceptual ideas which in turn generate effective organisational proposals is one factor which distinguishes gifted designers from those less so. In architecture, like sculpture or the graphic arts, two states of externalisation exist, *the model* and the work itself. Unlike the finished work, the model does not attempt to become the ultimate state of externalisation, however, but exists simply to represent it. But the status of the model incorporates two roles, firstly to represent the ultimate physical state of the finished work, but also and very importantly, to represent or to express the internalised ideas of the designer.

4

Traditionally, the former role of the model as representation is well supported in CAD systems. Sophisticated modelling and rendering techniques have achieved levels of representation which are almost indiscernible from the physical world. In its capacity to represent volumetric qualities, the model (whether physical or virtual) provides the ultimate referent. Many students think that in producing a highly rendered *realistic* CAD model, they have satisfied the objectives of their design project. Sadly, it is all too often the case that although the model might appear impressive, the essence of the design proposal is nowhere to be seen. The realism instead becomes what Bijl has called a *realistic deception* (Bijl, 1995).

Models used to communicate design intentions and ideas externally to others are often very different from design drawings or design models. From the first hesitant pencil scribblings, through conceptual proposals to development drawings, design representations serve an alternative purpose, to externalise or to express the ideas of the designer, not for others but for the designer alone. Mark Hewitt (Hewitt, 1985) makes the distinction between objective and subjective drawings. Whereas the former *present the building* the latter are made for the *edification of the designer himself*. This is an important distinction because Hewitt's subjective drawings are an integral element in the period of activity when a design is being formulated. It is then that the relationship between a designer's idea and its expression is explored and developed. In direct contrast to the subjective drawing, the objective drawing is prepared after the period of design formulation has ceased, and therefore plays no part in the *modification of ideas*.

Recognising the importance of graphical expression during design, the characteristics of expressions can be categorised into three broad groups related to the stage of development of the proposals. Graves, in relation to drawn expressions, has named these stages *referential sketches, preparatory studies and definitive drawings* (Graves, 1977). The referential sketches are the very immediate direct recording of influential ideas. These may be related strictly to the contextual environment of the project, or like Le Corbusier's carnets, may be combined with daily observations or travel notes. In relationship to the earlier discussion of conceptual generators, the sketchbooks become highly personalised records of the influences, often combined with highly schematic organisational partis. Referential sketches can also encompass textual descriptions and thoughts, scrapbook paste-ups, and of course generalised architectonic observations.

By the initiation of the so-called *preparatory study*, a tentative connection between conceptual generator and preliminary organisational parti begins. Confidence in the suitability of a proposal is impossible at this point, but it is important that initial proposals are *expressed* to enable their critical analysis and, therefore, the development of an enhanced understanding of a design project. At the stage of the preparatory study, some initial attempt is made to relate schematised diagrams of circulation, planning, structure, etc., to a suggested architectonic formal proposal. This indicates a designer's inherent ability to intuitively relate architectural form with structured understandings of its implication, or more importantly, the potentiality of forms related to desired structured relationships. During this stage of design, a rapid succession of proposals is externalised and related continually to the programme requirements and the conceptual generators. The nature and influence of such conceptual generators may vary continuously during this stage of design formulation, but a strong relationship between conceptual ideas and organisational proposals is highly important in generating an identity and direction.

Once the so-called definitive drawing stage is reached, the dialogue of concept and organisational parti has reached a level at which the designer is satisfied of its efficacy. However, beyond the level of basic schematic organisation and volumetric architectonic approach, a level of resolution is still absent. Although a satisfaction of the solution is achieved, further development of organisation and relationships is required.

It is at this stage, therefore, that a resolution of the basic criteria of structure, zonal planning, servicing, construction and volumetric composition is carried out. Post-rationalisation analyses of design precedents (Baker, 1989) powerfully demonstrate the degree to which this resolution can be carried out by gifted designers. It is at this stage particularly that higher level ordering techniques are used to enable and enhance this procedure. Proportional systems, geometric grid organisations and techniques of symmetry are among the many methodologies used to govern organisational refinement.

During the preparatory study stage of design formulation, the immediate generator and referent are the referential sketches (i.e. conceptual ideas). During the development of definitive drawings, the preparatory studies, or chosen architectural parti, take prominence as the generator and controlling influence. Whilst conceptual ideas are still significant in providing the ultimate anchor to the design, the relationship between definitive drawing and preparatory studies is more immediate in the designer's consciousness.

In all stages of design, it is the ability of the designer to express or to externalise his ideas to the limit of his understanding at that particular stage which is crucial. No attempt is made to exhaustively describe or resolve all aspects of the design. What is omitted in an expression is often as important as what is included. Dimensional accuracy is often absent – approximate dimensions are sufficient, with intuitive understandings of scale and proportional relationships being of greater importance. Partial models display similar characteristics. Often being very crude and having incomplete descriptions of elements, they are, however, effective tools to enable an appreciation of spatial relationships, for example. In all cases, a strong relationship exists between the components of an expression, and the designer's idea which this expression signifies. For example, in separate expressions, an identical graphical element may be used, but may signify two entirely different ideas. Therefore, despite attempts to standardise graphical descriptions with convention systems, a semantic specificity exists between designer and expression.

The activity of *analysis instigates change* and hence the development of design. In Clark and Pause's work (Clark and Pause, 1985), for example, the range of analytical criteria include the following: structure, natural light, massing, the relationship of plan to section, symmetry and balance, the relationship of circulation to use, the relationship between repetitive elements and unique elements, the relationship of individual units to the whole scheme, geometry, the extent to which elements have been formed out of additive and subtractive operations, the hierarchical structure, and the parti diagram.

We need to investigate the ways in which these and other criteria might be supported in terms of CAD principles. In the case of structural, energy, and lighting analysis, this would entail the use of already developed software in these areas, ensuring that the CAD data is both represented and presented in a form to which this *analytical software* can be applied. In looking at massing, the user needs to be competent in *volumetric block modelling techniques*. In describing relationships between plans and sections, and between circulation and use, this implies the ability to *overlay information* within the CAD environment. Repetitive elements can be represented effectively within CAD environments through the use of *symbols*. The description of relationships between units and wholes requires the understanding and use of more advanced CAD principles such as the expression of *parametric relationships and object-oriented techniques*. Geometry, symmetry and balance imply the understanding of basic CAD operations that either *transform existing objects*, or allow the *construction of new objects in relation to existing ones* in user-controlled ways. Addition and subtraction imply an understanding of how to use *boolean operations*. Hierarchical structuring implies knowing how to represent information at different *levels of detail*. Parti diagrams can be viewed in terms of user-defined *grid systems*.

Already we have begun to develop mappings between analytical criteria that are highly relevant to the process of designing, and CAD principles that require understanding in order to support design development. The above is by no means an exhaustive set of mappings. Clark and Pause represent just one source in this area of design. It is also beyond the scope of this book to arrive at some definitive list of mappings, as this will inevitably be subjective and variable amongst design practitioners. It is merely an attempt to adopt a certain approach and way into CAD that may be more palatable to design students than technology-driven approaches.

Analysis, therefore, should be seen as the binding link in a cyclical progression of idea – expression – analysis – idea ... end proposal. CAD needs to support critical dialogues between design ideas and their expressions. This was recognised by Schon in his studies of architectural design tutors' working methods, and which he described as reflection-in-action (Schon, 1983).

Drafting vs Modelling

Drafting is still associated with the common perception of the application of CAD to architectural design. This book will query this perception, and suggest that technology has now moved on to a position in which far more than mere drafting is now possible. CAD technology has progressed to a level in which it is possible to communicate design expressions representing early stage design ideas right through to detail drawings. This is quite different from CAD as an instrument for efficient production, or as a vehicle for the graphic presentation of the already designed building. Being able to use CAD systems fluently and three-dimensionally, is synonymous with being a good designer, rather than a draftsman.

CAD models in architectural design, therefore, need to be assessed not in terms of their quality of presentation, but as objects with which to carry out precise analytical functions. An understanding of the ways in which 3-D CAD modelling techniques can be used to support and reflect design thinking, can then lead to the development of a greater awareness of architectural design representation of space and form. The ability to express design concepts and to work them through from conception to completion within a CAD environment, without losing the initial liveliness, is a skill that will become a fundamental part of architectural education in the future. Knowledge of how to generate form, and then to transform and modify it in ways which maintain pertinent design relationships is central to this process.

A skilled CAD modeller should be adept at interpreting the right form of presentation for a model based on needs emerging from the design brief. The primary purpose of a CAD model needs to be established at an early stage in a project. With this in mind, an appropriate way of representing this model needs to be decided. The factors that determine a model's representation will depend upon the underlying data structure of the CAD environment, and this in turn will affect the user's ability to edit the form of the CAD object in response to subsequent changes in the design proposal. The case studies in this book will illustrate those CAD models with explanatory qualities, used to convey complex design relationships to fellow professionals. Such models often illuminate three-dimensional relationships not yet resolved.

Some of the 3-D CAD models shown later in the context of several case studies, were generated in order to study and refine important elements of a building, *as well as* to prepare final contract drawings and construction documentation. While architecture is very much a 3-D experience, there still seems to be a reluctance by some students and practitioners to venture into 3-D, often due to its perceived complexity. Architectural design students should think of CAD models as representations of essential design criteria, rather than as an inanimate collection of line drawings.

Significant increases in the performance of low-cost, desktop computing is now making it possible to move on from symbolic images towards more contextual and meaningful representations. A CAD-generated building model can be rendered from a common database of digital samples taken from the real world. The application of realistic materials textures to CAD-generated building models can then be linked to energy calculations, for example, using the chosen materials. The complete model may then be viewed in a more meaningful way through a total simulation of the life-cycle of the design proposal. The CAD model may also be used to explore environmental/energy considerations and changes in the balance between the building and its context, as part of a larger planning model of an urban site.

A common perception of CAD is still as a drafting tool in the post-design stages of work, rather than in its use in supporting 3-D design formulation activity. However, the scenario illustrated in **figure 1.1** is now commonplace in most CAD systems. Firstly, parts of a 3-D CAD model that need further refinement and detailing can be selected within volumetric regions. Within a selected region, vertical and horizontal section cuts can be made that generate 2-D regions that in turn can be further developed as more traditional detail drawings. In other words, 2-D plans and sections become by-products of 3-D models, instead of existing independently and separately from other drawings.

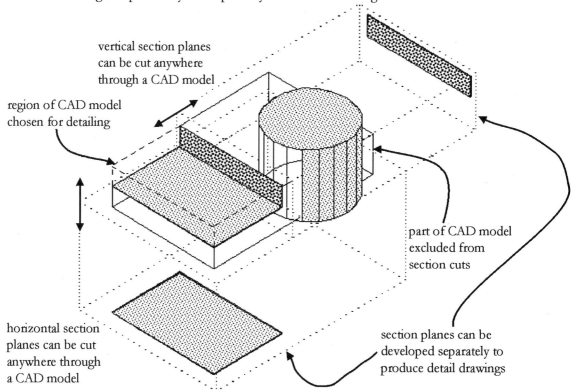

vertical section planes can be cut anywhere through a CAD model

region of CAD model chosen for detailing

part of CAD model excluded from section cuts

horizontal section planes can be cut anywhere through a CAD model

section planes can be developed separately to produce detail drawings

Figure 1.1: plans and sections are by-products of 3-D models.

Given that the above scenario is now possible, and is increasingly being adopted as a way of working in architectural practice, attention should now be given to exploiting existing CAD software in ways that enable the rapid expression of design ideas, in a manner which assists (not replicates) the designer in his intuitive analysis of those ideas. Recognition of the centrality of the idea – expression – analysis cycle which takes place during design activity is needed, and this theme will be continued in **Part 2** of the book. Before that though, it is worth thinking about the consequences and possibilities offered by the emerging technologies in design education.

A New Model for Interdisciplinary Design Education

Building upon the discussion so far, the following objectives and principles, some pedagogical and some technological, are seriously worth exploring further as a basis for the establishment of a new approach to the teaching and use of CAD in schools of architecture.

• *Professional Practice*
Design students need to be aware of the ways in which design schemes are currently being modelled and analysed in the design profession. The obvious way to achieve this is to investigate how CAD has been applied in particular leading-edge case studies. The CAD software systems used in design practice have changed radically over the last decade. There is now a growing awareness, and in some cases actual implementation, of much more integrated, computational environments, within which it is feasible for designers to develop their work. There is no reason in principle why such integrated environments should not be available to students too. One important consequence of this would be that we could then offer students new kinds of interdisciplinary design courses, which would not focus on discrete design studios, but instead, offer shared, networked resources, breaking down physical studio barriers, and providing integrated design experiences.

• *Design Collaboration*
Students should be encouraged to work more collaboratively, and become accustomed to exchanging design information with other design specialists throughout the course of design projects. Traditional barriers between professions should become invisible. Students should be introduced to the emerging powerful computer-based technologies. Though beyond the scope of this book, networking, both local and global, has a key role to play in facilitating this emerging collaborative design process. Design students can potentially now, via local area networks, work on shared design models, and explore, evaluate and present their designs using VRML (Virtual Reality Mark-up Language), JAVA, whiteboarding and video conferencing. A design scheme, at any stage of the design process, can be accessed by designers from a wide range of design disciplines, either to further develop the design scheme, to evaluate the present scheme, or to present the scheme to a client.

• *Integration of Software Tools*
Students should be exposed to a wide range of digital software tools that are currently being exploited in practice. This would prevent students from pigeonholing themselves in relation to particular software (e.g. architecture = drafting), and encourage an appreciation of other disciplines and their complexities. The scope of urban design, for example, has expanded through the application of techniques such as GIS (Geographic Information Systems) allowing interpretations that include social, economic and environmental dimensions. Object-oriented CAD environments now make it feasible to integrate conventional modelling techniques with analytical evaluations such as energy calculations and lighting simulations. These were all ambitions of architects and landscape designers in the 1970s when computer power restricted the successful implementation of these ideas. Instead, the commercial trend at that time moved towards isolated specialist design tools in particular areas. Prior to recent innovations in computing, closely related disciplines relevant to architectural design have been separated through the unnecessary development of their own symbolic representations, and the subsequent separate and fragmented computer applications. This has led to an unnatural separation between what were once closely related disciplines.

• *Online teaching resources*

Net-based resources and CD-ROMs should be exploited, e.g. photo-libraries, national building specifications and regulations, bibliographies, etc. Additionally, one would expect that in future, this type of material will become increasingly more interactive and informative, rather than being mere 'slide shows' that could easily be presented by more traditional means. Students should become accustomed to downloading net-based data to be incorporated into subsequent CAD modelling work. The pedagogical premise here is that design no longer begins with a blank sheet of paper, but potentially with a complex urban plan.

• *Information Exchange*

Students should develop an awareness of commonly used data exchange formats, and be able to decide upon appropriate forms for different uses of information. Without going into details here, since names and version numbers change rapidly, there are a range of commonly used CAD data exchange formats. This makes it increasingly feasible for users of CAD software to use different CAD software systems for different purposes, in the knowledge that the transfer of information between one system and another will be reliable and robust.

• *Software Analysis Tools*

Software support should be provided for parallel analysis of common design models at any stage of the design process. Analytical tools for energy simulation, lighting studies, spatial analysis, etc., need to be provided. Brief descriptions of several of these analytical areas, together with their uses in design practice, will be given in the following part.

This book explores the future role of a more holistic and integrated approach to the use of CAD in architectural design. With the aid of new types of digital environments, there are increasing opportunities to explore and evaluate design proposals which integrate a wide range of architectural aspects. The production of integrated design solutions which support the exploration and evaluation of design proposals is now possible. Concerns about the practice and teaching of architecture, which through increasing specialisations have shifted from a holistic picture of design, can now be remedied. The eclectic nature of design, which was always its strength in the past, can now be recovered.

Part 2: CAD Modelling and Analysis

Chapter 2: The Importance of Analysis in CAD Modelling

CAD models in architectural design are developed in order to communicate intended design proposals. Communication of intention, therefore, is central to CAD modelling in architectural design. An expression in the form of a CAD model during design activity is carried out in order to visualise, comprehend and criticise design ideas, such that modification of the idea can take place in the path towards a satisfactory design solution. This very act of criticism or analysis is what enables the development of ideas, and only by the expression of ideas is it possible to successfully analyse them.

Existing CAD systems focus on two specific aspects which are related to design work, the representation of form, and specific quantitative analyses. The effort involved in producing accurate and detailed CAD models, however, is often inappropriate for supporting the rapid expression and analyses that are required during early design stages. The quantitative analytical facilities often associated with 3-D CAD systems, such as the calculation of heat losses, for example, need to be applicable equally to schematic, early stage CAD models, as they are to detailed CAD models, since the most important decisions concerning the character and performance of buildings are made in the early stages.

At all stages of design formulation, the interaction and prominence of particular analytical criteria constantly changes, and it is impossible to determine which analytical criterion takes priority at which stage. There is a continual cyclical process of CAD model generation as shown in **figure 2.1**, in which successive CAD models are produced with analytical tasks in mind. In some design practices, such as Behnisch, Behnisch & Partner, CAD models would frequently alternate with physical models in taking on an analytical role (see chapter 25). In other practices, such as that of Frank O. Gehry, CAD models and physical models would have clearly defined roles to play at particular stages in the design process (see chapter 28). Whilst some analytical criteria, such as proportional relationships, for example, are predominantly analysed during later design stages (in the definitive drawing stage, for example), what is important is the recognition that design activity incorporates both intuitive (intangible) and formal (tangible) analysis in a manner which is transparent to the designer. Formal analysis typically requires the direct application of quantitative methods to CAD models, several of which are referred to in chapters 3 to 8. Intuitive analysis often involves non-computational methods, but when computational methods are used, the techniques are often those derived from design theoretical areas that relate to building form. The latter require the imaginative use of current CAD systems by design researchers, to describe formal relationships in CAD models such as the examples given in chapter 9. Whatever the stage of design, architectural designers execute all forms of analysis of ideas without prioritising one form of analysis above another. Designers intuitively manage the interaction of design criteria as an internalised activity, and therefore have direct control over the relationship of architectonic form and the optimisation of criteria.

Integrated Design Process

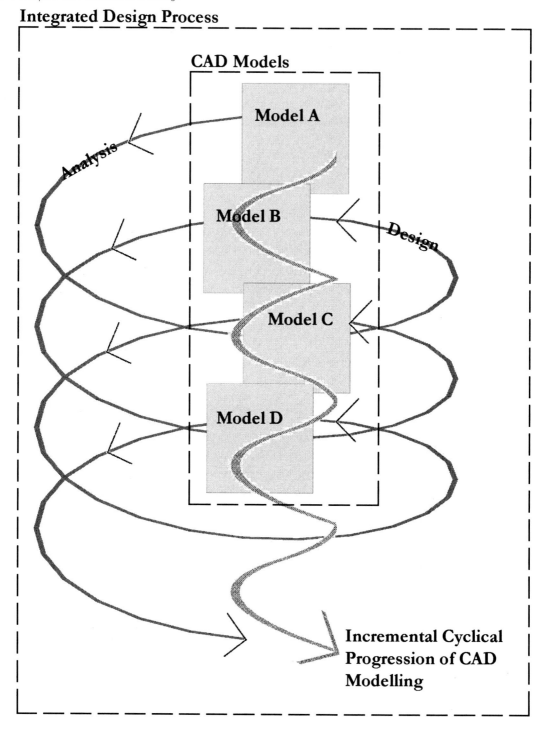

CAD Models

Model A

Analysis

Model B

Design

Model C

Model D

Incremental Cyclical Progression of CAD Modelling

Figure 2.1: the cyclical process of CAD model development in the context of design and analysis.

Criteria for Analysis

To support design activity with computational methods, we must examine in greater detail the methodology of analysis during design, and the criteria according to which analysis is carried out. By investigating how the methodology of analysis varies according to different criteria, we can derive a better understanding of the role of analysis in design formulation. The primary group of criteria can be classified as follows:

- Structure
- Zonal planning
- Circulation
- Servicing
- Environmental control

Each of the criteria in this primary group constitutes factors which are fundamental to the habitory purpose of architecture, and each in turn can be measured in a rational empirical manner against pre-determined aspects of a brief or programme. In their ability to be systematically assessed according to established benchmarks, they have in turn become a focus of many CAD analysis packages. For example, given an established heat loss level and data on the fabric of a proposal, it is a straightforward task to systematically calculate whether or not the fabric and the proposal achieve the required minimum standards. In the case of zonal planning, given pre-established relationship preferences and a set of proposals in a given structured format, performance gradings can be allocated to each in a similar fashion. If we now consider a second set of criteria they can be broadly grouped as follows:

- Volumetric massing
- Symmetry
- Cultural implications (iconology)
- Proportions
- Conceptual intention

All of the second set may be grouped under the description of compositional or aesthetic criteria, with associated concerns of balance, dynamism, contrast, orientation, emphasis, etc. Closer examination of how each of the two sets of criteria is analysed elucidates an important difference between them. Whilst the primary group of criteria can be considered *tangible* through their ability to be empirically measured, the second group of criteria are *intangible* architectonic qualities, and resist any form of scientific measurement. During design work these latter criteria are assessed intuitively by designers, who rely in turn upon their understandings of these qualities (idea-types) which are both inherent and developed through education. Often, analyses carried out on design precedents (Baker,1993; Clark and Pause,1985) are executed intuitively without making any distinction between the tangible and intangible nature of the properties which are deduced. But in the domain of computational assistance, the intangible criteria have until now resisted systematic, designer-independent, computational analysis.

As the development of a design progresses from preparatory study to definitive drawings, the nature of the expressions, in relation to the desire to intuitively carry out specific types of analysis, changes. During the preparatory study stage, expressions in the form of CAD models consist largely of schematicised descriptions of criteria, with perhaps only tentative suggestions of the architectonic forms which may realise these descriptions. However, as the definitive drawing stage is reached, designers become satisfied that the architectonic proposal incorporates the desired schematicised ideas. At this stage, a focus on architectonic composition occurs, emphasising the formal aspects of the proposals, but with any modifications constantly related to the changes which these may induce in the satisfaction of the criteria.

Comparative analysis is very important at this stage, since *superimposition* of a previous proposal with a development or alternative is a powerful analytical method. The comparative superimposition of two designs, whether it be previous solution and present solution, or present solution and precedent example, enables qualities to be highlighted through contrast and comparison in a manner which would not be possible through the isolated analysis of a single design alone (Rowe, 1947). Traditionally, comparative analysis is achieved through the use of tracing paper. In CAD systems, this would be supported by means of layering, a logical operation common to most CAD systems, described in chapter 15. Some of the analytical criteria to which the technique of comparative superimposition would be suited are described in chapter 9.

An expression of design ideas should be possible in both two- and three-dimensional formats, but further developments are still required in the interface between designer and CAD model, such that rapid expression can take place without the consciousness of system command structure obscuring the designer's concentration on ideas. Expressions should be possible without the necessity for dimensional accuracy or explicitness of description. Importantly, it is preferable that as little system *intelligence* as possible is applied in the allocation of conventions or meaning to objects, for example a slab element being understood as a floor in 3-D, or a shape of a specific size or format being interpreted as a building element. Semantic intention for elements should be at the discretion of the designer within CAD environments that allow the non-prescriptive expression of ideas.

It should be recognised that the three stages of design cannot all be adequately supported by computational facilities. Referential sketches, i.e. the expression of generative conceptual ideas and initial parti diagrams, are no more effective if expressed with the use of a computational sketch package, for example. In fact, they may be considered less so, because the consciousness of system command structure constantly acts as a filter between designer and expression. The immediacy of a sketchbook and pencil is undeniable. However, support for the latter two stages of design (preparatory studies, definitive drawings) do offer the opportunity of effective CAD support, but differences in format of ideas, format of expression and analysis, must be taken into account. With this framework in mind, the following few chapters will look at a range of case studies in which the expression of particular models was needed in order to support specialised types of analyses that are often encountered in architectural and engineering design.

In summary, the aim is to link the intentions of designers to specific CAD techniques. These intentions stem from the central analytical aspects of design schemes which subsequently drive the development of the building form. These include structure, lighting, acoustics, energy, climatic features, spatial analyses and design theory. The text, therefore, is goal-orientated rather than software-orientated. It aims to show not only how particular forms can be produced, but also the further implications of producing forms in different ways. The implications of CAD representations are extremely important in their relationship to design intentions. CAD possibilities are investigated, therefore, from a design viewpoint.

Chapter 3: CAD and Structural Analysis

There is an abundance of structural analysis software for evaluating schemes at various stages, particularly for the analysis of dynamic responses with large displacements in structural assemblies (Lee, 1999). For such analytical tools, each component in an assembly is assumed to have a lumped mass. Another type of structural analysis software, however, is used to evaluate the distribution of stresses or temperatures in mechanical components undergoing force or heat loading. Vibration analysis of components can also be carried out when they undergo dynamic loading. The latter types of analysis are carried out using *finite-element analysis* (FEA) techniques, originally introduced to calculate stresses in aircraft, and used to good effect in buildings such as the new Guggenheim Museum in Bilbao (see chapter 28).

Structural optimisation is another computer-based technique in which design functions such as stiffness, fabrication, weight, and often importantly cost, are optimised in the context of structural constraints. This numerically intensive technique has also been exploited in the case of the Guggenheim. This kind of software is, to date, typically only available on powerful workstation environments, primarily because of the need to support a range of interlinked software in an integrated computer system. Students, on the other hand, need initially to be able to understand and express structural design features *visually* within the context of the desktop systems they typically have access to. There is also scope for introducing students to the principle of linking computer programming techniques to CAD modelling techniques in the context of describing their own basic structural analysis equations. The latter CAD principle will be discussed in more detail in the course of the case study in chapter 23.

Case Study: Merchants Bridge, Castlefield,
Manchester, Whitby Bird & Partners

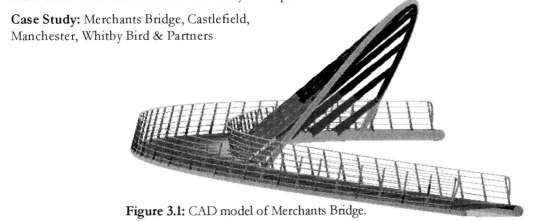

Figure 3.1: CAD model of Merchants Bridge.

As a case study in CAD presentation and visualisation of structural design ideas, the geometrically complex Merchants Bridge, in Castlefields, Manchester, was chosen as the focus of attention for a short undergraduate option project. Although the structural ideas were of central importance, and the CAD modelling of tubular extrusions along curved paths (see Part 4) was not without difficulties, other important design aspects were also represented. These included the site context of the bridge, set as it is amongst fifteen existing bridges, spanning 38.2m over the junction of the Bridgewater canal with the Rochdale canal. The constraints of a modest budget, ramps for disabled access, and strict clearance requirements over the canal, meant that for every 100mm of depth, the length of the bridge increased by 4m. The design solution was a thin deck structure (400mm), on a curving plan following existing desire lines of movement.

Figure 3.2: torsion effect on main tube between arch and deck.

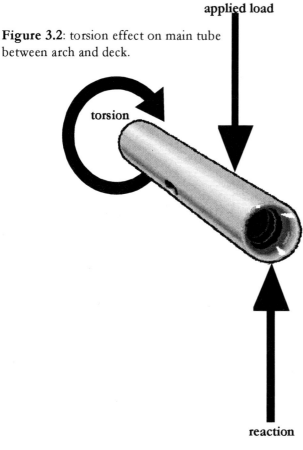

applied load

torsion

reaction

The bridge was supported from a single arch, itself restrained by the deck, so harnessing two mutually compatible structural systems. Inclining the arch away from the bridge counterbalances the deck, which curves in the opposite direction to the arch, endowing the entire structure with a dynamic, sculptural quality. The key structural concept, therefore, that required expression was the idea of the deck as a *torsion* structure. The curve on plan through a total of 62° produces *torsion in the deck* which, with its top and bottom plates and tubes in the leading and trailing edges, is a closed torsion box. The arch tube is restrained from out-of-plane buckling by the bending stiffness of the arms and the torsional stiffness of the deck.

Instead of simply having a vertical support under the arch on the west side of the canal, concern to *visually extend* the form of the arch resulted in a steel cantilever. The base of this returns below the arch, indicating the course of the structural forces involved. In effect, the resulting slender steel prop carries the larger proportion of the vertical load and limits deflection in the cantilever arm. The handrails were simple, flat, horizontal bars, set in panels and clipped to the structure. The topmost stainless steel rail is continuous and was welded on site.

The simple form of the bridge structurally relies on separate but interrelated actions:

- The stiffness of the deck means that the main span contributes in the carrying of the vertical loads (30% approx.) by normal bending action.

- Resolving forces in the plane of the arms into the plane of the arch produces bending in the arms and additional *torsions in the deck*. The curved deck acts as a tie to the main arch creating a crescent shape which as such responds more favourably to uneven loads than a simple tied arch.

Figure 3.3: resolution of forces generates torsion in deck.

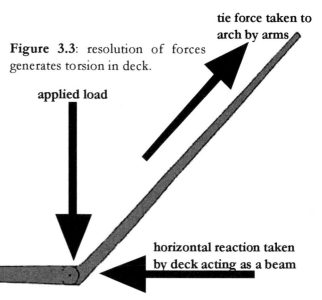

tie force taken to arch by arms

applied load

horizontal reaction taken by deck acting as a beam

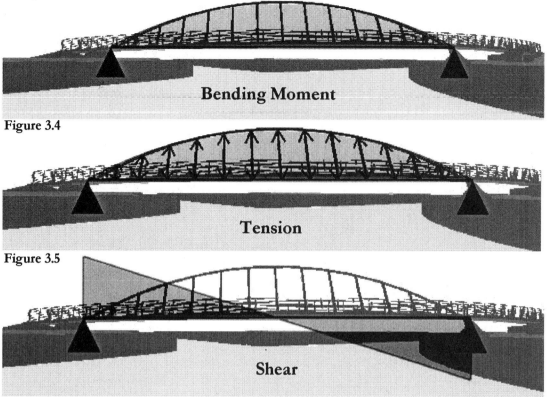

Bending Moment

Figure 3.4

Tension

Figure 3.5

Shear

Figure 3.6

The issue that needed resolving was how to express the structural forces involved in the scheme in the context of the CAD model itself, since this was the object of the exercise, rather than separately in the form of structural force diagrams and equations. It was found that the bending moment diagrams, tension forces in the arms, and shear force diagrams could all be illustrated and understood in a single 2-D plane in which the points of support were shown in elevation. The force diagrams could then be superimposed using the layering mechanism (see Part 4). A difficulty arose in the presentation of torsion, or more accurately, the torsional moment, which seemed to require a more dynamic form of presentation to illustrate its effect. The solution was to apply computer animation techniques to the static CAD model. To achieve this, it was sufficient to generate two 3-D CAD models, each at the extremity of torsional movement of the deck, and to allow the animation software to interpolate intermediary images. An impression of the effect can be seen in **figure 3.7**. In fact, the CAD model shown was too detailed for the communication of this structural concept, and better results were achieved when a more simplified model was animated.

Several observations can be made from this brief CAD modelling and visualisation exercise. Firstly, it should be noted that CAD systems for describing and generating the kind of complex 3-D curved geometric forms such as in **figure 3.1**, and animations such as in **figure 3.7**, are now commonplace and available on desktop computers. Structural analysis software, although more specialised, has the potential to be integrated into desktop systems such that the analytical component can be applied to abstractions of CAD models (e.g. elevation in this example), and the results of the analysis output visually directly in the context of the CAD model itself.

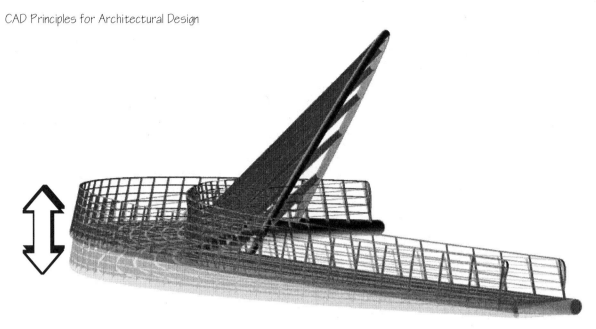

Figure 3.7: Torsion – The Key Concept.

As far as the design of the bridge was concerned, it is highly significant that the designers themselves actually contemplated applying the modelling and analytical capabilities of software from other disciplines, such as from aircraft design, for example, to architectural and engineering design. The computer analysis of aircraft stability, for example, makes possible structures that combine interdependent structural systems, which until recently was an inconceivable concept in architectural design. It turns out, however, that this was exactly the type of software that was used in Frank Gehry's design for the Guggenheim Museum, Bilbao (see chapter 28).

Bridge design is an area of design which over recent years has demonstrated the synergy of architecture and engineering, manifested strongly, for example, in the bridges designed by the Spanish architect, Santiago Calitrava. It is abundantly clear from such schemes that not only have engineering problems been solved, but architectural ideas expressed, even though the form of the structural system is always such a dominant influence in bridge design. In order to succeed in this approach, the demands on a designer are such that an architectural vision, expressed visually within a CAD environment, needs to be combined with analytical responsibilities based upon a knowledge of structures and construction technology.

This interaction between the expression of architectonic ideas in three-dimensional form, and the structural analysis that is required, can be greatly facilitated by the use of emerging CAD environments. Even at the conceptual design stage, powerful yet user-friendly structural analysis software can now be integrated with CAD systems. This is largely the result of the fact that the exchange of information across different software environments has improved in recent years, making it possible for the analytical software to numerically process the more geometric type of information typically provided by CAD systems. This improvement in communication between different software platforms promotes a greater emphasis on a more rapid analysis/synthesis/evaluation cycle, to use design methods terminology. This is turn supports the *reflection-in-action* recognised by Schon (Schon, 1983) in which a dialogue takes place between a designer's ideas and their graphical realisation.

Chapter 4: CAD and Lighting Analysis

Most CAD users are familiar with the increasingly sophisticated rendering software which allows the modelling of the effects of light on object surfaces. CAD rendering software allows users to position light sources of various types (e.g. point source, spotlights, ambient sources), and to define the colours, textures, shininess, and other properties of individual surfaces. Once all these factors have been defined, a range of rendering *algorithms* (computable calculation procedures) such as Gouraud shading, Phong shading, ray tracing and radiosity can be applied to the CAD model. Most rendering systems allow the user to select the method of rendering they wish to use, bearing in mind that the more sophisticated the rendering algorithm, the more computationally intensive are the calculations needed to render the scene. *Gouraud* shading has the effect of smoothing out the faceted appearance of CAD modelled curved surfaces. *Phong* shading is better than Gouraud for handling specular reflections (i.e. the reflections from highly polished surfaces). The *ray tracing* method generates individual rays of light from the CAD model to the viewpoint and can be used to highlight shadows as well as reflections. It is also capable of rendering transparent and translucent objects. The most advanced form of rendering is *radiosity*, in which each CAD object surface is defined in terms of how much light energy it emits, and how much it reflects.

These rendering techniques tend to be used by students to produce what they perceive as *realistic* renderings of CAD models, even though each of the rendering algorithms is based upon very specific mathematical models. A more analytical use of this software is to focus less on the complexity of the algorithms, and more on generating variations in shading over time periods, such as over days or years, for example. In this case, less sophisticated rendering techniques are sufficient to generate the required results. Sun-path information is now frequently built into most CAD software allowing users to carry out *shading studies*.

Case Study: Proposal for Yorkshire Artspace Studios, Stuart Craigen
Architecture students are often encouraged to submit design proposals for forthcoming projects and design competitions, particularly in a local context. One such scheme was to design an artists' studio in Sheffield's cultural quarter near to the impressive National Centre for Popular Music designed by Nigel Coates. The brief called for the building to offer an environment dedicated to artists specialising in craftwork including jewellery, sculpture and print-making. Stuart Craigen's proposal was characterised principally by studio blocks read as distinct blocks. These were held in a frame separating them from each other, and suspended over a large open plan lower ground level. Smaller studio pods were suspended in the gap between larger studio blocks. A CAD model of the proposal was produced as shown in **figure 4.1**, illustrating the direction from which lighting and shading needed to be analysed.

The studio spaces were to be lit principally by large glazed areas at the end walls of the studios. The south-east facing glazing was designed to be protected by solar control devices which shade the facade from direct sunlight during the summer months. One end wall was glazed/semitransparent, and faced into the circulation zone, which also had a glazed facade. The calculated average daylight factor for one of the large studios was 2.7%, indicating that *natural lighting* would provide most of the lighting requirements for this studio space. A strip of clerestory lights 500mm deep, with 1m of the strip exposed, the rest internal, adds an insignificant amount of *artificial lighting* to the average daylight factor. This adds more to the character of the space than to the actual *illuminance values*. Fluorescent lamps were chosen throughout this scheme because of their long life, low energy consumption, and good colour rendering characteristics making them suitable for most tasks. It was recognised that some artists may need to supplement this with task lighting specifically suited to their trade.

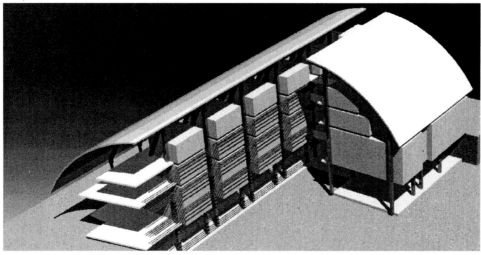

Figure 4.1: CAD model showing direction from which lighting and shading needs to be analysed.

The spaces between the studios and the walkways were to be lit with pendant downlights hanging over the walkways providing patches of light. Luminaires fitted into the side walls of the facing studios, shine across a void, and illuminate the walls of the facing studio with small patches of light of differing colour. These wall luminaires were mounted at the bottom edge of the ground floor studio where they could be easily reached for maintenance. Another row of wall luminaires were located in the parapet wall of the 3rd floor/roof of the 2nd floor studios, so that they could be accessed from the roof of the 2nd floor studios. A large open plan public/education art space formed most of the lower ground floor. It was to be brightly illuminated so that at night, light from the lower ground floor filters its way up the building, providing a strong contrast between the darker circulation spaces and the art spaces. This is reinforced by the fact that studios occupied after dark will also be brightly lit, and the light from these will penetrate through the translucent end wall onto the walkways and out of the building through the glass facade. The first step in the analysis of lighting for this project was to investigate the effects of natural daylight on the building proposal. This was done by means of *sun-path diagrams*.

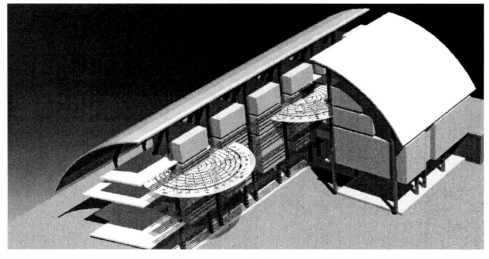

Figure 4.2: CAD model showing how parts of building cast shadows on specific areas of glazing. Sun-path diagrams show when a particular point is in shade, for different times throughout the year.

In a sun-path analysis, the studio spaces are shown as rectangles, whilst the centres of the sun-path circles are located over the plan centres of the studio glazing (centre of bottom edge of the rectangles). The southern wing of the building casts a shadow on the studio spaces behind. The shadow zones within the circles indicate that during the mornings (all year round), that particular area of glazing is in shade, but in the afternoons receives direct sunlight.

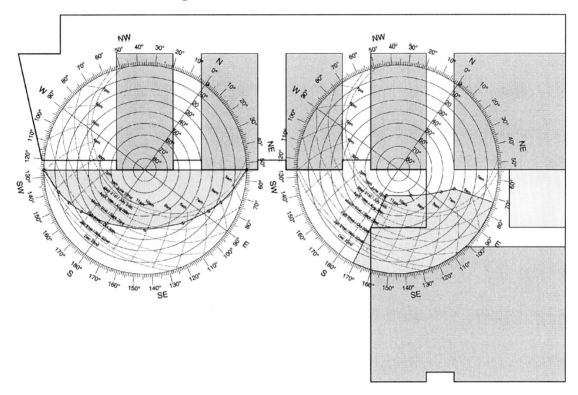

Figure 4.3: sun-path diagram showing effects of obstructions.

The left-hand sun-path diagram in **figure 4.3** shows that the external shading device is effective in covering the main glazing of one of the studios. The shaded sun-path area represents the times when the window is in shadow. As the shading device extends beyond the glazed area in both directions, the sun-path shadow zone finishes in a straight line through the centre of the diagram. The sun-path shadow zone indicates that during the mornings (all year round) that particular area of glazing is in shade, but in the afternoons receives direct sunlight.

An interesting feature of this particular analysis is the way in which the CAD sun-path information has been applied to CAD objects (sun-path diagrams) that are not part of the CAD model of the building form. These graphical objects have been introduced into the model purely to support the analytical natural lighting studies.

Regarding the analysis of artificial lighting, this was carried out as illustrated in **figure 4.4**. This time artificial lights are represented as cones of light intensity in section, and as concentric intensity circles in plan. This type of analysis was used to select appropriate lamps for patches of light to be created on the walkway, and for ensuring that the minimum amount of light required is provided, at points where individual lights merge with adjacent ones. Again, the *effects* of individual lighting elements are graphically represented in schematic ways in order to support the analysis.

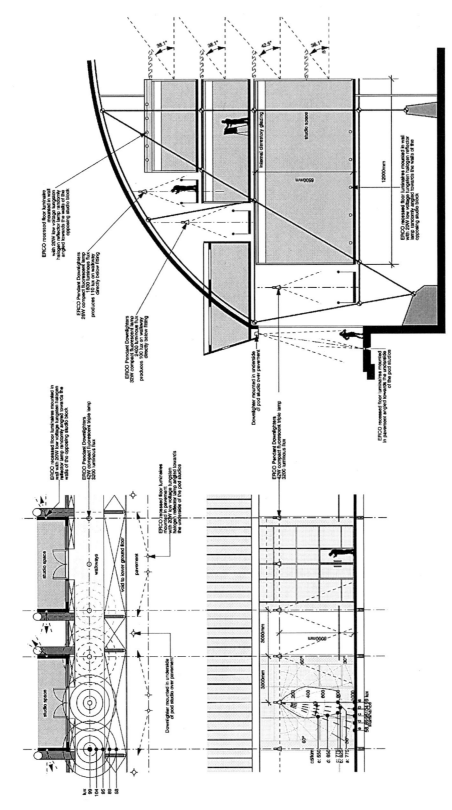

Figure 4.4: lighting characteristics of internal light fittings. Light intensity varies from centre point below fitting, radiating outwards.

24

Chapter 5: CAD and Acoustic Analysis

Some acoustic modelling programs can import 3-D CAD models and use them as a basis for acoustic models of spaces. Acoustic modelling programs work by generating thousands of rays which leave the source at all possible angles over a sphere and are reflected many times by the room surfaces. The properties of the room surfaces are combined with the information generated by ray tracing to produce predictions of the strength, time of arrival and direction of travel of acoustic energy in the room. The technique of *raytracing* sound 'rays' is exactly the same as that used in lighting. The predicted flow of acoustic energy is presented as a number of parameters which acousticians use to describe the loudness, reverberance, intimacy and clarity of the sound in a room.

One of the features of rooms used in acoustic modelling is that the room must be 'airtight' – otherwise some of the rays will escape, making the predictions inaccurate. Since surfaces are used to generate *specular reflections*, then curved surfaces cannot be used, and have to be represented in terms of a number of plane surfaces. CAD models used as a basis for acoustic models, therefore, must be constructed with this use in mind. These computer models can provide more detailed information about the acoustic behaviour of spaces than was previously possible using traditional methods. It is also now possible to *auralise* the responses of rooms. For instance, a sound source can be placed in a room (for example, a singer on a stage), and designers can then listen to the sound of that singer from any chosen seat in the room. To do this convincingly, the source recordings should be *anechoic* – that is recorded in an acoustically 'dead' environment. This is so that the acoustics of the recording room are not heard – only the acoustics of the CAD modelled room that has been auralised.

A major focus of architectural acoustics is on the acoustic analysis of large halls in public buildings such as auditoria, for example. The aim of this analysis is to provide optimum speech intelligibility and sound quality. Good acoustics in concert halls and theatres should enable sounds from the stage to be transmitted to the auditorium so that listeners can hear them clearly and without distortion. Echo reflections from hard polished surfaces in or around an auditorium can distort the sound so that it reaches the listener by two or three different routes. The sound waves travelling along different routes take slightly different times to arrive, and to the listener the sound seems distorted. Consequently, sound absorbent materials placed on the boundaries of the space (ceiling, walls, floors) are used to eliminate unwanted echoes. Many concert halls are now designed so that the tipped-up empty seats absorb the same amount of sound as would a person sitting in them. In this case the hall maintains its acoustic properties whether seats are empty or full.

Acoustical input is required in the construction of new buildings and during the refurbishment of existing buildings, whether they are general purpose or specialised facilities. A proper acoustical solution is particularly important for those halls where most activities take place without electro-acoustical sound reinforcement. However, favourable acoustical conditions are also quite important in halls where sound amplification systems are used. At earlier stages in the development of architectural acoustics, the acoustical design of halls was reduced mainly to providing an optimum reverberation time. However, further technical developments, and the experiences of people involved in operating halls have shown that it is not sufficient to consider only reverberation time in any acoustic analysis.

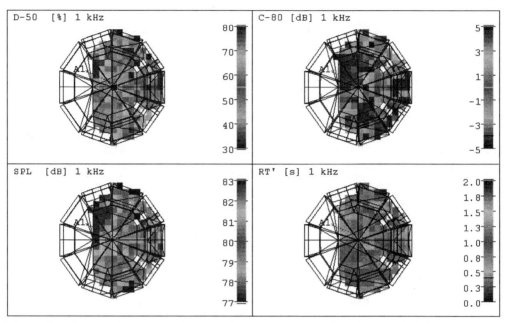

Figure 5.1: predicted acoustic parameters across the audience area for a hall modelled by Arup Acoustics.

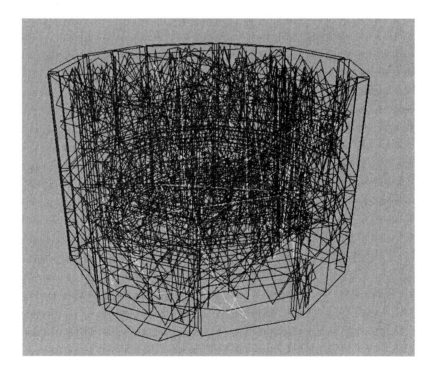

Figure 5.2: ray tracing across the audience area for a hall modelled by Arup Acoustics.

Auralisations which allow aural evaluation and *visual presentation* of predicted room acoustics are now possible on desktop computers. The acoustic response at any point typically involves the calculation of tens of thousands of reflections for each sound source. One acoustic property that is typically calculated is the binaural room impulse response, based upon a computer simulation of the acoustics of the human head. This calculation takes into account the acoustic reflections of nine octave frequency bands. Auralisations, output as sound and visually, allow the analysis of reverberation times, levels, speech intelligibility and clarity.

Acoustic quality related to the diffusion of the sound field is becoming as relevant as the analysis of detailed sound reflections. New criteria for acoustic analysis have been developed in response to studies of the relationships between objective acoustical parameters and subjective evaluations. A by-product of acoustic analysis techniques is that they have also improved acoustic measurement methods. CAD-based acoustic analysis is now making it more feasible to precisely predict the acoustic quality of particular building types such as auditoria. The next step is to further integrate acoustic analysis techniques with other design factors in order support design compromises between acoustic and other analytical requirements. One case where this would prove beneficial would be in the acoustic design of large halls with multi-purpose requirements, for example.

Case Study: Greater London Authority (GLA) building; architects: Foster & Partners; acoustic engineers: Arup Acoustics

The analysis of the acoustic environment of Foster & Partners' proposal for the GLA HQ building, scheduled for 2001, was very comprehensive. The geometry and finishes of the chamber will control the acoustic response of the space. The *elliptical plan* form of the chamber, combined with the requirement for mainly glass walls will have the effect of causing reflected sound to converge, resulting in a series of focuses. If these are coincident with a listener, the result will be a strong *hot spot*, and in some cases a clearly perceived echo. A series of acoustic 3-D computer simulations of the chamber were developed during various stages of the design development to investigate the acoustic response of the space.

From this development, a section has been derived to ensure that all sound which deflects off the glass walls is directed upwards away from all participants and the public gallery. This unwanted sound will then be absorbed by materials on the underside of the ramps and on the soffits of the floor plates as they cut into the chamber. The top of the chamber must be designed to absorb or *catch* unwanted sound. This zone is under continuing development. The area of the chamber wall that is defined by a *diagrid* forms a potential focusing surface. This is, to some extent, dispersed by a *spiral ramp* and associated balustrade. This will be investigated through further detailed analysis.

The approach to the design of the debating chamber of the GLA is based on the use of a *speech reinforcement system* with microphones and loudspeakers placed near the delegates. Reinforcement to the public gallery will also use small, distributed loudspeakers. Speech in the chamber will be clear, but with an aural sense of space commensurate with the scale of the room. The space will provide a good acoustic for speech-based events. The reinforcement system will aid all normal speech-based activities. The quiet background noise level will also mean the space will be good for natural speech events when spoken at an appropriate level. Whilst the chamber is not designed specifically for music, the shape and response will not preclude this activity.

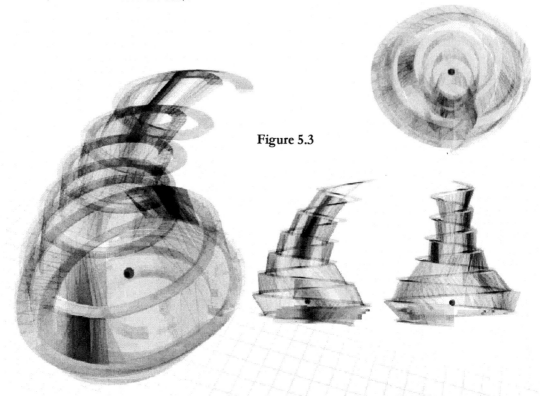

Figure 5.3

The illustrations in **figures 5.3** to **5.8** are the results of the acoustic analysis of schematic CAD models of the GLA proposal that indicate the direction and frequency responses of point sound sources. Line and surface sources can also be analysed in a similar manner.

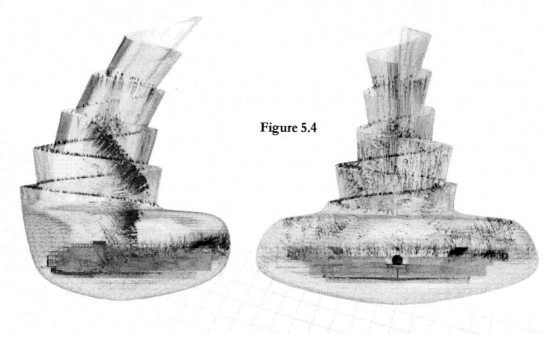

Figure 5.4

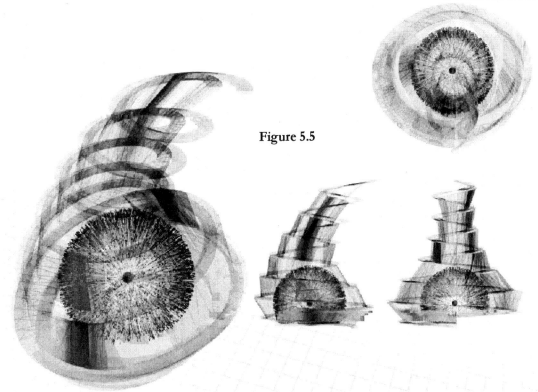

Figure 5.5

One of the acoustic properties under analysis was *envelopment*, the experience of being surrounded by sound, which relies upon lateral reflections arriving more than 80ms after the direct sound.

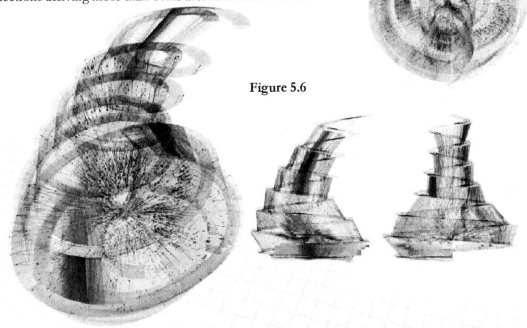

Figure 5.6

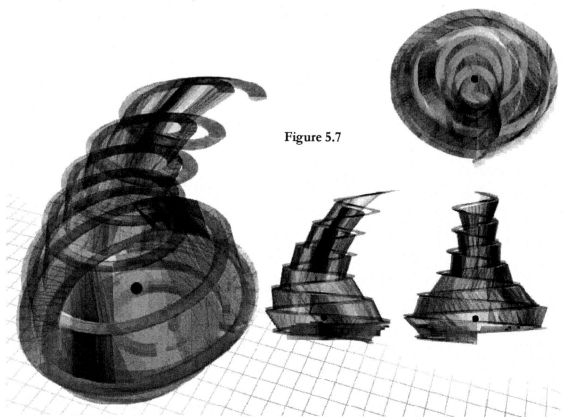

Figure 5.7

Another important acoustic property requiring analysis is that of frequency dependent reverberation. The results of such an analysis can help to equalise the reverberations in a space, provided time is also taken into consideration, as sound gets darker as it decays.

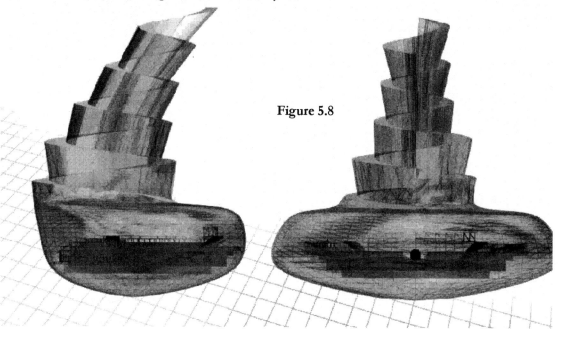

Figure 5.8

Chapter 6: CAD and Thermal Analysis

Some of the earliest CAD systems to have been developed were those that focused on the specific and discrete tasks of environmental analysis in order to assess the performance of building proposals. These tasks include environmental systems such as ventilation and lighting, for example, with heating and energy systems being of particular importance. Thermal analysis ranges from simple U-value calculations, through to complex simulations that dynamically model thermal properties. Typically these methods are used to assess and compare the thermal behaviours of different types of construction based upon standard procedures, such as those developed by CIBSE (Chartered Institution of Building Services Engineers), and ASHRAE (American Society of Heating, Refrigerating and Air-Conditioning Engineers). Material properties need to be specified by users as input data, and graphical output is often produced in the form of temperature profile graphs through the building fabric and surrounding spaces. Historically, the conventional CAD modelling of building proposals and their corresponding thermal analyses have required separate and unrelated forms of input and output, often causing a separation between architects, and specialists in services and environmental issues. The greater integration of computer software from these two areas now makes it feasible to visualise and analyse within the same computing environment.

Case Study: Sardis Roman Baths, Turkey, Max Fordham & Partners

Figure 6.1: CAD model of Sardis Roman Baths.

A roman baths was designed then built at Sardis in Southern Turkey as part of the filming of a television documentary. Max Fordham & Partners formed part of the design team on this project. A 3-D computer model of the proposed design was first constructed, and its geometry used as the basis for a mathematical model. The model was used to calculate temperatures, pressures and air movements in the baths using computational fluid dynamics (CFD) techniques. The results enabled the design to be tested, formed a discussion piece about the workings of roman baths for the team, and by varying physical features of the model such as housings for the furnace and location of flues helped guide the design process and justify some features of classical roman baths which seem at odds with modern engineering practice. A computer animation was also produced showing the geometry of the baths, a summary of how hot air and smoke circulate around the rooms to heat the baths and pictorial representations of the CFD results. An interesting feature of the CAD models shown overleaf in **figures 6.2** and **6.3** is the use of *transparency* in the rendered presentations which helps to visually superimpose building spaces that would otherwise be obscured.

The frigidarium (1) or cold room is unheated. It contains a cold plunge bath called a baptisterium (A).

The caldarium (2) or hot room is heated, often to above 50° C. Humidity is also kept high. The room contains a hot bath called an alveus (B).

The tepidarium (3) or warm room is connected to both the frigidarium and caldarium, and acts as an intermediate room for acclimatisation. It is heated to around 40° C.

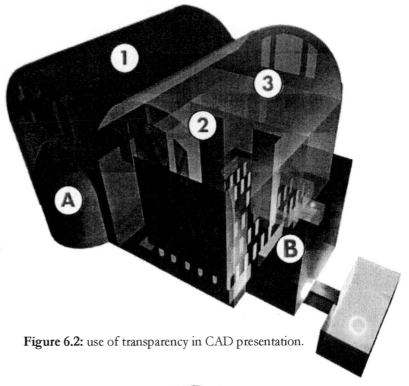

Figure 6.2: use of transparency in CAD presentation.

A wood fire is used to heat the baths from a furnace (a) outside. A duct runs underground from the furnace to the hypocaust (c, d), a void below the two heated rooms. The hot furnace gases provide underfloor heating.

A small additional furnace (b) allows the temperature difference between the rooms to be adjusted.

Hollow tubuli walls (e) in the hot room allow the gases to circulate up the sides of the room, exchanging heat through their walls.

Furnace gases are exhausted from the hypocaust through brick flues to the above.

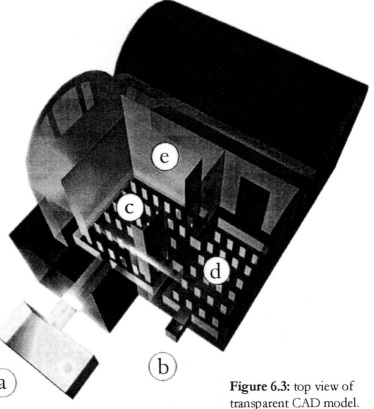

Figure 6.3: top view of transparent CAD model.

frigidarium
(cold room)

tepidarium
(warm room)

furnace

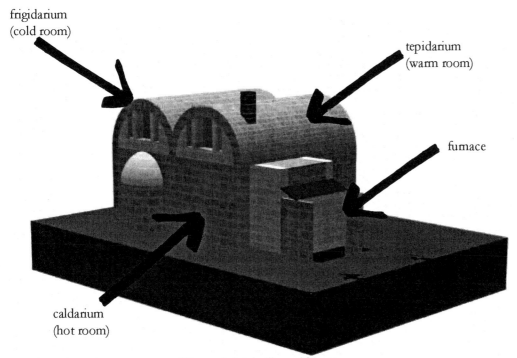

caldarium
(hot room)

Figure 6.4: labelling without transparency.

The design of this particular building form was based upon a tried and tested roman design solution which is well described by the following quotation:

'All the bath-rooms lay over a substructure (suspensurae) about two feet high, the ceiling of which rested on rows of pillars standing at distances of one and a half foot. The furnace (hypocausis), with the firing-room (propnigeum, praefurnium) lying in front of it, occupied the centre of the establishment. From here the heat was diffused through the basement, and ascended in earthen or leaden pipes (tubi) in the walls to the bath-rooms. The cold, tepid, or hot water required for the baths came from three tanks lying above the furnace, and connected with each other by means of pipes. The bath-rooms, over the basement, grouped round the furnace at greater or less distances, were divided, by the different degrees of heat attained in them, into tepidaria (sudatory air-baths), caldaria (hot baths), and frigidaria (cold baths). Tanks (piscina), or tubs (solium, alveus), occupied the centre of the caldaria and frigidaria; benches and chairs were ranged along the walls, or stood in niches; a flat tub (labrum), placed in a niche on the narrow side of the oblong calidarium, was filled with cold water for a plunge after the hot bath.' (Guhl and Koner, 1989)

Such a detailed description makes it possible to model the essential spaces and elements, but fine tuning in terms of thermal analysis is still needed to determine temperature distributions across spaces, together with important details such as the heat input by the furnace, for example. Once a CAD model based upon such a description has been completed, the path and temperature of the moving air can be modelled using *computational fluid dynamics* (CFD) methods. For CFD methods to work, the CAD representation has to be converted into a grid or mesh of points, and mathematical equations are then solved at each point. The results generate temperature profiles around surfaces or through passages.

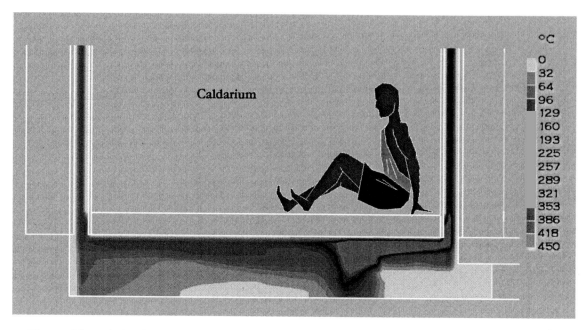

Figure 6.5: analysis of CAD model showing air from furnace entering into hypocaust at around 400°C, with average temperature in hypocaust about 100°C. Analysis also shows stratification.

In order to carry out a thorough energy analysis, several environmental factors also need to be taken into account in any computational representations that need to be completed prior to the analysis. These include the location information associated with the design proposal, as energy performance is directly affected by factors such as altitude, latitude and longitude, ground topography and surrounding structures, and local micro-climate. Standard weather data sets are now being increasingly used in design practice. The temperature of the external environment can be provided as hourly, daily, or monthly values. Other climatic data used in energy analysis include wind speed and direction, solar radiation, and humidity. Dynamic thermal simulation software can analyse energy issues relating to building fabric, mass flow, heating plant systems. The time steps of the simulation can vary from seconds to hours. The CFD calculations are applied to the simulation of air flow and building fabric heat transfer. A common form of graphical output consists of temperature distribution graphs, such as that shown in **figure 6.5** in relation to the air flow of one of the heated spaces. These graphs can be used equally well to study various building fabric properties such as insulation, for example. In more complex building forms than roman baths, they can also be used to evaluate alternative heating plant capacities, as well as the effects of their alternative positionings within the building.

Chapter 7: CAD and Bio-climatic Analysis

Case Study 1: Office Building, Hamzah & Yeang Architects

Ken Yeang of Hamzah & Yeang has been concerned for some time now with an ecological approach to design, which focuses more upon the systemic aspects of architecture than with aesthetic or social aspects, and places importance upon tackling the environmental interactions associated with the design problem in the correct manner from the start (Yeang, 1995).

> 'Before any design is turned into form, the designer might make explicit maps of the problem structure using the interactions framework. These maps serve to diagram the relationships that need to be understood in order to grasp the nature of the design problem. Activities, relationships, events, and situations could be expressed graphically in a form that contains their essential attributes, then combined to show their relationships.' (Yeang, op.cit.)

A recent outcome of this approach is a project for an institutional building along the equatorial belt. It is essentially two blocks separated by bridges, and has a single floor that spans over both blocks. The form is determined by a particular approach to bio-climatic architecture, in which the designers begin with the principle that design must start by optimising on all passive design strategies. Passive design strategies include design in relation to the climate of the place:

- by shaping of the building,
- by proper building orientation,
- by use of vegetation and landscaping,
- by wind and natural ventilation,
- by building colour,
- by facade design,
- by solar protection.

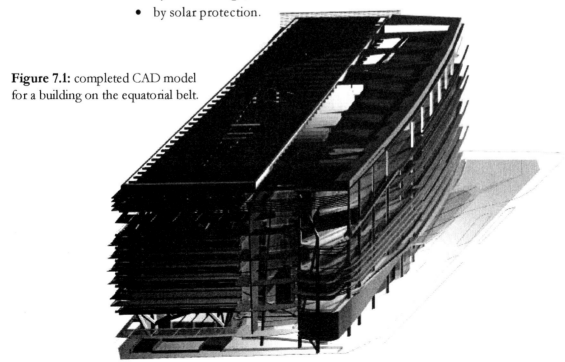

Figure 7.1: completed CAD model for a building on the equatorial belt.

In Yeang's approach, in which each of his design projects is viewed as a prototype for the next and a basis for experiment and innovation (Richards, 1993), the form evolves from conceptual diagrams that show the factors that influence the shaping of the building. Whether these are hand-drawn or produced within a computer environment is immaterial.

Figure 7.2: model of bio-climatic proposal.

His first modelling stage on this particular scheme was not computational but physical, and in fairly rough detail modelled at a scale of 1:1000. Only after this has been achieved were CAD drawings produced at 1:200, from which the CAD model shown was made. Once the environmental criteria have been addressed, the configuration itself generally followed the shape of the site.

Figure 7.3: model of bio-climatic proposal.

Case Study 2: Swiss Re Office Building, Foster & Partners

A more specific illustration of bio-climatic analysis is the computer simulation of the airflow around buildings by means of computational fluid dynamics (CFD) techniques. These effectively create a *computational wind tunnel* which enables faster analysis of different types of building form than would be possible with a physical wind tunnel. Even though CFD techniques have been used for many years now by building scientists, it is only relatively recently that this type of analysis has become possible on desktop computers, and wind analysis is just one of a range of programs available to architects and planners for environmental design and evaluation. Carrying out wind analysis on new building proposals leads to building layouts which provide relatively good outdoor micro-climates in the surrounding spaces, and reduces the climatic stresses on individual buildings, making detailed design less critical, and running and maintenance less costly. The following illustrations show the kind of visual output that can be obtained. They were produced by Foster & Partners for the Swiss Re reinsurance company office proposal, and show how the wind flow develops around the proposed structure in the form of flow streaklines.

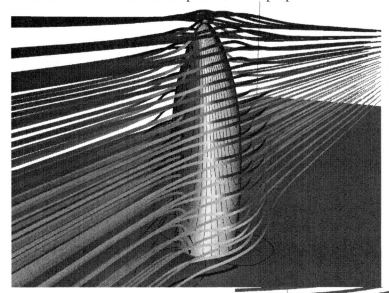

Figure 7.4: wind flow around Swiss Re proposal.

Figure 7.5: elevation view of wind flow.

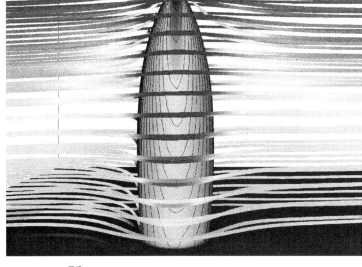

One of the arguments used by designers in the past against CFD simulations has been that they tended to produce more information than could be understood and used profitably in the design process. However, now that it is possible to three dimensionally *visualise* the results of analyses *within the context of the CAD model itself*, rather than interpreting masses of numerical data in the form of graphs, designers can minimise subsequent analyses and so save valuable design time.

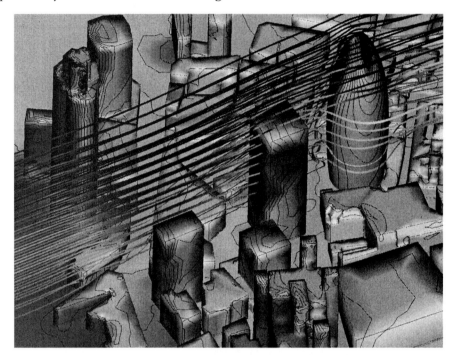

Figure 7.6: windflow through site.

Figure 7.7: wind flow through site.

This relatively recent development in bio-climatic software makes it possible for visualisations of the ways in which wind interacts with a proposed building form to affect the geometry of the built form, its orientation, structure and construction. The mathematical technique of computational fluid dynamics upon which such visualisations are based can potentially be a minefield to the uninitiated. However, it turns out that certain simplifications can be made which make this less of a worry for certain types of geometries. The first of these relates to the concept of the pressure coefficient, and the fact that the relationship between air flow and high-rise building forms is *independent of scale* (Wilson, 1982). It is appropriate to make this assumption in the case of Foster & Partners' proposal for the Swiss Re building, as the proposed height is 185m, and this would make it the tallest structure in the Square Mile of London.

Another acceptable simplification is to ignore the effects of neighbouring buildings, thus focusing on the form of the building under design. What appears to be emerging from this area of work is that in any simulation of wind upon buildings, it is sufficient to have only approximately modelled wind turbulence and wind profile, together with models of the major surrounding buildings. This leads to results which are *accurate enough for design purposes.*

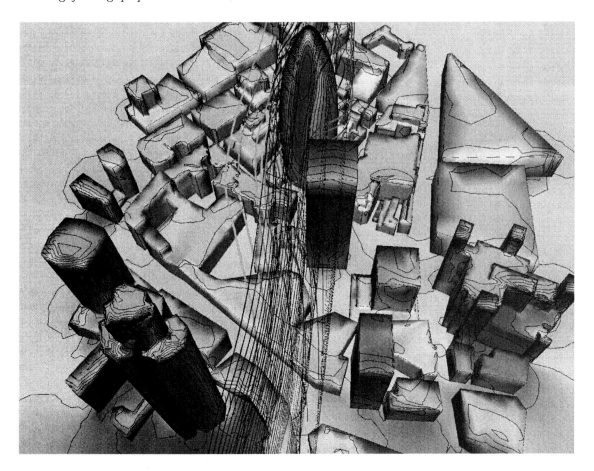

Figure 7.8: top view of wind flow around Swiss Re model.

Figure 7.9: wind flow analysis through schematic CAD models of surrounding buildings.

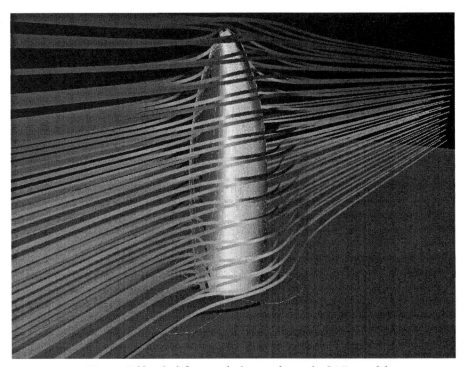

Figure 7.10: wind flow analysis on schematic CAD model.

Chapter 8:   CAD and Spatial Analysis

Space Syntax

Space syntax is a method of analysis originally developed by Bill Hillier at the Bartlett School of Architecture, London. It has primarily been applied to the analysis of urban space, but can also be used to analyse the spaces within buildings. The underlying principle in the application of this method to urban design is that the spatial layout of urban spaces affects patterns of movement and use.

Figure 8.1: urban plan.

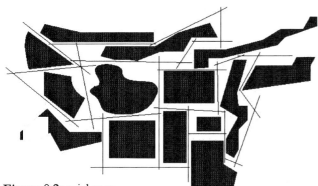

Figure 8.2: axial map.

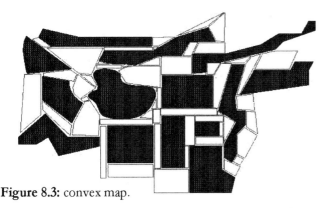

Figure 8.3: convex map.

The results of a space syntax analysis generate values for criteria such as the *intelligibility of space* which is a measure of the relationship between the overall urban space and local features.

Given a plan of an urban space such as that shown in **figure 8.1**, an *axial map* can be constructed, consisting of the fewest and longest straight lines that cover the entire plan (**figure 8.2**). Axial lines extend as far as a point is visible and directly accessible from a viewpoint. Alternatively, a *convex map* can be generated (**figure 8.3**), which is composed of the largest and fattest convex spaces covering the urban plan. Whether starting from an axial or convex map, the analysis proceeds by converting the map into a graph, and then calculating *depth* values from any point in the graph to any other point. If several spaces have to be crossed in order to reach a point, then the depth relationship between the two points is the *number* of spaces crossed. By numerically comparing the depth values of different spaces, this reveals the extent to which spaces are either *integrated* into or *segregated* from an urban environment. This technique has been applied to the analysis of the siting of new streets and roads within towns and cities, with the aim of improving the integration of certain areas.

Case Study: Possagno Plaster Cast Gallery, Carlo Scarpa

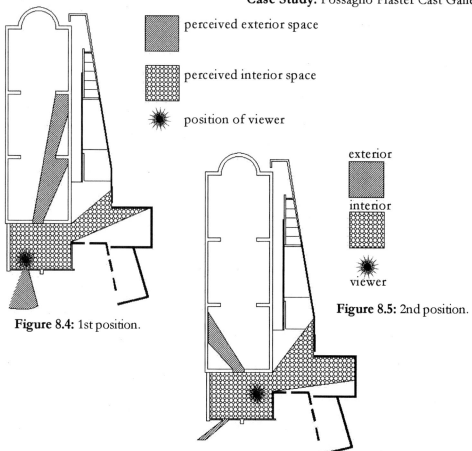

perceived exterior space

perceived interior space

position of viewer

Figure 8.4: 1st position.

exterior

interior

viewer

Figure 8.5: 2nd position.

A possible way of applying space syntax analysis to a building form instead of an urban space is shown in this example. The building in this case is a sculpture gallery. Given the plan of the building such as that shown in **figure 8.4**, a convex map can be generated, representing the cones of vision of the viewer from a particular point within the building. The cones themselves can penetrate through to the outside through openings and windows. As the viewer moves through the building interior, alternative visual maps are generated as shown in **figures 8.5** and **8.6**. The degree of variability of these maps as the viewer moves through the spaces could be one criterion for the spatial analysis of building types such as galleries, potentially providing information on required levels of interest or distraction in the building's spaces.

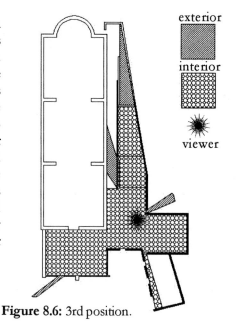

exterior

interior

viewer

Figure 8.6: 3rd position.

Shape Grammar

Shape grammar is another well-known technique for the analysis of the spatial properties in drawings. Shape representation of design objects in shape grammars is expressed as relationships between parts of shapes made up of lines (line primitives). Formal shape grammars consist of sets of relationships between symbolic entities, plus transformation rules for *instantiating* new symbolic expressions (Stiny, 1975). Shape grammars are implemented as sets of replacement rules, such that the shape on the left-hand side of the rule can be replaced by the shape on the right-hand side of the rule. Lines in shapes are not interpreted in any way as design objects. *Labels* may be attached to shapes to differentiate between similar shapes, often denoting their orientation. In **figure 8.8**, a label in the form of an asterisk is introduced in rule 1, but removed in rule 2.

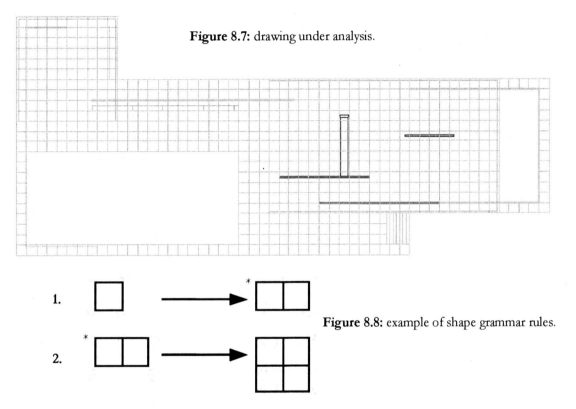

Figure 8.7: drawing under analysis.

Figure 8.8: example of shape grammar rules.

Shape grammars are based on the view that important properties of design objects can be abstracted from design drawings (usually plans), and understood in terms of a *syntactic structure*. Formal grammars can be devised which correspond to perceived abstract structures of designs (Krishnamurti, 1981). These grammars can then be used to generate new instances of designs which preserve properties of existing good designs (Knight, 1980; Koning and Eizenburg, 1981). The prescriptive nature of shape grammar rules reduces users of such systems to passive roles in the design process.

'In shape grammar systems, the mode of operation is to identify by pattern-matching opportunities to which the user reacts' (Wojtowicz and Fawcett, 1985), meaning that the user can say yes or no to the system instantiation of design changes. It is this characteristic of shape grammars in use which makes them more akin to expert systems than to CAD systems, and that area of research is beyond the scope of this book.

Shape grammars have most often been used to analyse well-known and completed design schemes, and it is claimed that they can also operate in a *generative* way, generating new instances of designs. The practice has been to study exemplars of good design, the past works of individual designers who are widely acknowledged to have been good designers, and to infer from their drawings the abstract relationships between line objects which they are believed to have employed (implicitly or explicitly). These relationships are then interpreted as particular grammars and implemented as rule systems. Thus we have examples of newly designed Palladio villas (Stiny and Mitchell, 1978), Frank Lloyd Wright houses (Koning and Eizenberg, op.cit.), generated by their respective grammars, long after these designers have died. In our present time, it is argued that we should be able to develop grammars that encapsulate the abstract structure of designs of contemporary good designers, and that these grammars could make good designs widely available to others who would not otherwise have access to the services of good designers.

If shape grammars can detach themselves from particular instances of design such as Palladio villas, then we can envisage how they might be made more generally useful. Objects could be viewed more generally as lines with certain properties: linearity (straight, curved); intensity (thick, thin); continuity (dotted, dashed, solid); length (linear measure). These properties describe instances of lines and may have given values or their values may be *parameterised*, i.e. values found from some relationship to values of other properties. Shapes could be considered as assemblies of one or more lines which are bound together by relationships that exist between them, such as connected lines, angle relationships and distance apart. Relationships instance shapes. In the general formalism of shape grammar, line objects and their relationships can be represented in a symbolic form in an algebraic environment, so that shapes can acquire mathematical properties such as symmetry, and can be subjected to algebraic functions, add, deduct, etc. to effect shape transformations. A given set of relationships targeted at a selected class of line objects constitutes a shape grammar, implemented as a set of replacement rules.

One way in which shape grammars could prove useful without being prescriptive in design contexts would be if they enabled users to modify existing rules and add new rules. This would then have the effect of enabling designers to formulate their own grammars and add their own rules. Designers could then potentially evolve their own design languages, employing formal definitions that give them access to the power of computers. This proposal for evolutionary rule-based systems requires a non-trivial extension to current work on shape grammars. Single systems that can support implementations of different shape grammars and permit users arbitrarily to change the rules still pose fundamental questions.

Chapter 9: CAD and Design Theory

The aspect of design theory that CAD is most suited to supporting the analysis of is that of the arrangement and ordering of forms and spaces. The scope and potential for the application of CAD to uncovering relationships within design precedents, is far greater than is presently exploited within schools of architecture. Irrespective of any design function, purpose, context or meaning, students should *'be able to recognise the basic elements of form and space and understand how they can be manipulated and organized in the development of a design concept'* (Ching, 1996). Typically, a formal analysis starts with a CAD model of the generic form, which can be either a rectilinear plan or a volumetric 3-D model. Subsequent analysis then attempts to show how particular design factors lead to transformations of this form in order to clarify and understand a scheme, rather than showing how the designer designed it (Baker, 1989).

Case Study: Villa Stein, Le Corbusier

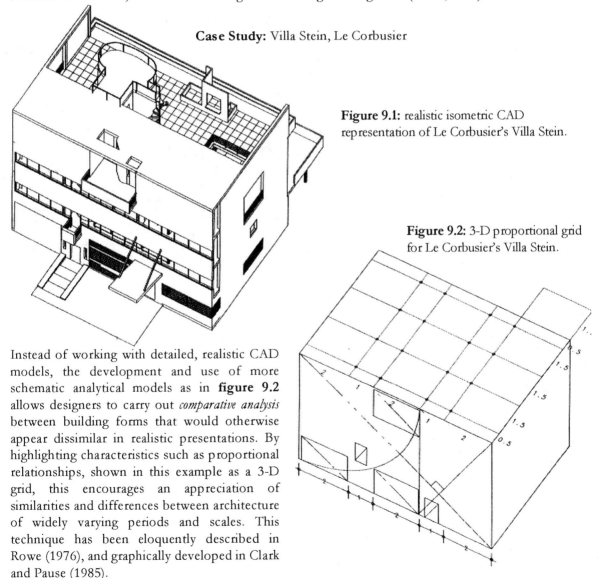

Figure 9.1: realistic isometric CAD representation of Le Corbusier's Villa Stein.

Figure 9.2: 3-D proportional grid for Le Corbusier's Villa Stein.

Instead of working with detailed, realistic CAD models, the development and use of more schematic analytical models as in **figure 9.2** allows designers to carry out *comparative analysis* between building forms that would otherwise appear dissimilar in realistic presentations. By highlighting characteristics such as proportional relationships, shown in this example as a 3-D grid, this encourages an appreciation of similarities and differences between architecture of widely varying periods and scales. This technique has been eloquently described in Rowe (1976), and graphically developed in Clark and Pause (1985).

45

Baker places importance upon the analysis of geometric properties of form as a method of uncovering *generating lines*, which architects such as Le Corbusier held were the basis of subsequent design actions (Baker, op.cit.). These generating lines become rhythmic features within schemes upon which Baker bases his analyses of movement and circulation. Analysis of these lines can also be based upon more overtly geometrical features, such as in terms of the proportional relationships between them. The proportional relationships (sometimes referred to as scalar ratios) that have been most often used in architecture are those that lie between 1:1 and 2:1. Transition in terms of scale between buildings and larger urban projects, for example, requires careful planning and detailing to achieve this design objective. Design development based upon the human perception of scalar difference has been exploited by architects, and one relationship in particular that has often been used is the *golden section*.

The Golden Section

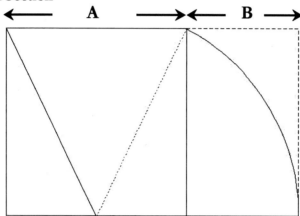

Figure 9.3: geometric construction of the golden section.

$$A : B = (A+B) : A \sim 1.618$$

A golden rectangle can be constructed by drawing an arc, centred on the midpoint of one side of a square, from one of its corners, as shown in **figure 9.3**. The golden section can also be derived from the Fibonacci series which is as follows:

$$1, 1, 2, 3, 5, 8, 13, 21, ...$$

Each member of the series is derived by the addition of the two previous members. The division of a member of the series by the value of the previous member converges to 0.618, the factor that is added to any unit of length to produce the golden section value of 1.618. The golden section is just one of many proportional relationships that can be used as the basis for analysis of salient design-theoretic features within CAD models of built form. Proportional relationships in turn are just one category of analytical criteria that are referred to in work on formal design theory. Clark and Pause (op.cit.), for example, developed a framework for analysis which includes the following features: structure, natural light, massing, the relationship of plan to section, symmetry and balance, the relationship of circulation to use of the building, the relationship between repetitive and unique elements, the relationships between units and wholes, geometry, determining additive and subtractive components of a scheme, hierarchical organisation, and parti diagrams. Whichever analytical criterion might be the focus of attention, the superimposition of diagrammatic analyses upon CAD-generated models can support the extraction of salient relationships in a design scheme. Within a CAD environment, this superimposition can be carried out either in plan, section, or as suggested in **figure 9.2**, in relation to complete 3-D models.

Case Study: Villa Savoye at Poissy, Le Corbusier

The application of the analytical criterion of golden section proportion to plans and sections of the Villa Savoye gives rise to the schematic diagrams in **figures 9.4** and **9.5** respectively. Such diagrams are potentially more meaningful than the illustrations of finished buildings frequently found in books on architectural history which usually leave students guessing as to the design process that went into them. In this case, it appears to be the case that the golden section is a strong feature of the scheme. Of course it would have been possible to discover this feature using manual drawing techniques with rulers and compasses, but when CAD functionality allows users to construct arcs and to find geometric features such as midpoints with comparative ease, then it would be remiss of CAD users not to take advantage of it.

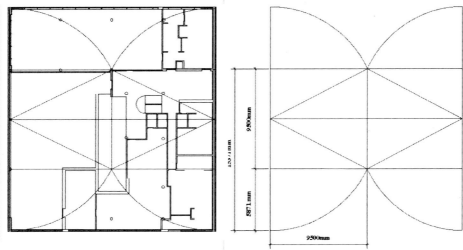

Figure 9.4: golden section in plan analysis of Le Corbusier's Villa Savoye.

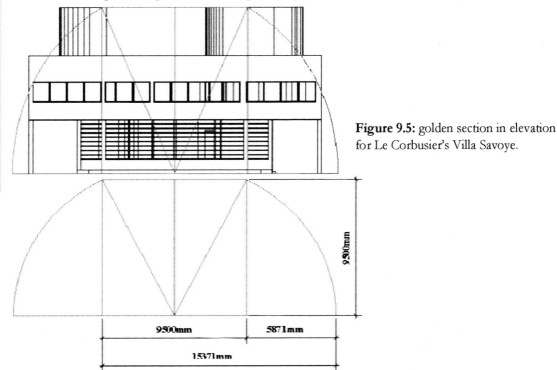

Figure 9.5: golden section in elevation for Le Corbusier's Villa Savoye.

The Modulor

The discovery of the golden section relationship in the Villa Savoye is not entirely surprising given that Le Corbusier himself developed a proportioning system based on the Fibonacci series which he called Le Modulor. Le Modulor consists of two interrelated geometric series, the red and the blue. The red is the primary series. The initial value of the red series is 1830mm. The ratio by which each member increases is 1.618, and the series also works backwards. A member of the blue series is twice as big as the corresponding red as indicated in **figure 9.6**. A red series member is the arithmetic mean of the two blues on either side. Each blue is the harmonic mean of the reds on either side.

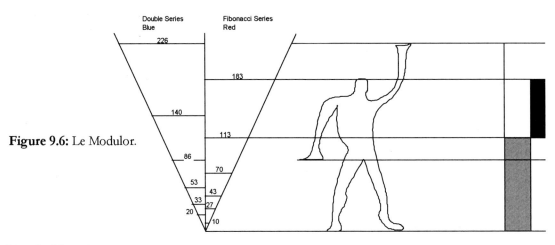

Figure 9.6: Le Modulor.

The Plastic Number

Hans van der Laan (van der Laan, 1983) developed a proportional system based upon the following series:

$$1, 1, 1, 2, 2, 3, 4, 5, 7, 9, 12, 16, 21, ...$$

In any sequence of four terms, the fourth is the sum of the first two. As terms increase, the ratio between successive terms approaches 1.325. This is called the *plastic number*. In contrast to the golden section as used by architects such as Le Corbusier primarily in plan, section, and elevation, van der Laan claimed that the plastic number has 3-dimensional qualities which manifest themselves the strongest when applied to the design of 3-D junctions in which elements from different planes meet in 3-D space. There are only eight terms in the plastic number series (each of which is a rational number), since these are what is perceptually distinguishable.

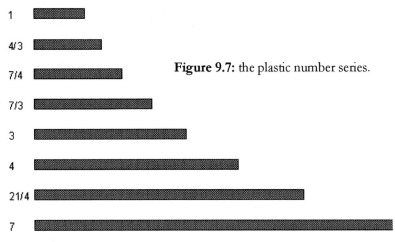

Figure 9.7: the plastic number series.

The use of proportional systems in both analysis and design generation is just one technique concerned with those aspects of design expression that articulate the parts of buildings. Articulation enables designers to relate whole building objects to smaller parts, and ultimately to an elementary part that acts as a unit of size (van der Laan, 1983). Van der Laan refers to architectonic spaces borrowing forms from other building objects such as walls.

Krier (Krier, 1988) describes a range of design operations that need to be controlled by means of proportional systems. He states that it is essential that analogies between key parts need to exist in any building composition, but that compulsive restriction to particular proportional systems is unnecessary. The following models (**figure 9.8**) illustrate key configurational possibilities within commonly encountered proportional systems.

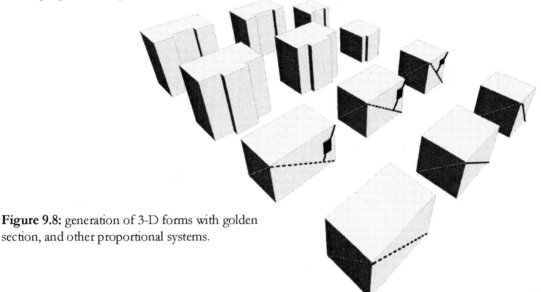

Figure 9.8: generation of 3-D forms with golden section, and other proportional systems.

Moving from front to back, firstly diagonals define the extent of surfaces, and constitute reference markers for further placement of objects. Openings such as doors and windows can be placed with reference to these 3-D construction lines. Additionally, porticos and recesses can be added as masses derived directly from the form of the existing structure. In design generation in which proportional relationships can be expressed, therefore, it appears that there needs to be computational support that constrains placement and scaling *parametrically*. The spaces between built forms are also constrained according to the same principles. Parametric design, and the expression of user-defined constraints upon CAD models, are important aspects of CAD modelling that will be discussed in later chapters.

Both this and previous chapters have attempted to show that design development evolves within analytical contexts that require expression as much as the form of the design itself. Until comparatively recently, the application of CAD to architectural design was only ever considered in terms of the representation of the final form, an activity associated with the post-design stage. Two key ideas upon which this book is based should by now be apparent. Firstly, that the analytical context of a design object will always influence the conceptual ways of thinking about, modelling and presenting this object. Secondly, that computing technology has now progressed to a position in which it becomes feasible for designers to integrate analysis with CAD modelling, thus allowing the effective communication of design ideas in CAD environments at a much earlier stage in the design process.

Part 3: CAD Objects

Chapter 10: 2-D Objects

In most CAD systems, lines are typically defined by endpoints, plus something that happens inbetween them. In architectural practice, architects make use of continuous straight or curved lines of varied thickness, colour, dotted and dashed lines, and blank lines. It is evident, however, that in many cases, particularly in the earlier stages of a design, architects are not very concerned about the exact locations of the endpoints of lines (they tend to sketch). An inherent feature of most CAD systems is that the position of lines with respect to other lines is determined solely by means of endpoints. This is somewhat restrictive in that it forces designers to make a commitment to the exact positioning of graphical elements, often before the locations of these elements has been decided within the design scheme. If the reader thinks that this is a somewhat minor criticism of current CAD software, then he should read the seminal work on sketching written by Paul Klee for his students at the Bauhaus (Klee, 1925) in which it is made abundantly clear that elements as apparently straightforward as lines exist within analytical contexts that determine how they should be interpreted. The four main contexts that Klee develops are proportionate line and structure, dimension and balance, gravitational curves, and kinetic and chromatic energy. Although the purpose of this part of the book is to work with the objects that are provided within the kind of CAD systems that most students and designers have access to, there should be no reason to limit the rich and varied range of expressions that designers like to use in their work. It should emerge later in the book, in the context of some of the more advanced case studies, such as in Frank Gehry's Guggenheim Museum scheme in Bilbao (chapter 28), that CAD environments are now emerging in which a greater degree of expression is possible.

Working within the limitations of desktop CAD systems, therefore, point location is the critical beginning of any drawing operation. The problem is how to get points to be where you intend them to be. There are essentially two responses to this question. The first comes from architectural practice, and the second is the one actually used by the majority of CAD systems. In architectural practice, one first draws straight lines of any length anywhere on the drawing surface and then positions further points and lines by specifying geometric constructs and distance values. The most commonly used constructs are perpendicular and parallel, facilitated by the conventional use of T-squares and set-squares. Drawings produced in this way are influenced by the chosen geometric constructs, but are dimensionally infinitely variable.

Of greater importance in architectural sketching, therefore, is to be able to express relationships such as *two lines are parallel and displaced by a certain amount*, or *two lines are orthogonal to each other* for example, without worrying about particular co-ordinate locations. Such general relationships can of course be expressed in most CAD systems *at the time of drawing* particular lines with particular endpoint co-ordinate values. However, once lines have been drawn, the reader should bear in mind that it is very difficult to maintain the *consistency* of an intended relationship should the properties of a line change. Typically, the only way to do this in conventional systems is to re-describe (by the deletion of existing lines and by the addition of new ones) that part of the drawing in which the relationship occurs. Ideally, one would prefer a CAD system to maintain such consistency, i.e. if the drawing changes, the relationship should still be valid. This disparity between the ways in which designers would like to create graphical expressions on the one hand, and the types of objects and operations that CAD systems actually provide on the other, has been the subject of much research (Szalapaj, 1988; Bijl, 1988), but is beyond the scope of this particular chapter. It is, however, an issue that doesn't go away easily, and one that will reappear in some of the later chapters where complex design relationships need to be maintained in large-scale design projects.

Lines

The basic 2-D object in any CAD system is the line. The straight line is used most frequently, and therefore has the widest range of attributes such as thickness, style, colour, and end markers such as arrowheads. Since the majority of drawings produced in architectural practice are still 2-D, many practices have developed strong conventions concerning the ways in which lines of different styles and colours are associated with different layers, which in turn are associated with different kinds of architectural objects such as services, structural elements, etc. A major issue in the construction industry is to attempt to standardise the line types used in order to improve communication of information between design specialists.

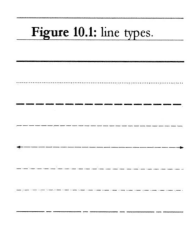

Figure 10.1: line types.

A range of 2-D graphical objects composed out of lines are usually provided within CAD environments. These include rectangles, polygons, circles, arcs, and curves such as Bezier and spline. Drawing a Bezier curve involves clicking on control points not actually on the curve, but which define the intersection point of two tangent lines to the curve. With splines, the control points themselves sit on the curves. Ellipses, hyperbolas and parabolas are special types of curves known as *conic sections* since they are derived from planes cutting cones in 3-D. These will be investigated in more detail in the following chapter. Circles, ellipses, hyperbolas, parabolas, Bezier curves, B-spline curves can all be represented very efficiently in CAD environments by means of NURBS (Non-Uniform Rational B-Spline) curves.

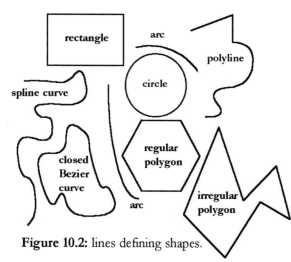

Figure 10.2: lines defining shapes.

The drawing opposite shows a typical eaves detail constructed primarily out of lines and hatched, rectangular areas, which indicate materials such as the brickwork, for example. Hatching is particularly useful for drafting such details even though many CAD systems now offer more sophisticated shading patterns. The reason for this is that since hatch patterns are basically just lines, this makes it easier to transfer drawings into other CAD software using standard exchange formats such as DXF and DWG. Bit-mapped shading instead of hatching will only transfer correctly if the different systems have the same shading libraries.

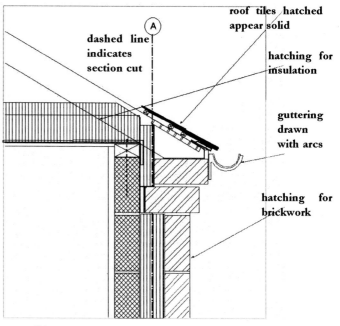

Figure 10.3: CAD detail with hatching.

Grids

Grids are used to predefine the parts of a drawing surface that offer candidate locations for points in a drawing. Drawing then consists of planting points on selected grid locations and linking points with lines that are not necessarily on the grid. Grids represent some logical ordering of dimensions that may correspond to the physical properties of objects that constitute a building, such as a structural system or a co-ordinated component system. Grids may also come about as a consequence of properties of the drawing surface itself, as in the case of computer graphics displays with associated pointing operations. Drawings produced by means of a grid are influenced by the dimensional system of any given grid.

The virtue of a grid, for the person doing the drawing, is that the dimensional system governing the possible location of points is visible and, by locking a point on to a grid, the point can be positioned exactly. For this virtue to be effective, a grid pattern needs to be regular and, for visual clarity, the interval between grid points or lines as seen on the drawing surface needs to be as coarse as the intended drawing will permit.

There is a distinction between the physical presence of a grid on a drawing surface and the real-world dimensions which the grid represents, as in scaled drawings. The physical grid interval needs to be as large as possible, whereas the real-world dimension of the interval needs to be small enough to provide the dimensional variability appropriate to the building objects represented in a drawing. This tension results in the need to change the grid interval value as the scale of a drawing is changed. As the scale is increased, finer detail becomes visible requiring a smaller grid interval.

As for grid regularity and size of interval, typically square grids with uniform intervals of 300mm and 100mm are used for house design. Irregular grids are of course possible, but they would bias the possible arrangement of lines in a drawing. Finer intervals lose clarity at the scales at which general plan layouts of houses are normally drawn (1:100 and 1:50).

Some building construction systems need regular rhythms of dimensions which can be abstracted and represented as grids. These produce tartan grids and, less commonly, non-orthogonal grids.

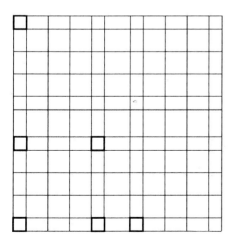

Figure 10.4: tartan grid.

Figure 10.5: non-orthogonal grid.

When different interests are represented in a drawing, such as a structural system overlaid on a general plan layout, different grid patterns can be overlaid on each other. For example, a tartan grid can overlay a square grid, where the tartan may be a subset of the square grid.

A drawing can represent a building that has parts with varied structure or geometry that call for different grids. This can be seen in the final case study of this book, the Guggenheim Museum by Frank Gehry (see pages 190–204). In this case there are discontinuous grids patterns or grid orientation over the surface of a single drawing.

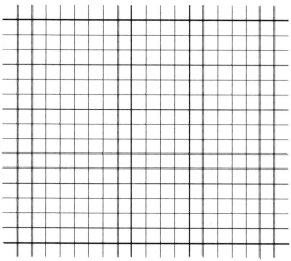

Figure 10.6: superimposed grids.

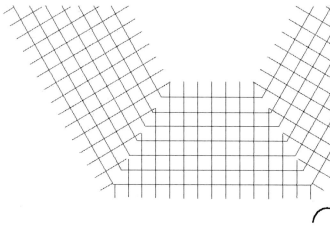

Figure 10.7: discontinuous grids.

In the Beaux Arts approach to architectural composition, great emphasis was always placed upon studies of the plan, since it was viewed that the plan of a building established two of the three dimensions in space, and implied the third, thus lending itself to thinking in three dimensions (Curtis, 1926). It was viewed that every organic plan arrangement could be broken down into a few elementary types of compositions. The combinations of these compositions formed the *parti* of the building. The parti effectively constitutes a grid upon which building elements can then be placed. The classification of the possible types of composition was derived from the combinations of axes that enclose space, as shown.

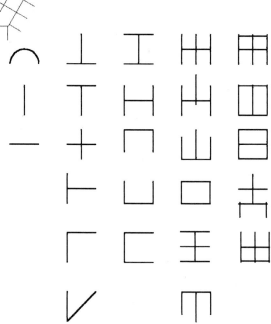

Figure 10.8: parti diagrams.

2-D Symbols

If a complex 2-D CAD object (i.e. not a primitive object such as a line or rectangle, for example) is used repeatedly in a drawing, then a more efficient way of working is to create a *symbol* out of this complex object, rather than just copying and pasting the same element all the time. Detailed elements such as furniture, for example, are typical symbols. A major advantage of using symbols is that when modifications are made to a symbol, all *instances* of that symbol in the drawing file correspondingly change. If only copies of the original object had been used, then each copy would need to be edited separately in order to achieve the same changes. Most CAD systems have a special interface for editing existing symbols or creating new ones out of graphic elements. Once symbols are to be inserted into a drawing, they will obviously need to be positioned correctly by moving and rotating them accordingly. If the CAD system is an *object-based* or *hybrid* system, then inserting a window symbol into a wall, for example, will automatically create an opening for the window to fit into. If the CAD system is purely *geometric*, then the opening will need to be created first by the user.

window type-1 symbol   **window type-2 symbol**

door, sink, and toilet symbols

Figure 10.9: use of symbols in 2-D CAD drawing.

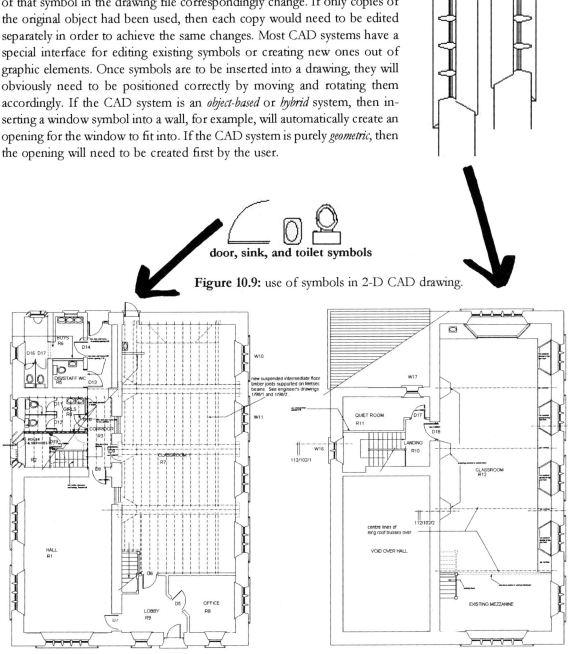

Dimensions

Many CAD generated drawings are still 2-D drawings in which heavy use has been made of the abilities of CAD systems to accurately calculate the *dimensions* of lines, distances between points, and angle values, for example. The resultant numerical values, together with the lines that indicate their extent, themselves then become graphical objects which can be moved, scaled, etc. Much attention has been paid to the different possible ways of setting out dimensions on drawings. Dimension values can be located above or on dimension lines, for example. The dimension lines themselves lie between *witness lines*, which indicate the start and end locations of the dimension. The dimensioning of a construction drawing for a school extension is shown below. In a drawing of this nature, much use has also been made of *arrowed lines*, which point to objects in order to label them in some way. It is also common to use *leader lines*, consisting of two segments for this purpose. Whilst working on such a drawing therefore, particularly if the scheme is of a complex nature, it may be necessary to separate the dimensions from the lines that represent building elements, by means of *layers*.

Figure 10.10: dimension line types.

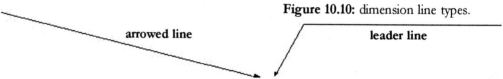

Dimensioned drawings typically exist as part of a set of drawings linked by means of sections taken through them and indicated by means of labelled *section lines*.

Figure 10.11: labelled section lines.

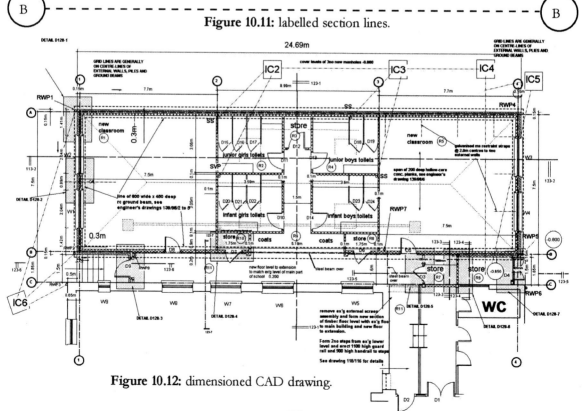

Figure 10.12: dimensioned CAD drawing.

Chapter 11: 3-D Objects

Planes

Mathematically, a plane is defined in terms of three non-collinear points, assuming that the plane so defined is flat and has no boundaries. In CAD practice, planes as 3-D objects always have some thickness, however minimal this might be, and are also bounded objects. To construct such a plane, therefore, involves firstly generating a 2-D form such as a rectangle or polygon, and then *extruding* this form by some amount. The 2-D form will give the plane its shape, and the extrusion its thickness.

The lines that represent the vertical edges of a building are *perpendicular* to the ground plane. A line and a plane are perpendicular if they intersect and the line is perpendicular to every line in the plane that passes through the point of intersection.

Typically, the walls of buildings are vertical and lie in parallel planes as shown below. Floors and walls usually lie in *intersecting* planes that are perpendicular to each other. Any two planes are perpendicular if one of the planes contains a line that is perpendicular to the other plane. If lines and planes intersect without being perpendicular, then they are usually referred to as *oblique*.

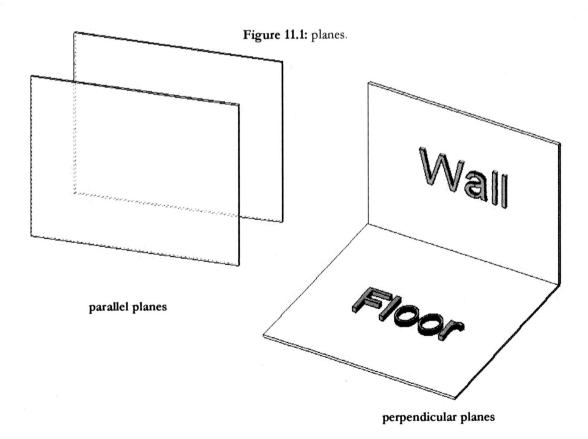

Figure 11.1: planes.

parallel planes

perpendicular planes

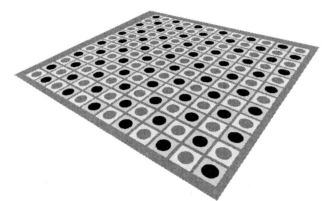

Figure 11.2: plane in perspective view.

Just as lines in 2-D have properties of thickness, style, and colour, so too can planes be rendered or textured in various ways. When viewed in perspective projection, an immediate impression of depth is created. It should be noted that the computer screen itself effectively represents a viewing plane onto a 3-D model. Most CAD systems usually offer a fixed number of predetermined positions of this viewing plane such as *front, back, left, right, top, bottom, left isometric, right isometric, left rear isometric, right rear isometric.*

Many CAD models can be modelled essentially out of planar elements such as extruded rectangular forms, and objects such as wall elements which are essentially vertical planes. Floors and flat roofs are modelled out of horizontal planar elements. The modelling of modern architecture lends itself to this approach. The following images are isometric views of just such a model of the well-known Fallingwater house by Frank Lloyd Wright.

Figure 11.3: two isometric views of Fallingwater.

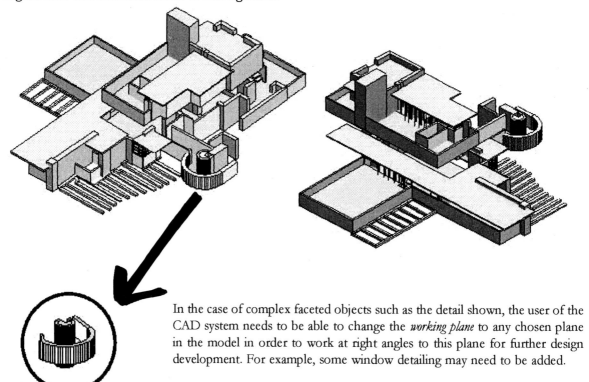

In the case of complex faceted objects such as the detail shown, the user of the CAD system needs to be able to change the *working plane* to any chosen plane in the model in order to work at right angles to this plane for further design development. For example, some window detailing may need to be added.

Volumes

In most CAD systems, there are typically a range of predefined 3-D volumes which can be generated merely by specifying particular parameters such as length, width, height, radius, etc. It is usually possible to model these objects directly in 3-D without typing in actual values, but by using the mouse to *stretch* the objects out to the required dimensions.

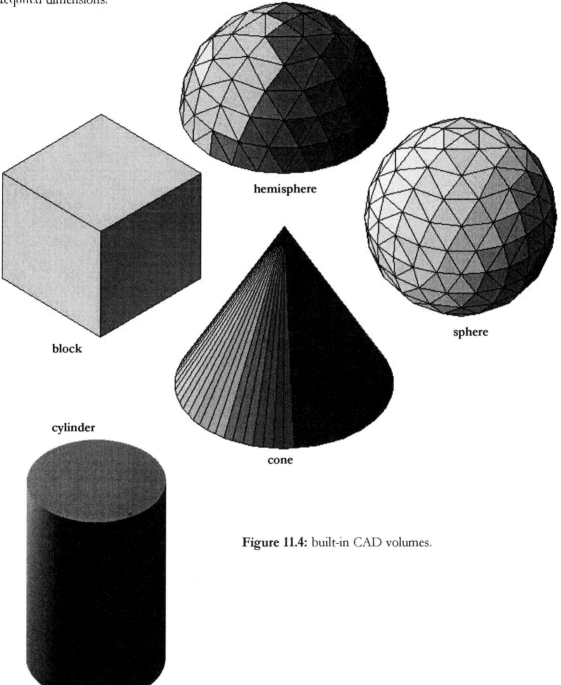

Figure 11.4: built-in CAD volumes.

Quadric Surfaces from Conic Sections

The surfaces described in this section are only a subset of all possible surfaces, but they are of great interest mathematically, geometrically, and, more importantly, as will be seen from the case study in chapter 20, architecturally. A conic section is the 2-D shape that emerges when a plane cuts a cone at various angles. If any of these shapes is then swept around an axis, a 3-D surface of revolution is generated. These 3-D objects include spheres, ellipsoids, hyperboloids, and paraboloids. Although cones and spheres are usually available in most CAD systems as graphical primitives, the others, often, are not. The user therefore needs to generate them by applying the graphical operations described in the next chapter to the available graphical primitives. In those CAD systems in which these surface objects are directly available, they are all probably represented as NURBS (Non-Uniform Rational B-Splines) surfaces. A NURBS surface is analogous to a NURBS curve in that it can be controlled by means of control points, and hence easily manipulated. For **figures 11.5 to 11.8**, numbered lists of CAD operations needed to generate particular forms are given in the lower right-hand corner of the page. Key steps have been illustrated and numbered. The remainder have been left as an exercise for the reader.

Sphere

When a cone is sliced parallel to the base, the intersection forms a circle. When the circle is swept about an axis, the resulting surface is a sphere.

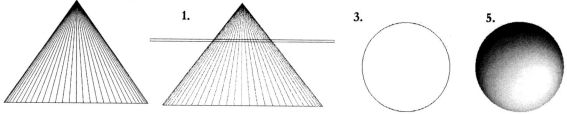

Figure 11.5: generating a sphere from a conic section.

Ellipsoid

When a cone is cut at an angle to the base which is less than the slope of the edge of the cone, the cut forms an ellipse. When this ellipse is swept about an axis, an ellipsoid is formed.

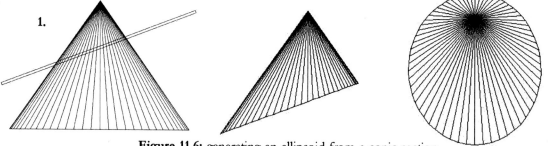

Figure 11.6: generating an ellipsoid from a conic section.

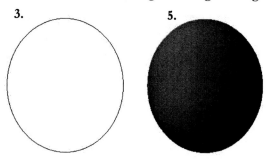

1. **Position cutting plane in elevation**

2. **Position cutting plane in plan**

3. **Circle or ellipse obtained from cut**

4. **Sweep circle or ellipse**

5. **Sphere or ellipsoid formed by sweeping**

Hyperboloid

When a cone is sliced perpendicular to the base of a cone, the profile of the cut section forms a hyperbola. When the hyperbola is swept about an axis, the resulting surface is a hyperboloid.

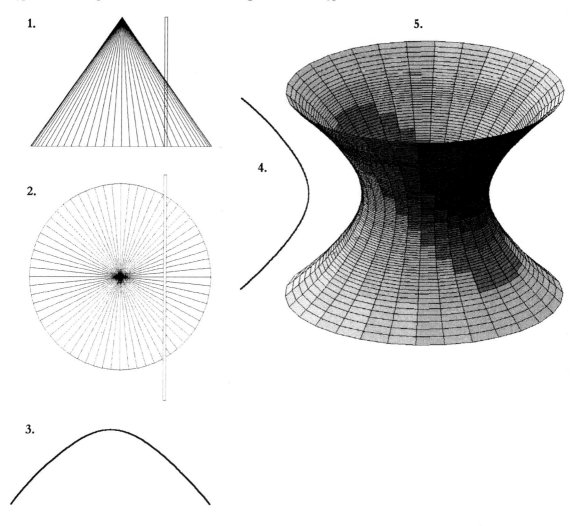

Figure 11.7: generating a hyperboloid from a conic section.

1. Position cutting plane in elevation

2. Position cutting plane in plan

3. Hyperbolic curve obtained from cut

4. Hyperbolic curve rotated 90°

5. Hyperboloid obtained by sweeping

Paraboloid

When a cone is sliced parallel to its side, the profile of the cut section forms a parabola. When the parabola is swept about an axis, the resulting surface is a paraboloid. Again, just as with the hyperboloid, there is some effort involved in generating this CAD object from other, existing objects such as the cone. This also involves the application of some of the operations described in more detail in the following chapter, such as rotate and sweep.

5.

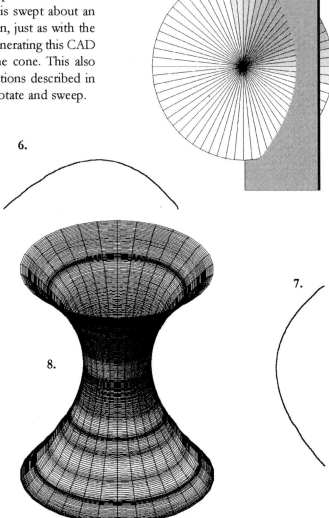

6.

1.

2.

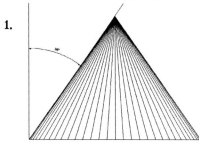

3.

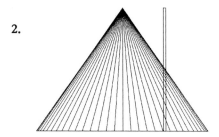

8.

7.

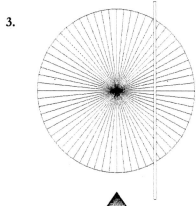

4.

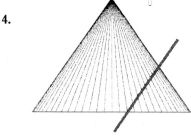

Figure 11.8: generating a paraboloid from a conic section.

1. Measure slope of cone

2. Position cutting plane in elevation

3. Position cutting plane in plan

4. Rotate cutting plane parallel to cone

5. Top view of cutting plane and cone

6. Parabolic curve obtained from cut

7. Parabolic curve rotated 90°

8. Paraboloid obtained by sweeping

3-D Symbols

The principle in the use of 3-D symbols is similar to that of 2-D symbols. Users can construct composite 3-D objects such as furniture, for example, and then define those complex objects that will be used frequently in different parts of a CAD model to be 3-D symbols. Again, if any changes are made to the geometric form of a 3-D symbol, all *instances* of that symbol in the drawing file correspondingly change. As with 2-D symbols, revisions to 3-D objects can be dramatically reduced by using symbols, since one revision will affect all symbols of the same type within the same CAD model. Another practical advantage of using symbols is that this effectively reduces the memory size of CAD models, since the only information that needs to be stored in memory is the geometric description of just one symbol, together with the origin point locations for each symbol instance. As CAD users become more proficient in the use of symbols, they will realise that all kinds of useful additional non-graphical information, e.g. manufacturer, cost, size, etc. can be associated with a symbol's description. The issue of integrating non-graphical with graphical information is extremely important in CAD work, and in large-scale construction projects in which a multitude of non-graphical details need to be passed on to contractors (see chapter 27).

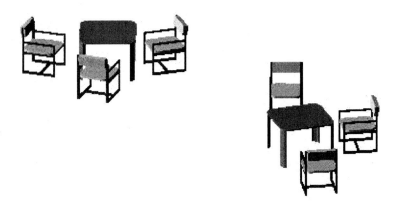

Figure 11.9: repetitive objects instantiated using 3-D symbols.

Part 4: CAD Operations

Chapter 12: Geometric Transformations

The following transformations are all illustrated with reference to 3-D CAD objects, but they are equally applicable to 2-D CAD objects.

Move

The move transformation will move a selected object by a specific distance. A positive or negative value will signify the direction of movement. Positive usually means moving an object to the right along the x-axis, upwards along the y-axis, or counter-clockwise in a polar co-ordinate system. Negative values will have the opposite effect. This transformation will change the position of an object but leave its orientation unchanged.

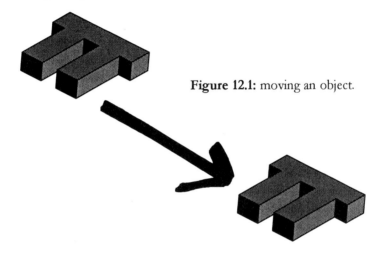

Figure 12.1: moving an object.

Rotate

A CAD object can be rotated by a chosen angle value. With reference to a selected 2-D plane, a positive angle value will typically rotate the object in a counter-clockwise direction, and a negative angle value will rotate the object in a clockwise direction. Rotation preserves the shape of an object, but changes both its position and orientation.

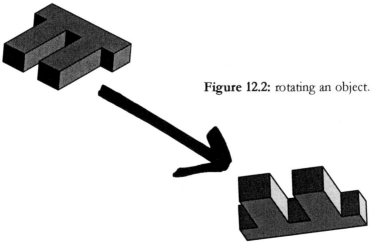

Figure 12.2: rotating an object.

Scale

Typically, any CAD object can be scaled in size relative to its x, y, or z co-ordinate values. If an object needs to be scaled proportionally, then the scale factors should be equal across all co-ordinates. A scaled object will either be bigger or smaller than the initial object, but its orientation will be the same.

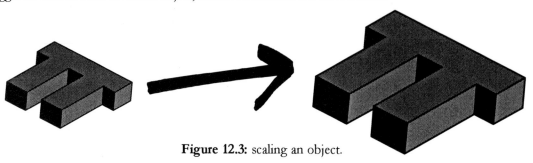

Figure 12.3: scaling an object.

Reflect

A CAD object can be reflected, or mirrored, by indicating an axis about which the reflection takes place. This axis can be a side of the object itself, or offset by a distance. A reflected object is still the same shape as the initial object, but its position and orientation is changed.

Figure 12.4: reflecting an object.

Shear

The shear transformation will maintain an object's *topology*, i.e. number of vertices, edges, and faces as well as their connectivity relationships, but still produce a distortion. Typically, shearing takes place with reference to an axis, and if one of the edges of the object is on this axis, this edge will stay fixed. In other words, shearing is an operation that can potentially control which parts of an object are fixed, and which are movable.

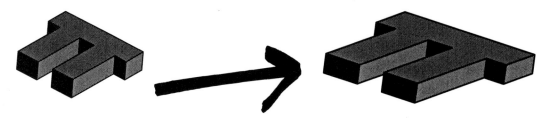

Figure 12.5: shearing an object.

Chapter 13: Topological Transformations

Extrude

In the extrude operation, a 2-D object in plan projection can be extruded to a specified height value. If the 2-D object was drawn in elevation, then the extrusion will determine the depth value. In some CAD systems, this operation is described as *constructing a surface projection* rather than extrusion, since volumetric objects are created by projecting a 2-D surface through 3-D space.

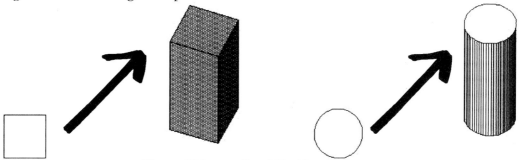

Figure 13.1: extruding 2-D objects.

Extrusion is the simplest and most common way of transforming a 2-D into a 3-D object. It is typically used to create simple block models of urban spaces by scanning in an image of a site plan, tracing around polygonal objects (e.g. the boundaries of houses), and extruding these polygons upwards to give an impression of height.

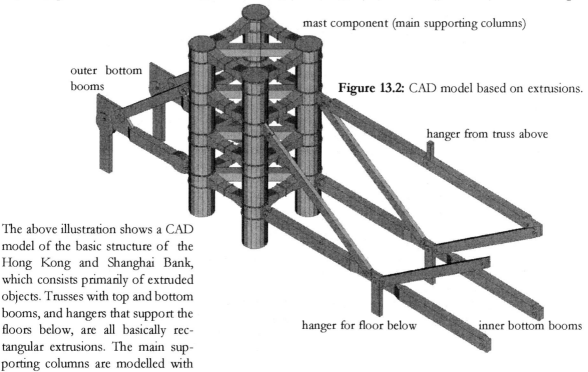

mast component (main supporting columns)

outer bottom booms

Figure 13.2: CAD model based on extrusions.

hanger from truss above

hanger for floor below

inner bottom booms

The above illustration shows a CAD model of the basic structure of the Hong Kong and Shanghai Bank, which consists primarily of extruded objects. Trusses with top and bottom booms, and hangers that support the floors below, are all basically rectangular extrusions. The main supporting columns are modelled with circular extrusions.

Sweep

The sweep operation takes a 2-D object (or several 2-D objects) and converts it to a 3-D object by rotating it around a vertical axis. The sweep operation cannot be used on 3D objects, but it can be used on various selected 2D objects. It does not matter if the initial object is open or closed.

The axis of rotation can usually be precisely positioned in most CAD systems by introducing a locus point either on the object itself, or offset from it. This locus point can then be included as part of the description of the object to be swept prior to invoking the sweep operation. If such a point isn't used, then the origin point of the object is chosen. Very often, the user of the CAD system will not know until after the operation exactly where this origin point is, since it was supplied as part of the description of the object internally by the CAD system when the object was drawn. Typically, the default origin point is in the lower left-hand corner of most objects.

The axis of rotation is always vertical relative to the screen, no matter which view has been selected. Once a 3-D object has been created using the sweep operation, the properties of this newly created object can usually be modified. These will include height, pitch, radius, start angle, sweep angle, and segment angle. The latter determines the number of facets in the swept object. If the segment angle is large, an object will appear more faceted. If the angle is smaller, the object will appear smoother, but the redraw time for the object will increase as there will now be more lines in the object's representation.

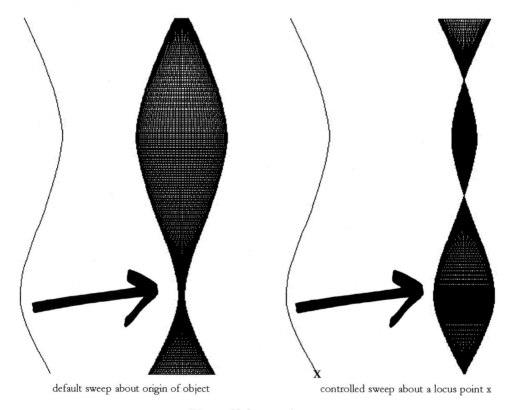

default sweep about origin of object   controlled sweep about a locus point x

Figure 13.3: sweeping a curve.

Loft

Lofting creates a smooth surface by blending between a series of selected shape curves. These curves define the *cross-section* or *profile* of the lofted surface at particular intervals. In the example below, the cross-sections are all roughly circular. Rail curves may be used to position the cross-section curves accurately. Strictly speaking, the rail curves are not part of the lofting operation, but can sometimes be included in order to further control the edges of the surface. Once the cross-section curves have been chosen, the edges of a smooth lofted surface are created automatically by fitting smooth curves through the selected curves.

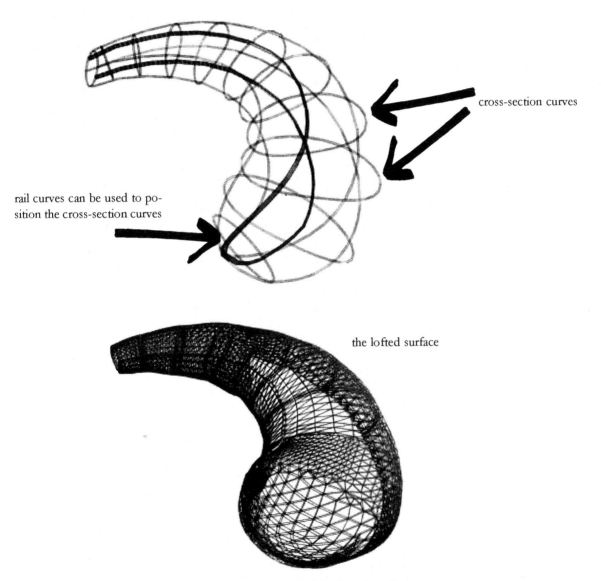

cross-section curves

rail curves can be used to position the cross-section curves

the lofted surface

Figure 13.4: generation of a lofted surface from curves.

Chapter 14: Boolean Operations

Boolean operations are named after George Boole, an English mathematician who described logical operations in terms of mathematical symbols. A Boolean operation typically affects two objects at any one time, and is the basis of the binary systems that underlie most of computing. Boolean operations are absolutely fundamental in CAD, and allow the creation of complex forms and compositions by their successive application to objects that may initially be quite simple. Several of the later case studies illustrate just how important they are in generating form (e.g. chapter 20). Learning how to think in terms of applying successive Boolean operations to generate a particular form is essential for CAD users. The Boolean operations that can be performed between the 2-D objects A and B are as follows:

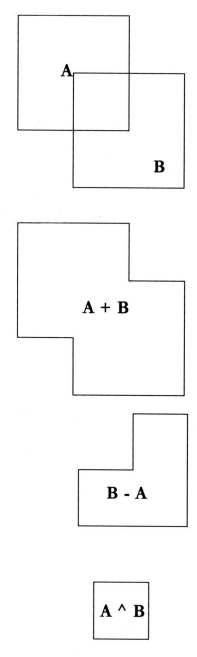

Add (sometimes referred to as Union) joins objects A and B together.

Add combines overlapping objects (polygons) and deletes line segments in the overlapping region. In terms of the CAD system, the first object (polygon) selected is the altered object (polygon) that remains after the operation. The second object (polygon) is deleted.

Subtract subtracts the second selected object (a 2-D polygon in this example) from the first.
- Subtraction (A−B) subtracts object B from A
- Subtraction (B−A) subtracts object A from B (illustrated opposite)

Intersect leaves the difference between objects A and B. Intersection deletes all but the overlapping portions of the two objects (polygons). The first object (polygon) selected is the altered object (polygon) that remains after the operation. The second object (polygon) is deleted.

Figure 14.1: 2-D Boolean operations.

Boolean operations in 3-D work similarly to those in 2-D. The Boolean operations that can be performed between 3-D objects are as shown:

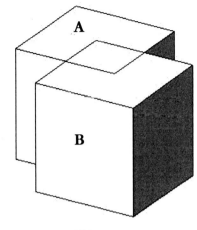

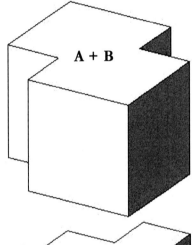

Add

Figure 14.2: 3-D Boolean operations.

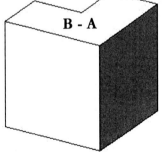

Subtract

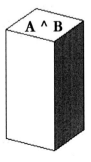

Intersect

Chapter 15: Logical Operations

Grouping

Grouping is an operation that is particularly useful when there are many objects, either 2-D or 3-D, that need to be *grouped* together as if they were one object. This grouped object can then be transformed in various ways, e.g. through movement. Subsequent changes to any member of the group can only be carried out if the group is *un-grouped*, thus allowing individual objects to be selected.

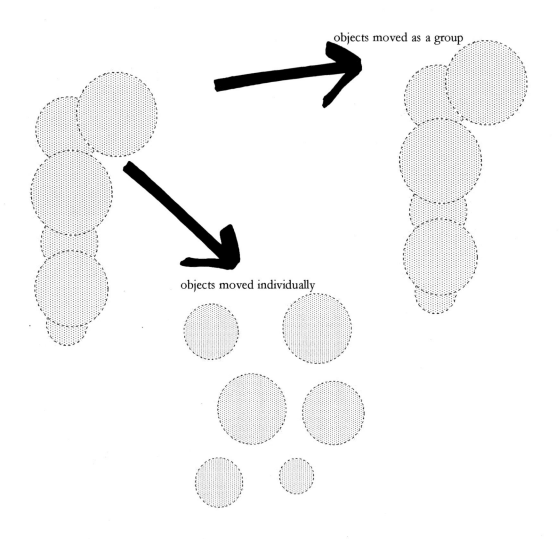

objects moved as a group

objects moved individually

Figure 15.1: grouping 2-D objects.

Typing

Typing is a way of grouping objects according to a user-defined type or category of objects. A *type* is sometimes referred to as a *class* or *kind* of object. Typing allows users to describe a drawing in terms of its parts, so that further things can then be done with these parts.

In the zoning plan layout for a school extension below, the user might need to know the amount of glazing associated with Phase I of this project proposal, either just to view it, or to go on to do something else, such as a costing calculation, for example. Types in CAD systems are often associated with non-graphical information in a database, which makes it possible to carry out analytical calculations such as area, cost, u-value, etc.

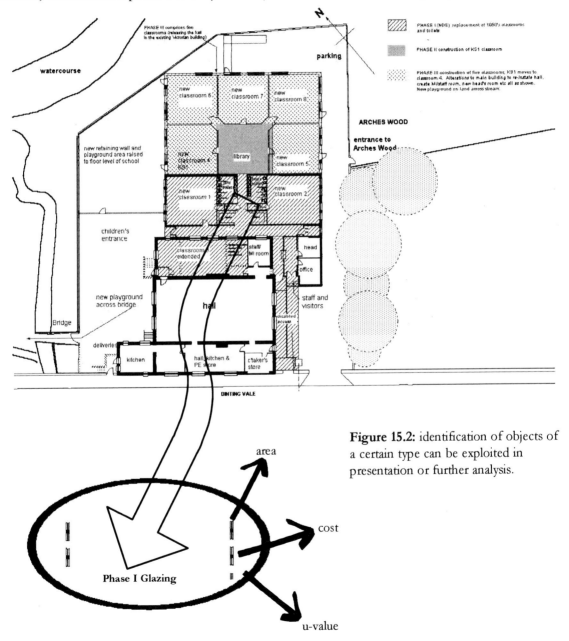

Figure 15.2: identification of objects of a certain type can be exploited in presentation or further analysis.

The exploitation of the typing mechanism within CAD systems offers the greatest potential for users to control the ways in which they use drawing information for other purposes. A simple example would be to count the number of objects of a certain type, and then to use this count value to calculate a total length or area value. Another example would be to associate type names with cells in a spreadsheet to produce scheduling information, for example. One could envisage recording type information in order to track the quantity and location of objects for facilities management purposes. Inventories of building components could potentially be maintained interactively as the drawings were developed.

A common strategy, therefore, for relating objects in a CAD environment is to use some kind of typing in the descriptions of composite CAD objects, and then to define functions expressed in programming languages, based upon these type definitions. In an ideal CAD environment, descriptions of functions or tasks should be as general as possible, and relatively independent from one another. This is analogous to the definition of methods that are specific to particular views of objects in the object-oriented programming paradigm. Ideally, typing should be targeted solely at the kinds of expressions that can be employed in descriptions, without limiting particular instances of expressions. Examples of general types are: names, numbers, logical constants, logical variables, etc. Domain-specific types should preferably be constructed by users and designers. The user declaration of abstract data types, however, may not be a straightforward task for designers with little experience of programming. General typing, together with a basic set of operators that can be applied to types of expressions, inevitably places the onus on the user to know how to employ types and operators for purposes of constructing task descriptions. Computer programming within CAD environments that support typed expressions, therefore, potentially opens up new and different way of investigating design problems. The downside is that designers may also have to become competent programmers too.

Layering

Layering is concerned with the organisation of drawings. Layers (or levels) provide an organising structure for information and objects in a computer drawing. This concept is similar to using several sheets of tracing paper, with specific information on each sheet that can then be printed in various combinations. Any layer can be made invisible to simplify a drawing presentation. This makes the drawing environment flexible. The appearance of a drawing can be controlled by the user through the layering mechanism. This has consequences for the overall drawing process, from the construction to the printing of documents. Appropriate use of layering can also decrease the screen redraw speed if less information is visible.

When a new document is opened, it automatically has just one layer created which will also be the active layer. If there is more than a single layer in a document, an object is automatically placed in the layer that is active when it was drawn. Objects can usually be moved relatively easily from one layer to another by cutting and pasting. Architectural practices often develop strongly coded practices in which different layers correspond to different kinds of drawings (e.g. services, cladding, etc.) in which each layer is associated with a particular colour. Once several layers have been established, the user can then control the visibility of any layer by setting it to be either visible or invisible. An invisible layer is always visible when it is the active layer.

When a user initially sets up a drawing, they need to make conscious decisions about how they want to separate and organise information. This often depends upon the types of project that is being modelled, and the ways in which information on these schemes has to be presented. Commonly, layers are used to represent floors at different heights within multi-storey buildings.

Figure 15.3: layering.

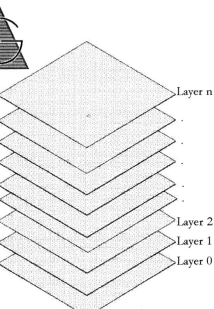

Part 5: The Development of Architectural Form from CAD Objects

Introduction

The purpose of this and the following four chapters is to show how the CAD objects introduced in Part 3, in conjunction with the CAD operations described in Part 4, can be used in a fairly straightforward manner, to generate a wide range of structures commonly used by architects and engineers. Although this part is not intended to be a guide to structures, and aims only to illustrate how some commonly used architectural forms might be modelled within CAD environments, it should show how a wide range of architectural forms can be generated in terms of a relatively small set of CAD operations. In keeping with the theme of this book, the reader should be aware that the design intention, which in this case is structural, should be borne in mind as CAD models are developed. In the case of structures, this will manifest itself in terms of maintaining relationships between thicknesses of elements and spanning dimensions, for example. For more detailed structural information, the reader should look at the excellent books *Surface Structures in Building* by Fred Angerer (Angerer, 1961), and *Buildings for Industry, Volume One: Plans, Structures and Details* by Walter Henn (Henn, 1961), as well as the web-based *An Ideabook for Designers* (Ketchum and Ketchum, 1997). No claim is made for completeness, therefore, regarding the structures chosen, since they are for illustrative purposes only. Only the essential structural features are shown in the CAD-generated images. Details such as openings and cladding elements have been omitted. Chapter 20 is a little different in that, as well as working with more complex CAD objects such as hyperboloids and paraboloids, it attempts to connect basic CAD modelling techniques with the description of a contemporary case study, namely, the fascinating remodelling of the nave of Gaudi's Sagrada Familia Church. This theme of connection with the actual use of CAD in practice will be continued in the remainder of the book.

It seems appropriate to begin the examples of shapes and forms with the folded plate because it is the simplest of shell structures. The main feature of a folded plate is that it is formed from plane surfaces, and these are comparatively easy to model within CAD environments. In many of the following examples, as in the illustrations showing the generation of quadric surfaces in chapter 11, numbered lists of the CAD operations needed to generate particular forms are provided. Some (but not all) of these steps are also illustrated and numbered.

Chapter 16: Folded Plate Structures

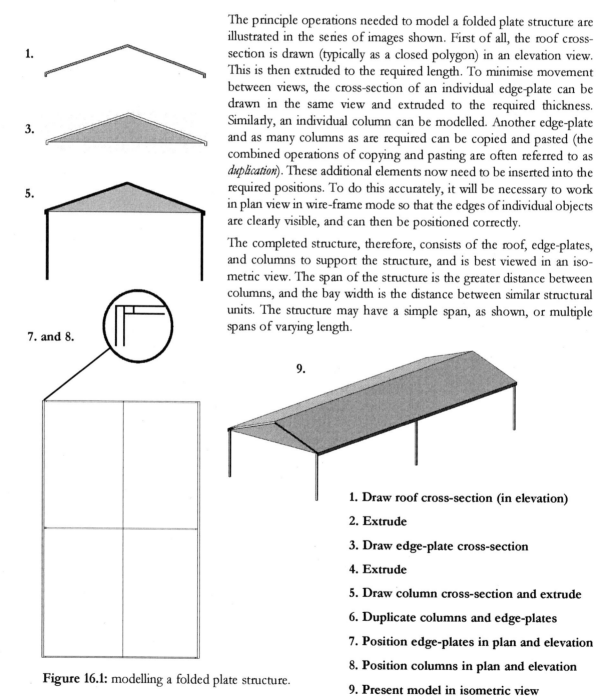

The principle operations needed to model a folded plate structure are illustrated in the series of images shown. First of all, the roof cross-section is drawn (typically as a closed polygon) in an elevation view. This is then extruded to the required length. To minimise movement between views, the cross-section of an individual edge-plate can be drawn in the same view and extruded to the required thickness. Similarly, an individual column can be modelled. Another edge-plate and as many columns as are required can be copied and pasted (the combined operations of copying and pasting are often referred to as *duplication*). These additional elements now need to be inserted into the required positions. To do this accurately, it will be necessary to work in plan view in wire-frame mode so that the edges of individual objects are clearly visible, and can then be positioned correctly.

The completed structure, therefore, consists of the roof, edge-plates, and columns to support the structure, and is best viewed in an isometric view. The span of the structure is the greater distance between columns, and the bay width is the distance between similar structural units. The structure may have a simple span, as shown, or multiple spans of varying length.

Figure 16.1: modelling a folded plate structure.

1. Draw roof cross-section (in elevation)

2. Extrude

3. Draw edge-plate cross-section

4. Extrude

5. Draw column cross-section and extrude

6. Duplicate columns and edge-plates

7. Position edge-plates in plan and elevation

8. Position columns in plan and elevation

9. Present model in isometric view

Exactly the same CAD principles and sequences of CAD operations as in the previous example can be applied to each of the following forms:

Three Segment Folded Plate
This is a folded plate structure with three segments for each barrel.

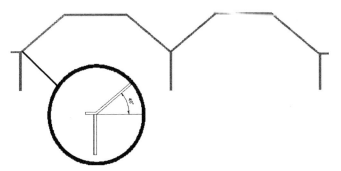

Figure 16.2: modelling using angle constraints.

When drawing the roof cross-section, it may be necessary to *constrain* the angle at which the roof is drawn. Angle constraints are commonly supported in CAD environments by allowing users to specify the angles that they require. Most CAD systems recognise when elements are being placed either horizontally or vertically, and allow users to lock on to these orientations by default.

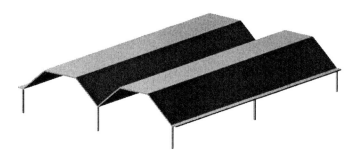

Z-Shell

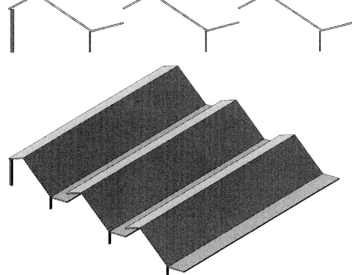

Each of the roof units has one large sloping plate and two edge plates arranged with space between the units for window openings.

1. **Draw roof cross-section (in elevation)**

2. **Extrude**

3. **Draw column cross-section**

4. **Extrude**

5. **Position columns in plan and elevation**

6. **Present in isometric view**

Figure 16.3: modelling a Z shell structure.

Walled Shell

In this structure, gable walls meet and support roof plates, avoiding the use of columns. Drawing the gable walls in elevation and then extruding is the easiest approach. Presentations using exploded views are useful in this case, showing that a structural unit is an empty box rather than a solid volume.

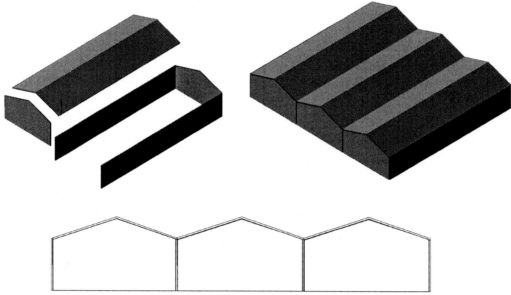

Figure 16.4: presentation of a walled shell with exploded views.

Canopy

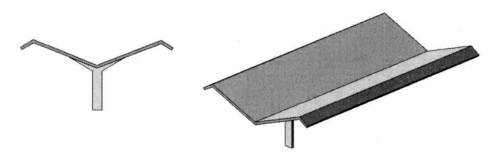

Figure 16.5: modelling a canopy structure.

The roof canopy shown above has four parts, and works structurally because of torsional resistance between the two cantilevered parts, echoing the same structural principle as the case study in chapter 3. The sequence of CAD operations listed here will generate both the canopy and the walled shell form.

1. Draw roof cross-section (in elevation)

2. Extrude

3. Draw wall/column cross-section

4. Extrude

5. Position wall/column

6. Duplicate and place multiple elements

7. Present in isometric view

Tapered Folded Plates

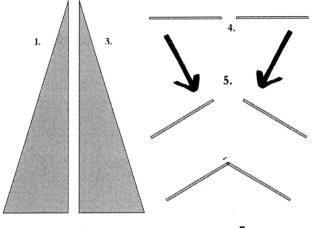

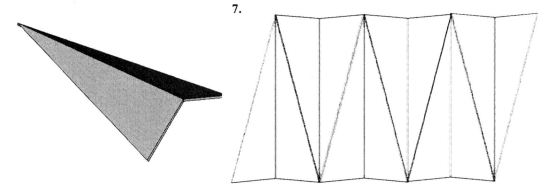

Folded plate structures can be constructed out of tapered elements, and one of many possible combinations is shown here. The tapers are themselves formed from triangular elements in this case. An exercise left for the reader here is to generate a CAD model in which all the smaller depths are situated at the same end, so that the entire structure forms a circular ring.

Figure 16.6: modelling tapering structures.

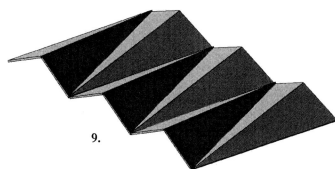

1. Draw triangular element (in plan)

2. Extrude

3. Copy and reflect this extruded element

4. Present in elevation view

5. Rotate each element about inside edge

6. Move and group elements together

7. Duplicate and rotate composite elements

8. Elevation view (wire-frame and rendered)

9. Rendered isometric view

Folded Plate Truss

A *folded plate truss* is a space structure with a complex structural action. There are horizontal ties across the width only at the ends of the building, and the structure acts as an edge supported shell. The thrusts from the triangular crossed arches are carried lengthwise to the ends. The top chord of the inclined truss is formed by the ridge member. The bottom chords are the ties at the base of the side gables and the diagonals are formed by the sloping valleys at the intersection of the gables and the triangular plates.

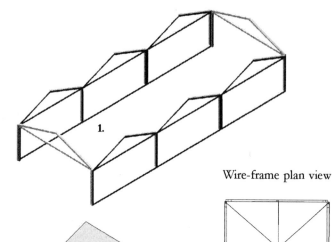

Wire-frame plan view

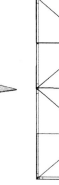

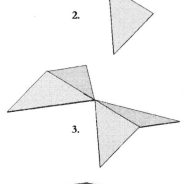

End elevation

End roof plates

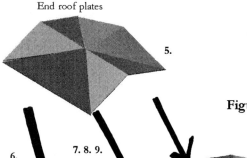

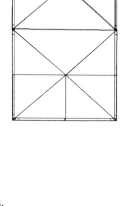

Figure 16.7: modelling truss structures.

1. **Construct frame from simple extrusions**

2. **Model triangular plate, copy and reflect**

3. **Reflect about ridge**

4. **Model gable end-plates**

5. **Model triangular plate in gap**

6. **Duplicate end roof plates and reflect**

7. **Duplicate end roof plates**

8. **Replace gable end with triangular plate**

9. **Insert middle roof section**

Chapter 17: Barrel Vaults

Barrel vaults are well suited to covering rectangular areas, since structurally the arch form reduces stresses and thicknesses in the transverse direction. The curve of the cross-section of a barrel is usually a semicircle. Other curved sections can be used such as an ellipse, a cycloid, or a sector of a circle as shown below. Strictly speaking, barrel *shells* span between end-plates, and barrel *vaults* are supported along their longitudinal edges.

The structure modelled in **figure 17.2** is a single barrel vault with edge beams. The shell projects beyond the edge-plates showing the shape of the shell. Structurally, the edge-plates could be replaced by portal frames or braced formwork, allowing more light into the structure, and would be modelled accordingly.

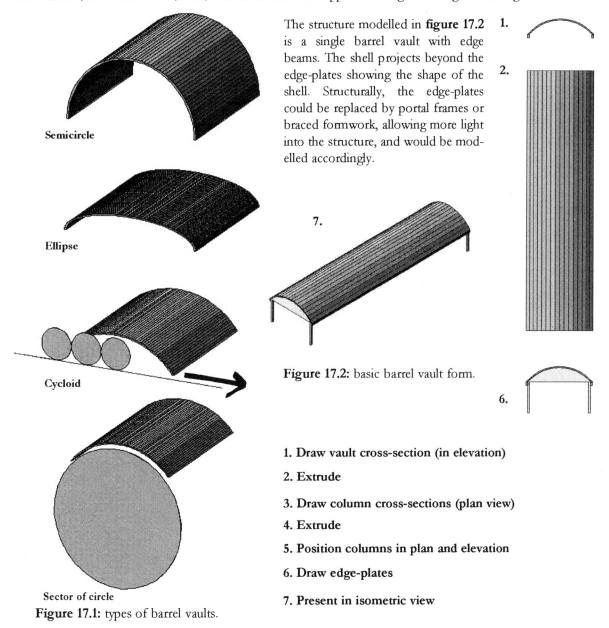

Semicircle

Ellipse

Cycloid

Sector of circle

Figure 17.1: types of barrel vaults.

1.

2.

7.

Figure 17.2: basic barrel vault form.

6.

1. **Draw vault cross-section (in elevation)**

2. **Extrude**

3. **Draw column cross-sections (plan view)**

4. **Extrude**

5. **Position columns in plan and elevation**

6. **Draw edge-plates**

7. **Present in isometric view**

Multiple Barrels

If more than one barrel is placed side by side, the structure is a multiple barrel structure and if more than one span, it is called a multiple span structure. The structure below shows a multiple barrel vault with edge beams and stiffeners above the roof.

Shells without Edge Beams

For barrel vaults with unstiffened edges, an elliptical cross-section is superior to a circular section, as the greater curvature of the ellipse makes the shell stiffer at the lower edge. A semicircular shell will be more rigid than one with only a sector of a circle.

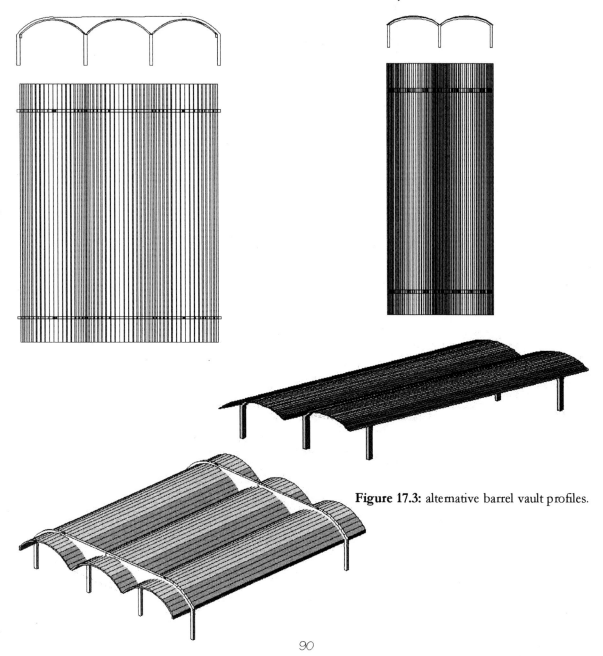

Figure 17.3: alternative barrel vault profiles.

Figure 17.4: isometric view of barrel vault form used in Sardis Roman Baths, Max Fordham & Partners (see chapter 6).

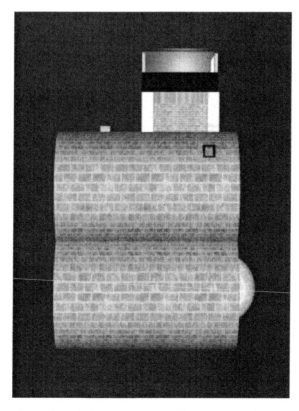

Figure 17.5: top view of barrel vault form used in Sardis Roman Baths, Max Fordham & Partners (see chapter 6).

The modelling of the following two types of barrel shells are left as exercises for the reader.

North Light Shell

A north light shell can be thought of as an inclined cylindrical shell and usually covers several bays. Each shell is supported on the following one except the last which rests on the end wall.

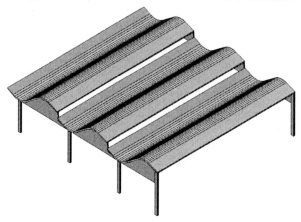

Figure 17.6: CAD model of north light shell structure.

Corrugated Shell

Barrel shells in the form of corrugations have the same area at the top and bottom of the shells, and are suitable for continuous structures where, in the case of concrete shells, for example, a maximum area is needed at the bottom of the shell at the support. Instead of alternative concave and convex circles of the same radius, the curves may be alternate circles of long and short radius. There are innumerable combinations of curves, or curves and folded plates to serve particular aesthetic or structural functions.

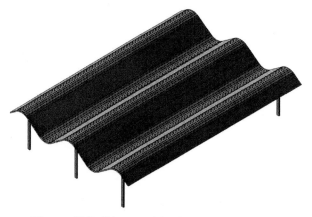

Figure 17.7: CAD model of corrugated shell structure.

Chapter 18: Domes

Domes are ever popular architectural forms, from the Pantheon and Hagia Sophia, to the Millennium Dome at Greenwich, London, designed by the Richard Rogers Partnership with Buro Happold Engineers. The transparent hemispherical Reichstag Dome by Norman Foster Architects is also worthy of an analytical case study in itself, combining as it does the functions of drawing natural daylight down into the chamber, whilst at the same time expelling the hot air generated by politicians.

Domes are essentially space structures that can be generated by sweeping curves of any shape about a vertical axis, e.g. **figure 18.1**. The surface resulting from the sweep operation has double curvature, and the resulting structure is structurally stronger than a single curved surface, such as a cylindrical shell. A simple dome generated by sweeping an arc is part of a sphere. However, domes can be generated with other curved profiles, such as an ellipse, parabola, other conic sections, or random curves such as those shown in **figure 18.6**.

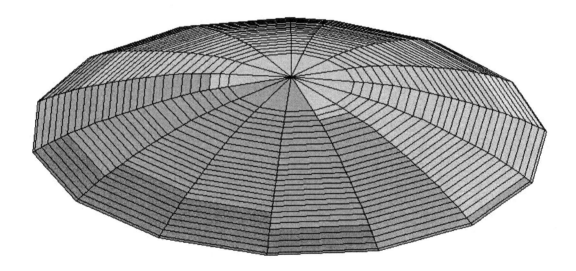

Figure 18.1: CAD-generated shallow dome form.

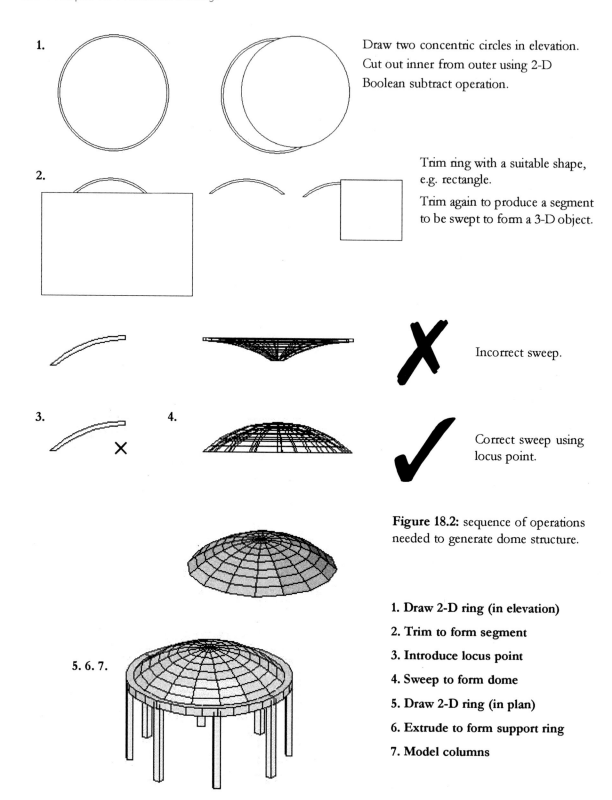

1. Draw two concentric circles in elevation. Cut out inner from outer using 2-D Boolean subtract operation.

2. Trim ring with a suitable shape, e.g. rectangle.

Trim again to produce a segment to be swept to form a 3-D object.

Incorrect sweep.

3. **4.** Correct sweep using locus point.

Figure 18.2: sequence of operations needed to generate dome structure.

1. Draw 2-D ring (in elevation)

2. Trim to form segment

3. Introduce locus point

4. Sweep to form dome

5. Draw 2-D ring (in plan)

6. Extrude to form support ring

7. Model columns

5. 6. 7.

Hemispherical Dome

A hemispherical dome has the structural property that it can be placed on top of walls and made continuous with them. The dome itself can be generated by the sweep operation, much as in the previous example. The supporting structure in this case was initially cylindrical, with eight similar shaped openings cut out from it by means of Boolean subtraction operations. The final form can be composed into a unified object by means of Boolean addition.

Figure 18.3: exploded view of hemispherical dome form and supporting structure.

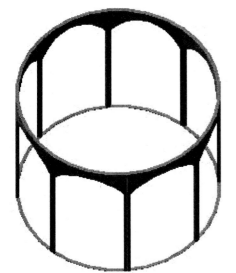

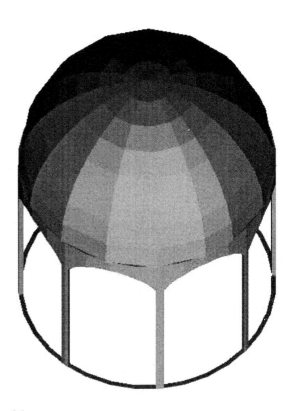

Figure 18.4: isometric view of hemispherical dome on top of supporting structure.

Alternative Dome Profiles

An elliptical dome generates a low-rise structure with a vertical tangent at the edges, and is therefore structurally very sound.

Figure 18.5: CAD-generated elliptical dome form.

This flying-saucer shaped dome in **figure 18.6** shows that domes can be generated by sweeping curves of any shape about a vertical axis. In this case, the axis of the sweep is offset from the curve itself.

Figure 18.6: CAD-generated free-form dome form.

The dome in **figure 18.7** is generated from a segment of a circle. Again, as in the previous example, the centre of the circle is not on the axis of the sweep operation, and hence a hole is produced in the centre of the dome.

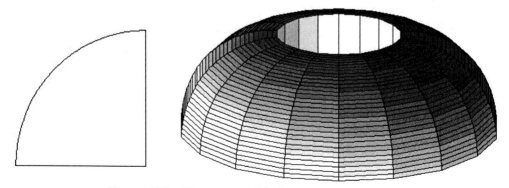

Figure 18.7: CAD-generated hollow dome form.

Folded Plate Domes

These domes are constructed out of planar CAD objects corresponding to structural elements such as slabs and plates. Particular types of folded plate dome structures depend upon the size of the angle between plates. From both a CAD and a structural point of view, folded plate domes are easy to construct.

Tapered Element Dome

In this type of structure, tapered objects can be generated in plan and then tilted towards the apex of the dome. An alternative and simpler way of generating the same form is to sweep a triangular profile about a locus point, and then to control the number of tapered elements in the structure by redefining the segment angle value of the swept object.

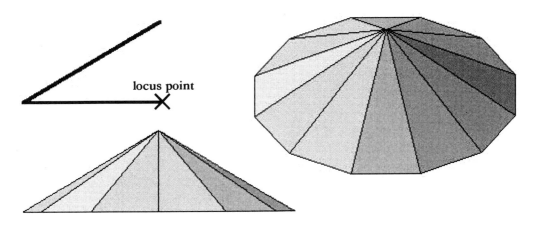

Figure 18.8: tapered element dome form.

Square Plan Dome

The simplest way of modelling a dome which is square in plan is to generate the dome form by sweeping, and then to truncate this form in plan by means of Boolean subtraction of volumetric blocks.

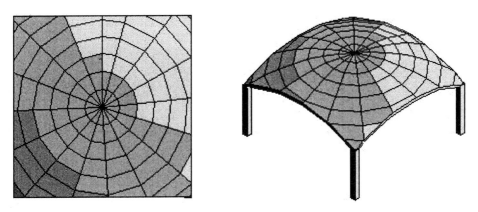

Figure 18.9: square plan dome form.

97

Faceted Dome

Faceted domes consist of a number of planes such that angled ribs are formed between them. One way of constructing such a dome as a CAD model is to position the planar elements relative to a sphere, just as construction lines are used to position line segments. A decision needs to be made as to which part of the planes touch the sphere. This is a laborious modelling process, and involves working in multiple views in order to position each of the planar elements correctly. Alternatively, it is possible to exploit specialised space structure configuration software to generate such forms, even though much of this software is still co-ordinate based, and places responsibility on users to produce a great deal of numerical input before any 3-D graphics can be generated. However, such software does allow users to specify the kind of surface that needs to be covered, the shape (e.g. triangular, hexagonal, etc.) and size of the covering elements, and, since this software is used primarily for structural analysis, the loading information at particular points. A structural mesh can then be generated *parametrically* on the basis of this information.

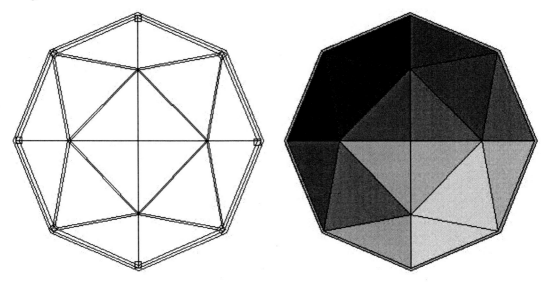

Figure 18.10: faceted dome form.

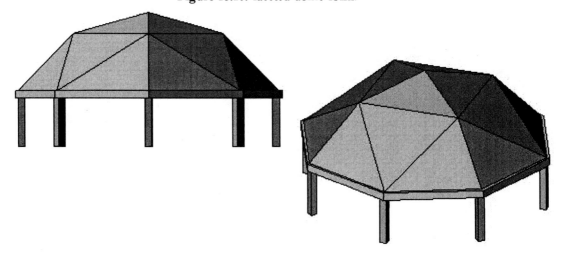

Chapter 19: Intersection Shells

Intersection shells are composed of parts of the structures described in the previous three chapters. Structurally, intersection shells are generally more stable than the individual elements themselves, since stability is achieved through the composite action of the intersecting elements. The structural efficiency of an intersection shell depends upon the angle of the intersection of the intersecting surfaces. A sharp angle between the intersecting surfaces will produce a natural rib that is stiffer than the surfaces on either side.

Intersection Dome

This structure is a dome formed by using triangular pieces of a cylindrical shell arranged in the form of a square. It is a more logical way of generating a dome that covers a square area than the one illustrated in **figure 18.9**. Starting from a hollow cylindrical form, a series of Boolean subtractions generates the triangular pieces needed for the dome.

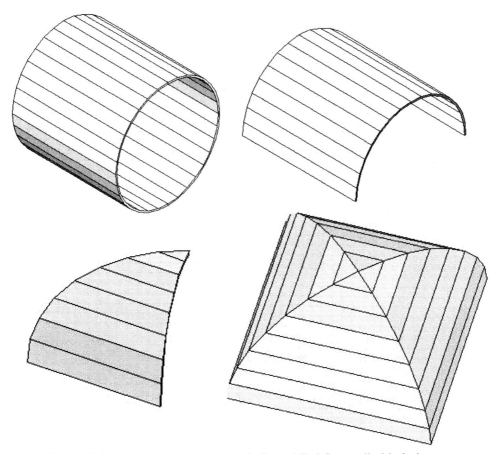

Figure 19.1: dome form intersection shell modelled from cylindrical pieces.

Shallow Intersection Dome

The shallowness of an intersection dome depends upon the angle between the intersecting elements, which is in turn affected by the rise of the shell. The elevation profile of the intersection dome in **figure 19.1** is shown in **figure 19.2**. An elevation profile of a shallower intersection dome form is shown in **figure 19.3**, together with its corresponding isometric view.

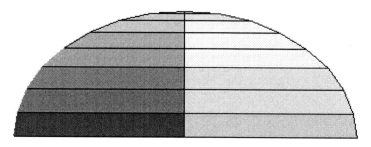

Figure 19.2: sharper intersection dome form.

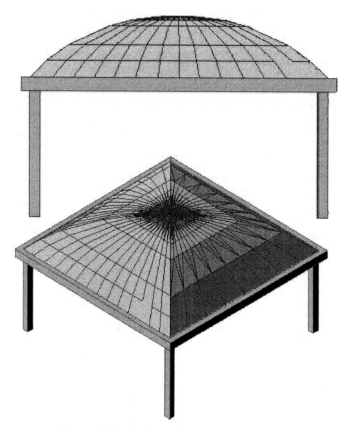

Figure 19.3: shallower intersection dome form.

Folded Plate Intersection Shell

Just as with simple folded plates, the profile of one element can be drawn in elevation. This can then be extruded to a required length. The extruded form can then be duplicated and rotated 90° to the initial form.

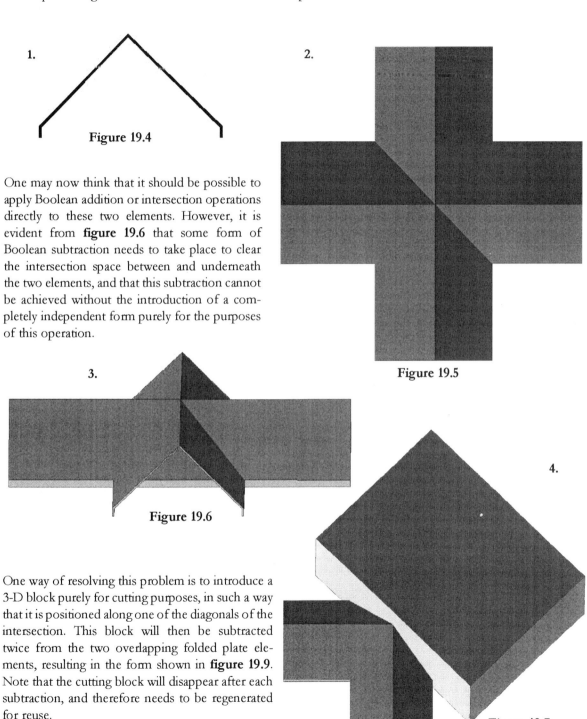

1.

Figure 19.4

2.

One may now think that it should be possible to apply Boolean addition or intersection operations directly to these two elements. However, it is evident from **figure 19.6** that some form of Boolean subtraction needs to take place to clear the intersection space between and underneath the two elements, and that this subtraction cannot be achieved without the introduction of a completely independent form purely for the purposes of this operation.

3.

Figure 19.5

Figure 19.6

4.

One way of resolving this problem is to introduce a 3-D block purely for cutting purposes, in such a way that it is positioned along one of the diagonals of the intersection. This block will then be subtracted twice from the two overlapping folded plate elements, resulting in the form shown in **figure 19.9**. Note that the cutting block will disappear after each subtraction, and therefore needs to be regenerated for reuse.

Figure 19.7

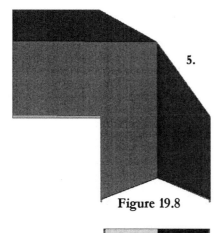

5.

Figure 19.8

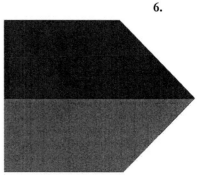

6.

Figure 19.9

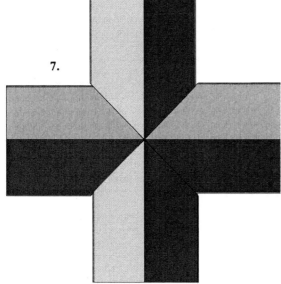

7.

Figure 19.10

This individual element can then be repeated four times in a circular (often referred to as *polar*) array with the centre at the tip of the pointed end. Finally, to ensure that the four components combine into an integrated structure, Boolean addition can be applied to successive elements. It should be stressed that whenever Boolean operations are involved, accuracy of placement of the two elements involved in the operation is crucial, as any slight deviation from correct positioning will often result in a loss of symmetry of the resulting element, thus making it an awkward form to replicate and continue working with.

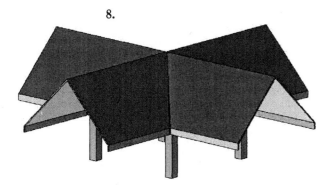

8.

Figure 19.11

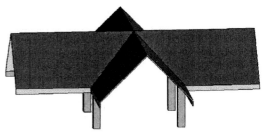

Figure 19.12: view showing that the way through the shell has now been cleared.

Barrel Vault Intersections

This structure is similar to the previous one with barrels instead of folded plates, such that four cylindrical barrels intersect to form a central dome.

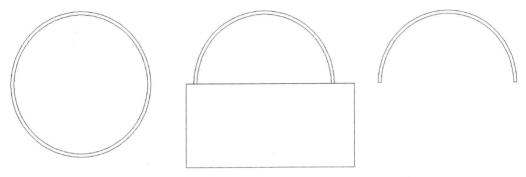

Figure 19.13: modelling of barrel elevation prior to extrusion.

Figure 19.14: barrel vault intersection in plan.

Figure 19.15: barrel vault intersection in isometric view.

Groined Vault

The groined vault is an intersection shell that can be modelled from four triangular pieces of cylindrical shells, using the same method as in the previous two structures. The pieces are aligned on a square plan so that each side has an arch. Structurally, groined vaults are very strong because of the relatively large angle at the intersections of each of the four shell elements.

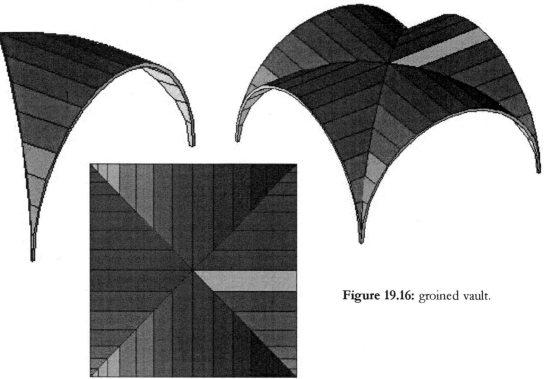

Figure 19.16: groined vault.

Polygonal Groined Vault

This structure is similar to the previous one, except that there are more cylindrical elements. The five-sided polygonal vault structure has been modelled with stiffening elements around the outside of the structure. Polygonal vaults with a greater number of sides can be modelled in a similar manner.

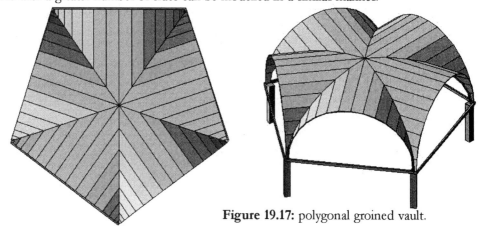

Figure 19.17: polygonal groined vault.

Chapter 20: Ruled Surfaces

Ruled surfaces, as the name implies, are curved surfaces constructed out of straight elements. The sets of straight lines within a curved surface are called the *generators* (or *generatrices* – see overleaf) of the surface. Perhaps the simplest example of such a surface is the cone. The most interesting such forms from an architectural point of view are *helicoids*, hyperbolic paraboloids (or just *paraboloids*), and elliptic hyperboloids of one sheet (or *hyperboloids* for short, and to be distinguished from elliptic hyperboloids of two sheets, which are composed of two parts separated in 3-D space).

The main practical advantage of using ruled surfaces is that they are easy to construct. For concrete structures, for example, they require relatively simple formwork. Since ruled surfaces are composed entirely of straight lines which have both start and end points, they have also been exploited by stonemasons through the use of *templates*. A template is a thin plate cut to a desired profile, and used to mark off surfaces during machining or cutting. The template defines a series of start and end points, each of which is cut out, one by one until the desired surface is generated. Ruled surfaces allow stone working to be carried out off-site, and so precisely that there is no need to refer to adjacent pieces before being fixed into place. The same advantages also apply to mould-making (e.g. for artificial stone) and to model-making.

A helicoid can be described in terms of a line which simultaneously rotates and translates about a central axis (**figure 20.1**). This is a common form found in architecture, often as spiral staircases, for example.

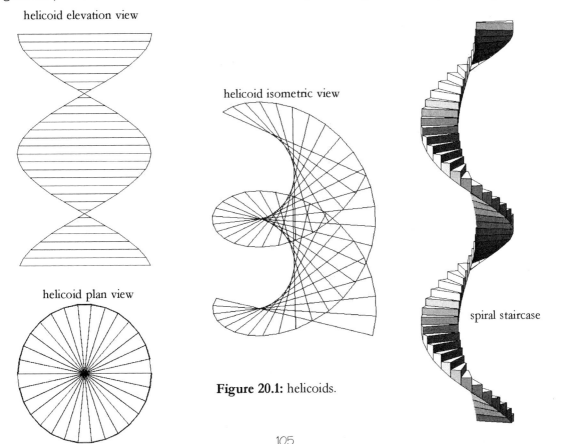

helicoid elevation view

helicoid plan view

helicoid isometric view

spiral staircase

Figure 20.1: helicoids.

Before moving on to the remaining ruled surfaces, the reader should be aware of common terminology related to the way in which ruled surfaces are created. Firstly, a moving straight line is often referred to as a *generatrix* in the sense that it generates a surface. The line that determines the direction in which the generatrices travel is called the *directrix*.

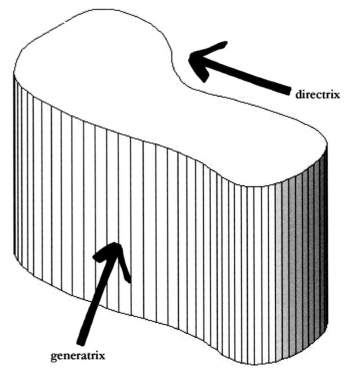

Figure 20.2: terminology of ruled surfaces.

A hyperbolic paraboloid is shown in **figure 20.3**. In this case, the generatrix, which can change in length as it moves, is controlled by two non-coplanar directrices, which can also vary in length. Any section through the surface taken along a generatrix will always be a line. A section through any other part of the surface will be a curve.

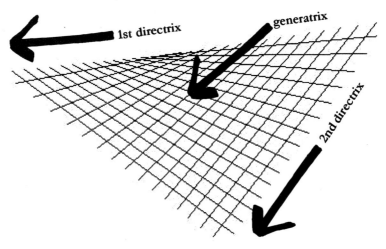

Figure 20.3: hyperbolic paraboloid surface.

The form shown in **figure 20.4** is an elliptic hyperboloid of one sheet (hyperboloid). In this ruled surface, the upper and lower circles constitute the directrices, and angled generatrices move between them. If the generatrices were vertical, then a cylindrical ruled surface would be formed. The shape, size and separation of the directrices can all vary, as can the degree of slant of the generatrices. The hyperboloid shown below in **figure 20.4** with circular directrices can also be produced by rotating a hyperbola about a central axis.

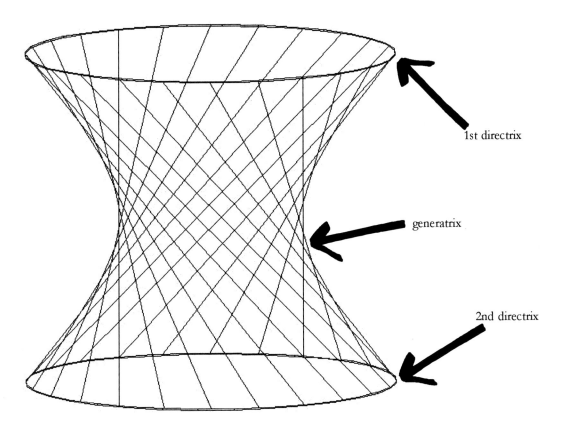

1st directrix

generatrix

2nd directrix

Figure 20.4: hyperboloid.

The surface of a hyperboloid, therefore, can be generated by two different methods:

- by sweeping a straight line about a vertical axis.
  This method can produce circular and elliptical hyperboloids, but is a memory-intensive CAD operation.

- by sweeping a hyperbola around a vertical axis.
  Circular hyperboloids can easily be produced this way. Scaling the resulting hyperboloids differently in x or y can then produce elliptical hyperboloids.

The Application of Boolean Operations to Ruled Surfaces

Case Study: The Sagrada Familia Church; Architect: Antoni Gaudi,
CAD remodelling: Serrano, Coll, Melero, Burry et. al.

All of Gaudi's drawings of the Sagrada Familia Church were burnt during the Spanish Civil War, and detailed 1:10 plaster cast models of the nave were broken. It is only comparatively recently when these models were restored that it became evident that their geometries were such that CAD remodelling was recognised as the best way of progressing with the construction of Gaudi's fantastic church. This whole project is described in Serrano, Coll, Melero, Burry (1993) and Serrano, Coll, Melero, Burry (1996).

The CAD modelling of the facades and horizontal elements of the Sagrada Familia relied heavily on the application of Boolean operations to hyperboloids considered as solid 3-D volumes rather than as surfaces. The basic principle of successive Boolean subtractions of hyperboloids from a solid block is illustrated in **figures 20.5–20.7**.

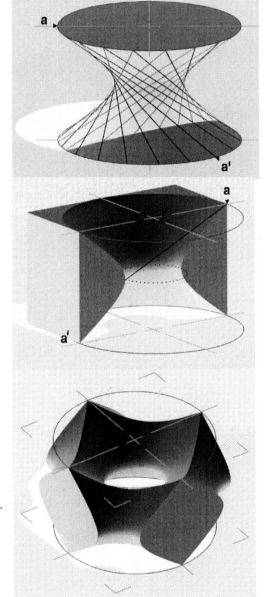

Figure 20.5: hyperboloid.

Figure 20.6: hyperboloid cut from a solid by means of boolean subtraction.

Figure 20.7: form generated by subtracting five hyperboloids from a solid block (one at each corner, and one in the centre).

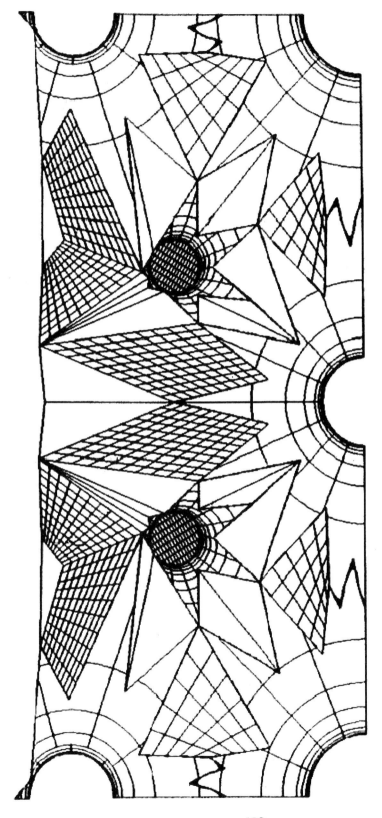

Figure 20.8: wire-frame CAD-generated image showing use of paraboloids and hyperboloids in one of the horizontal elements of the nave of the Sagrada Familia Church.

The facade of the nave of the Sagrada Familia, for example, includes parapets, arches, and circular and elliptical windows. Each of these parts turns out to be a different form of hyperboloid, and each is symmetrical about a longitudinal plane through the facade, so that internal surfaces are similar to the external ones. For example, the modelling of one half of a wall in the facade would begin from a 3-D object known as a paralellepiped. A parallelepiped is a six-sided prism, all of whose faces are parallelograms. This object would then be shaped by means of a succession of subtractions of individual hyperboloids. Once one half of the wall was modelled, the other half could be obtained simply by copying and reflecting the first half.

The buttresses of the facades were modelled in terms of paraboloids with a more complex system of generation than the simple subtraction of hyperboloids. The data that defines the directrices and the generatices of the paraboloids is obtained from the geometry of the hyperboloids. It should be evident that if the hyperboloid in **Figure 20.4** is turned on its side and viewed in plan, a square cut from this plan across the saddle of the hyperboloid will produce a paraboloid similar to that in **Figure 20.3**. Consequently, smooth transitions are made from parabolic buttresses to hyperbolic arches: a generatrix of a hyperboloid can at the same time be a directrix of a paraboloid. This principle was also used in the modelling of the horizontal elements such as that shown in **Figure 20.8** opposite. In the wire-frame illustration shown, paraboloids combine to form the bulk of the surface, whilst hyperboloids penetrate this surface to form openings. The two circular forms in the centre are where vertical columns are attached. The modelling of the columns themselves is illustrated later in this chapter.

The great window of the church is 7.5m wide and 15m high, so in terms of thinking about the construction process, it needed to be subdivided into smaller pieces, each weighing less than two tons. The cut lines were applied along generatrices, and this was convenient in another respect, in that decorative elements needed to be added later, and also along the lines of the generatrices. A uniform thickness for all the pieces was chosen to be 15cm. In terms of CAD modelling, this thickness is obtained by *creating extrusions or surface projections* inwards and perpendicular at each point of the external surface. Sometimes it was necessary to increase this thickness slightly in order to avoid problems associated with the application of Boolean operations to *coincident surfaces*. It is often preferable for objects to overlap each other prior to the application of Boolean operations, as otherwise strange outcomes can arise.

The following five pages illustrate how the columns which support the main nave aisle balconies and roof were modelled. An individual column rises upwards from a plan section which is derived from eight concave and eight convex parabolas at its base, and moves upwards towards a Doric section at the top. The main principle behind this shape transformation is the counter-rotation of equally shaped sections, which have varying relationships relative to where they are positioned. According to Burry:

> *This (base) profile doubles on itself and acts helicoidally for each stage of the column but in opposite senses: one minutely rotates clockwise up the length of the column, the other anticlockwise. The column is that solid common to the two opposing helicoids, that is, the material left by the interference between the two.'*
> (Burry, 1993)

In the case of the columns, therefore, instead of using Boolean addition or subtraction, the resultant column form is the *Boolean intersection* of two sections as they rise upwards. The column appears to grow as the sections move upwards. Gaudi generated a variety of columns based upon this same geometric principle. The main columns in the Sagrada Familia are sized in accordance with the loading and more resistant materials are used for greater loads.

Key Sagrada Column Sections

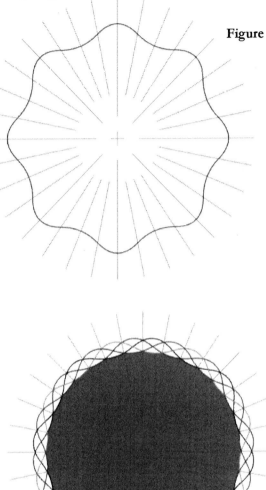

Figure 20.9: column section at 0m (plan view).

Figure 20.10: column section at 8m (plan view).

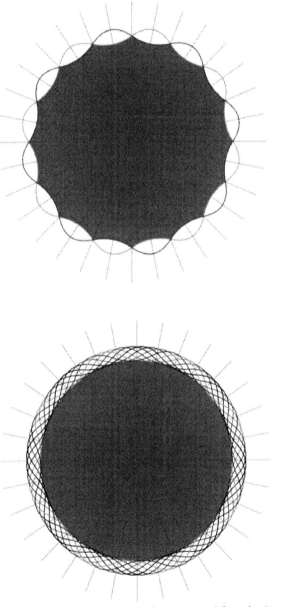

Figure 20.11: column section at 12m (plan view).

Figure 20.12: column section at 14m (plan view).

Key Sagrada Column Extrusions

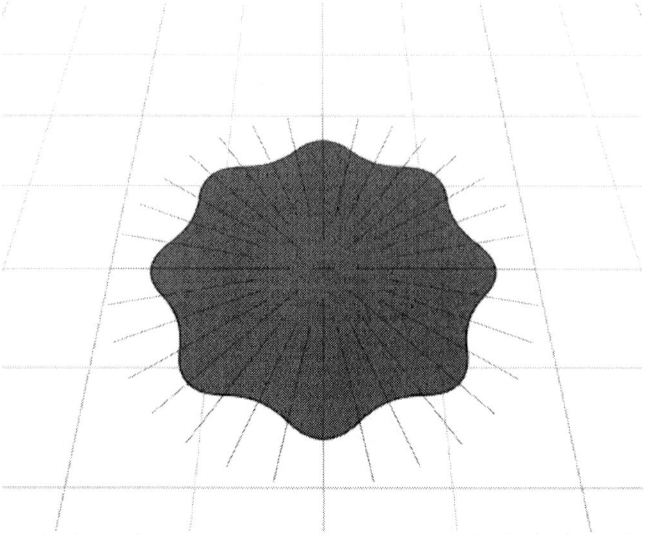

Figure 20.13: column section at 0m (perspective view).

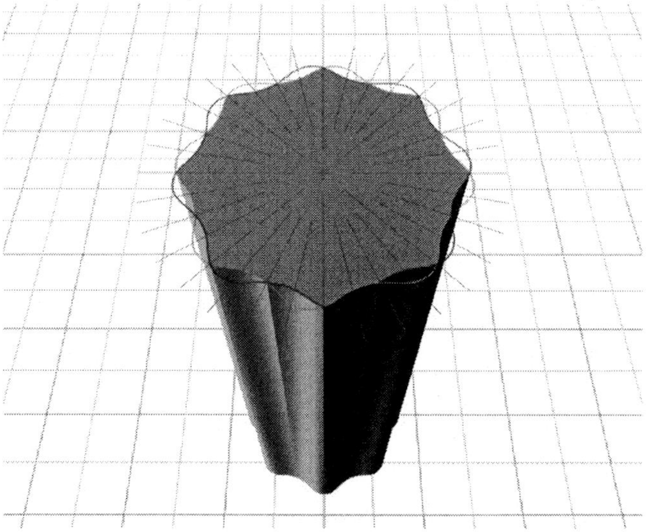

Figure 20.14: column from 0m to 4m (perspective view).

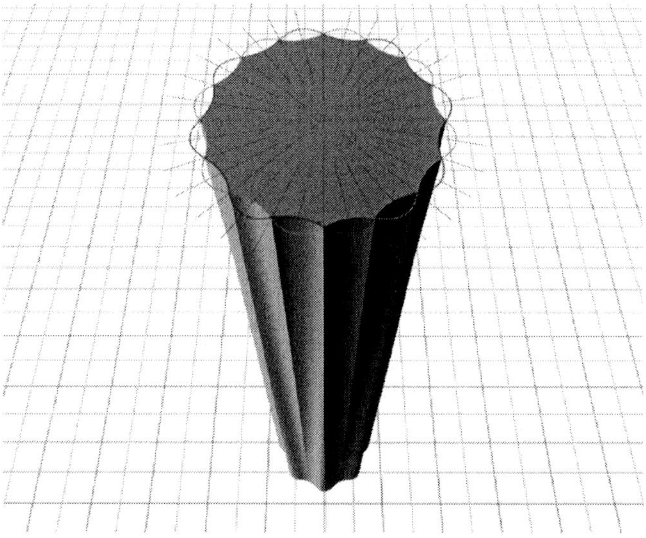

Figure 20.15: column from 0m to 8m (perspective view).

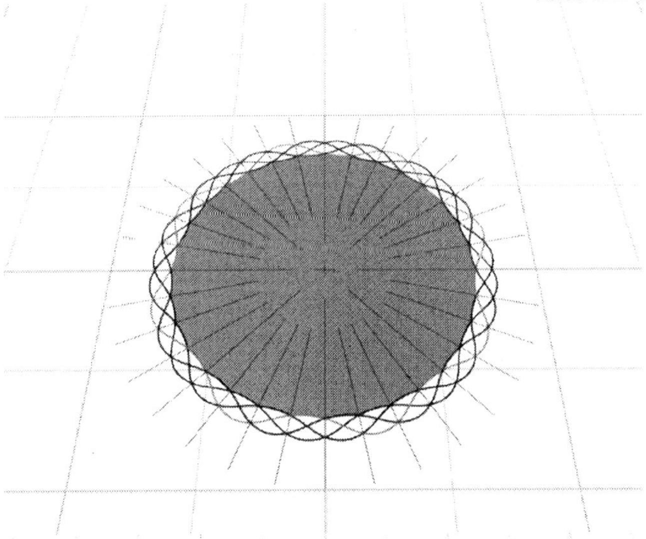

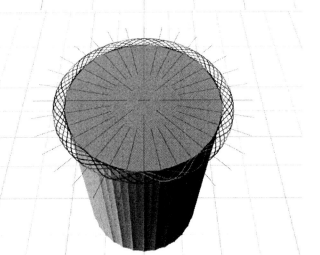

Figure 20.16: column section at 12m (perspective view).

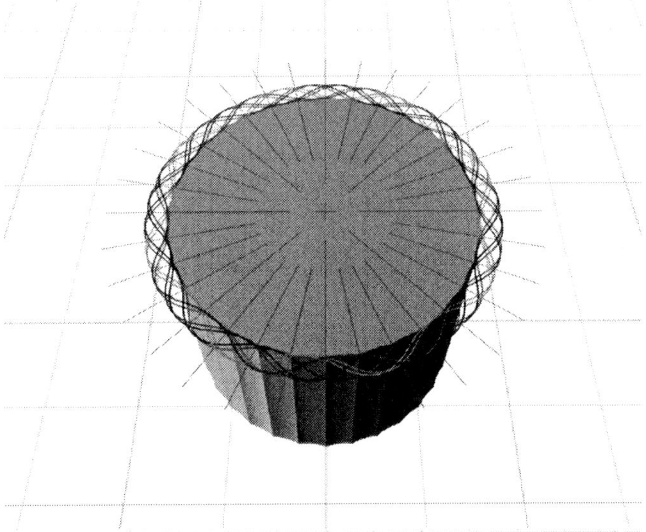

Figure 20.17: column from 12m to 13m (perspective view).

Figure 20.18: column from 12m to 14m (perspective view).

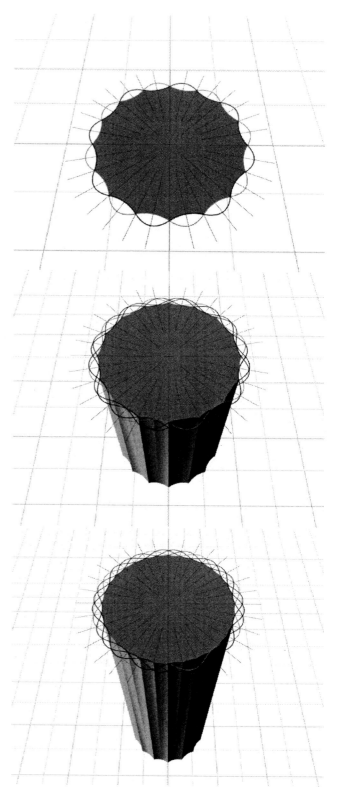

Figure 20.19: column section at 8m (perspective view).

Figure 20.20: column from 8m to 10m (perspective view).

Figure 20.21: column from 8m to 12m (perspective view).

Entire Sagrada Column

Figure 20.22

Section through Sagrada Familia Church

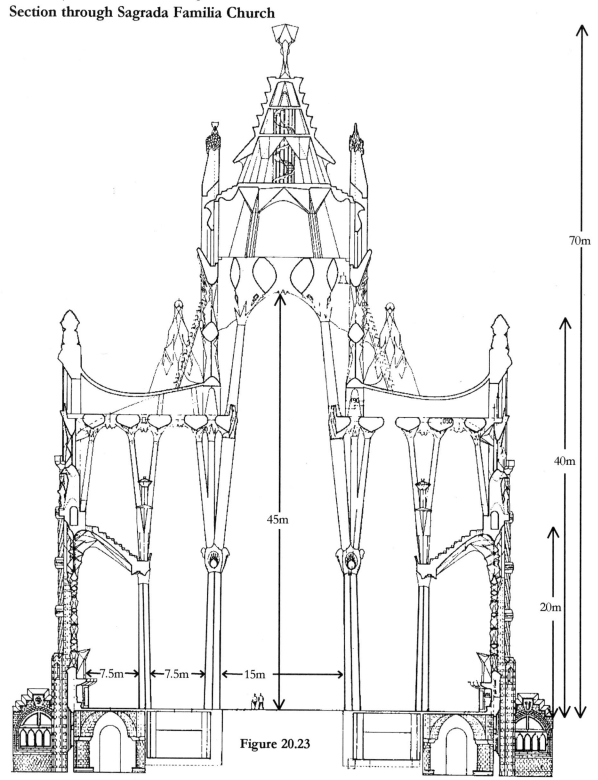

70m

40m

20m

45m

15m

7.5m

7.5m

Figure 20.23

Plan of Sagrada Familia Church

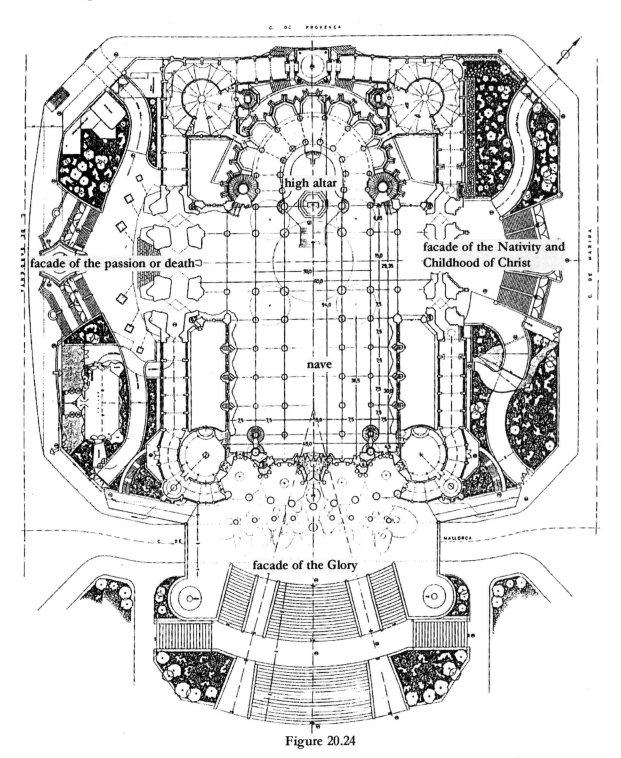

Figure 20.24

Historical Evolution

Gaudi took over the construction of the Sagrada Familia Church in 1883 from the architect Fancisco de Paula del Villar y Lozano. The site was at that time on the outskirts of Barcelona, and Villar had begun the project a year earlier from a cruciform Gothic ground plan. Gaudi continued with these plans until the completion of the crypt in 1887. The exterior walls of the choir were built between 1887 and 1893. After this, work continued on the facade of one transept until Gaudi's death in 1926. During this latter period, there were several interruptions to the project and Gaudi made several changes to the plan. It was only in 1925 that Gaudi introduced his new structural system for the nave which was radically different from earlier proposals. It had taken Gaudi about 30 years to get to the point where he abandoned buttressed Gothic structure in favour of what he perceived to be a more organic approach based upon hyperboloids and paraboloids. During this time, he reinvented the now well-known funicular models, the central principle of which is that the ideal form of compression structure is a funicular curve. His funicular models consisted of weights on cords creating tension forces, which, when inverted, transform into compression.

Although Gaudi's drawings were burnt and models smashed during the Spanish civil war, work continued since then based upon surviving material and records, the main focus being the construction of the second transept. It is only as recently as the 1970s that more emphasis was placed on converting the nave models into coherent and accurate building documentation. Before the recent introduction of the CAD processes described, this type of work was carried out by physical model makers who could not hope to achieve the level of accuracy required for building construction.

Analysis for Construction

Apart from the modelling of the complex geometry of the Sagrada Familia Church, the CAD environment was also used to carry out a wide range of analytical tasks that were crucial to the construction process. These included the following:

- a facility which enabled CAD models to be rapidly and accurately sectioned. This was used to determine the location of reinforced concrete within curved facades and roof vaults to comply with the seismic design code.

- volumetric and mass property evaluation tools were used to ensure that each individual piece was within crane lifting tolerances, and by calculating the centroid of each piece weighing up to two tonnes, lifting points were designed for orientation purposes.

- a finite element analysis (FEM) module was used to determine load paths in surfaces otherwise too complex to be investigated through conventional methods.

- a parametric variation facility to support the analytical work of interpreting Gaudi's models, in which continual adjustments to different but related geometries are made.

- a computer numerical control (CNC) facility to support automated manufacture in that the CAD environment generates precise numerical control output to drive five-axis milling.

Some of these analytical features are now becoming commonplace in large-scale construction projects, and these will be investigated in more detail in the context of some of the later case studies, and in chapters 27 and 28 in particular. Before moving on to some of the more advanced conceptual and analytical features of CAD modelling in practice, the next chapter will continue the theme initiated in this chapter of associating basic CAD objects and operations with the forms of actual design projects.

Figure 20.25: rendered CAD-generated image in one of the horizontal elements of the nave of the Sagrada Familia Church.

Chapter 21: Modelling with CAD Objects and CAD Operations

The previous chapter attempted to make a connection between the formal CAD modelling of particular complex surfaces known as ruled surfaces in terms of CAD objects such as hyperboloids and paraboloids, and one of Gaudi's major architectural achievements. The further architectural examples in this chapter will illustrate how buildings of apparent complexity can be constructed by applying the basic CAD operations described in Part 4 to the CAD objects in Part 3. The intention of all of these examples is to show the design student the ways in which a range of well-known architectural forms, some simple and others more complex, can be generated from basic CAD objects and operations. In other words, that there is a core set of CAD principles underlying the development of architectural form, however complex these forms might be.

Case Study 1: Welsh Assembly Proposal, Richard MacCormac
An essential element of the decision to create a National Assembly for Wales was the provision of a new building to house a debating chamber together with a range of other facilities. The architects for the new building were to be appointed following a design competition which set out a functional specification for the building within a budget of £12m. The brief called for high standards of environmental performance, and the use, wherever possible, of sustainable materials.

Amongst the competition entries was a scheme by Richard MacCormac, an architect who has been concerned in several earlier projects with the importance of geometry in building. Some of his more recent architecture has also featured abstract geometrical forms, such as the Ruskin Library at Lancaster University, for example. His recent unbuilt proposal for the Welsh Assembly in Cardiff has similar properties. In the CAD modelling of this scheme as part of the competition presentation by Virtual Artworks, a series of successive CAD models in the following illustrations show the relative positioning of the different elements in an additive manner, beginning with the simple roof plane shown in **figure 21.1**, which is essentially a slab element formed by simple extrusion.

Figure 21.1: roof canopy modelled by simple extrusion.

Figure 21.2: addition of curved wall with openings produced by Boolean subtraction.

In **figure 21.2**, the curved wall can be modelled directly using a curved wall tool, after which opening elements can be inserted into the extruded wall. A more primitive method is to extrude a closed 2-D curve, and then to apply successive Boolean subtraction operations.

In **figure 21.3**, an ellipsoid form is introduced. An ellipsoid can be formed by sweeping an ellipse as described in chapter 11. In this case, the top of the ellipse is sliced off by means of Boolean subtraction, and openings for glazing introduced by means of the same CAD operation.

Figure 21.3: addition of ellipsoid form of debating chamber with openings.

Figure 21.4: addition of glazing element.

In **figure 21.4**, a separate curved glazing element is introduced between the ellipsoid form of the debating chamber and the initial curved wall element.

Finally, the modelling is completed with the addition of office spaces behind the glazed element and abutting onto the curved wall. The surrounding buildings can be modelled very simply as extruded blocks with minimal rendering. People can be added by sumperimposing scanned photographs upon the final CAD image using image processing software.

Figure 21.5: addition of office spaces and surrounding context.

Case Study 2: Yorkshire Artspace Project, Mohammed Asri
The following four illustrations show the application of the CAD technique of lofting described in chapter 13 to the generation of a complex building form.

Lofting creates a smooth surface by blending between a series of selected curves of varying shape. The plan of **figure 21.6** shows the lofted form as it tapers according to its cross-sectional curves. These curves are also visible as structural elements that encircle the form at intervals in **figure 21.7**. The rail curves in this example traverse the form lengthwise. Both the cross-sections and the rail curves are also visible in the interior views shown in **figures 21.8** and **21.9**. The smooth surface generated by the lofting operation is visible as a triangular mesh, a computationally efficient way of representing surfaces, although curved meshes sometimes produce slightly more realistic results.

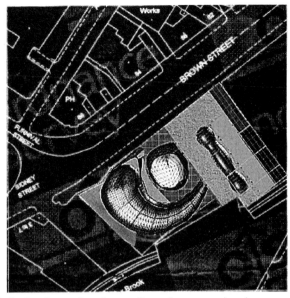

Figure 21.6: site plan of lofted volume showing scaling of cross-sectional curves.

Figure 21.7: lofted volume bounded by triangular mesh.

Figure 21.8: interior of lofted space with cross-sectional and rail curves.

Figure 21.9: interior detail of lofted space.

Case Study 3: Floating Theatre Pavilion, Fumihiko Maki

The Floating Theatre Pavilion designed by Fumihiko Maki is situated on a canal in Groningen, the Netherlands. It is essentially an open stage, sheltered and enclosed by a translucent white polyester canopy. It consists of a delicate membrane stretched over tubular steel members configured in the form of a spiralling double helix. This dramatic structure is supported on a concrete barge 25m long and 6m wide. A starting point for modelling this complex and dynamic form is to set up a 2-D construction line grid as shown in **figure 21.10**. The long thin rectangles on either side indicate the seating areas.

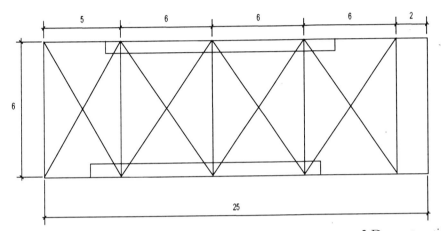

Figure 21.10: 2-D plan construction line grid.

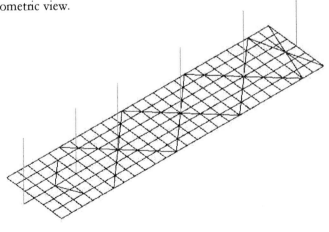

Figure 21.11: 3-D construction line grid, isometric view.

3-D construction lines need to be drawn to function as *reference lines* for the more complex elements. If the CAD system doesn't offer lines that can be drawn directly in 3-D space, then it is possible to simulate them by drawing them first in 2-D, extruding them slightly, and then positioning them. Once anticipated 3-D construction lines have been drawn, these lines can then be grouped together as one element, preferably in the same layer with a default colour attribute. This will ensure that the construction lines function as reference lines only, and do not become incorporated in the rest of the model. A 3-D construction line grid is shown in **figure 21.11**, with a metre grid superimposed onto the plan.

Figure 21.12: 3-D construction line grid in elevation.

To model the tubular spiral curve which is the central component of this structure, the user needs to be able to create a 3-D curve, and more specifically, a 3-D B-spline helix. 3-D CAD objects such as B-*splines* are only available within more advanced CAD systems, and allow users to construct complex forms such as the spiral in this example, by keying in required *parameters* such as top radius, base radius, height, and pitch. Once the first spiral curve has been created, a second one needs to be modelled by manipulating a mirrored copy of the first curve. By utilising defined pivot lines in elevation, the two curves combined form double spirals, which will then form the base for the roof membrane.

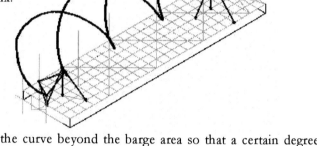

Figure 21.13: double spiral form constructed from 3-D B-spline helix.

Further modification is necessary to extend the curve beyond the barge area so that a certain degree of overhang is created for the roof. This is done by creating another B-spline curve, and fusing this with the existing spiral by means of Boolean addition to create a single entity.

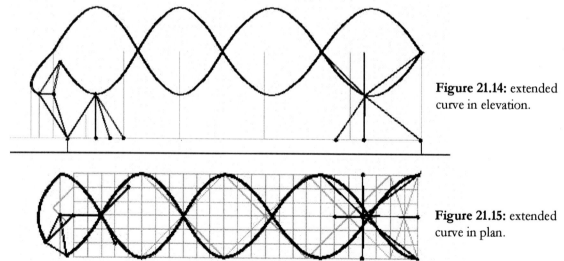

Figure 21.14: extended curve in elevation.

Figure 21.15: extended curve in plan.

In reality, each of the spiral curves is not just a single extrusion, but rather a combination of three similar spiral rods, located adjacent to each other, and connected by triangular steel plates. In order to model these three spiral rods, more construction lines need to be generated to properly place the rods. Once this has been done, a triangular plate can be modelled to attach the three spiral rods together. The end plates could be modelled in a regular x/y projection (e.g. elevation), then extruded to the required thickness along the corresponding z-axis. However, as the spirals move along an irregular axis, to have the plate copied to other locations is extremely difficult, requiring excessive numerical calculation, and consuming a great deal of time. A simpler approximation, therefore, is to use a circular cross-section instead of a triangular one.

The surface membrane roof system can be created by identifying the border elements of the surface, and letting the CAD system interpolate between these elements. To do this successfully, additional curvilinear lines need to be constructed to form the enclosing borders of the anticipated surface. A surface can then be created by identifying a series of enclosing border elements.

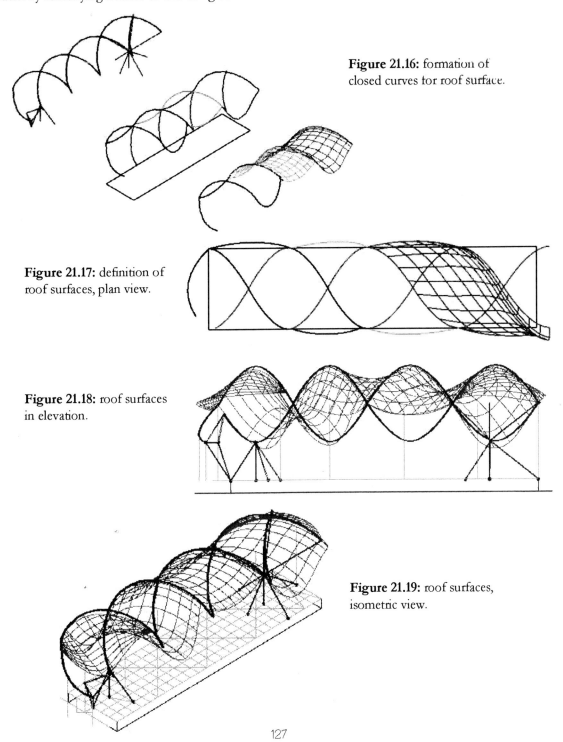

Figure 21.16: formation of closed curves for roof surface.

Figure 21.17: definition of roof surfaces, plan view.

Figure 21.18: roof surfaces in elevation.

Figure 21.19: roof surfaces, isometric view.

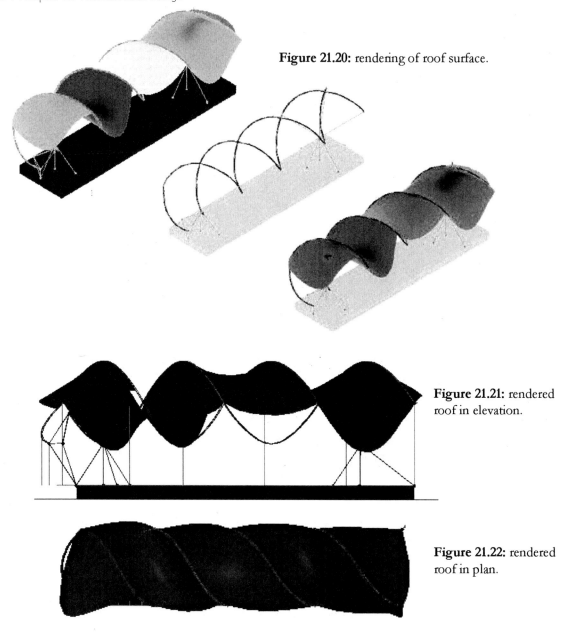

Figure 21.20: rendering of roof surface.

Figure 21.21: rendered roof in elevation.

Figure 21.22: rendered roof in plan.

Other important parts of the structural system are the cylindrical supports for the double spiral systems that distribute the load to the barge. In summary, the process of modelling the form of the floating pavilion involves five main steps:

- setting up the 3-D construction line grid,
- modelling the spiral curves,
- constructing spiral rods from the spiral curves,
- modelling the roof surface membrane,
- modelling a set of cylindrical elements as structural supports.

Part 6: Parametric Design

Chapter 22: The Propagation of Form through Parametric Expression

Case Study: Waterloo International Terminal, London, Nicholas Grimshaw & Partners

Figure 22.1: view of train platforms from concourse of existing train station.

The £130m international terminal at Waterloo, London, is a railway station on a complex site that handles up to 15 million passengers a year, and was completed within budget and on time in May 1993. The most impressive feature of the scheme from a CAD perspective is the massive curved train shed which gradually expands towards the station end. The complexity and variation in the size and shape of the structural elements involved in the train shed was possible because of the application of structural analysis CAD techniques, the essential feature of which was the ability to represent *parametric relationships*. A *parameter* is a variable to which other variables are related, and these other variables can be obtained by means of *parametric equations*. The main parametric relationships involved in this project were concerned with the description of the structural form, in which the span and curvatures of individual arches were related. These relationships in turn determined the detail of the trusses.

The asymmetry of the trusses derives from the position of a single track tight onto the western edge of the site, and the resulting need for the structure to rise more steeply at this point, to clear the trains. The basic structure is that of a flattened three pin bow string arch. Because of the asymmetrical geometry of platforms, the centre pin was moved to one side, allowing the arch to rise steeply on the west side to clear the structural envelope of the train, and a more gentle incline over the platforms on the east.

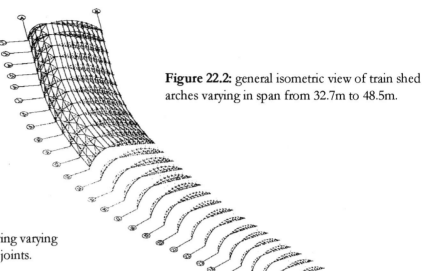

Figure 22.2: general isometric view of train shed arches varying in span from 32.7m to 48.5m.

Figure 22.3: a plan view showing varying roof truss sizes and expansion joints.

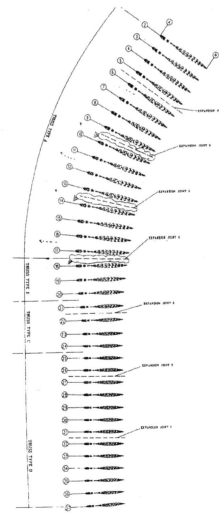

The arched roof of the train shed follows the curve of the railway and increases in span down the length of the station to accommodate the increase in the width of the platforms. The roof is supported by a series of three pin arches. Each arch and the related cladding are different as the roof changes width along the curved tracks. The variability of the arches is illustrated in plan in **figure 22.3**, and in isometric in **figure 22.2**. Using conventional CAD modelling techniques, a single arch form could be modelled, then duplicated 35 times down the length of the track (there are 18 pairs of arches, i.e. 36 in total, curiously numbered 2 to 37), with adjustments for the curvature of the track in plan. A laborious process of resizing individual trusses and arches would then need to be carried out.

Rather than model each arch separately, therefore, a single *parametric* model of an arch was modelled, such that it encoded the underlying design rules for the whole family of arches. The complete roof model then became a series of *instances* of this parametric arch, each with a different value for the span parameter.

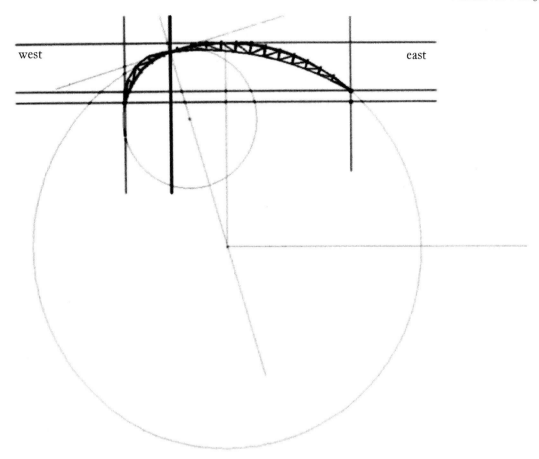

Figure 22.4: construction line grid defining truss geometry.

Sections through the train shed were determined by the need to restrict height and to accommodate trains as they arrive. **Figure 22.4** shows the response to the important design constraint of an arch on the west side with a much steeper curve than on the east side to allow trains to arrive right underneath it. A complete three-pinned arch is composed of two bow-string trusses. As indicated in **figures 22.4** and **22.5**, the longer trusses have tension rods on the inside, whereas the shorter trusses have tension rods *on the outside*. The cladding on the (western) short truss side is all glass, whereas the (eastern) long truss side is clad in stainless steel decking to reduce solar gains.

By expressing parametric relationships between graphical objects in a CAD model, it becomes possible to simply describe a whole family of possible outcomes. This fundamental CAD principle is just what was needed in the case of Waterloo, in which a range of structural arch forms, similar, yet variable in terms of scale, dimension, and position, could be described. The parametric expression of relationships between graphical objects is a way of modelling a complex set of design relationships that would be very difficult to model using conventional CAD techniques. However, given that most desktop CAD systems now have an associated computer programming environment, it is at least possible for CAD users themselves to set up parametric relationships within these environments, even if the same systems have no direct means of parametric expression. More discussion on the ability of users to define and extend CAD functionality in this way will follow in the next chapter.

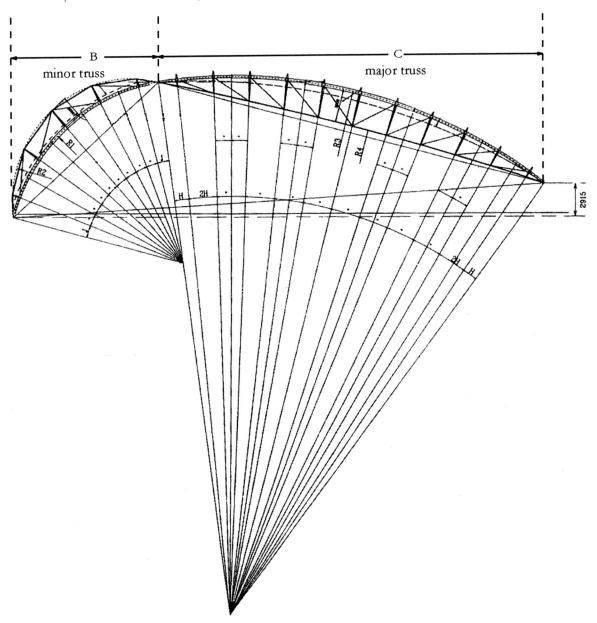

Figure 22.5: minor and major trusses spanning lengths B and C respectively.

The two primary elements involved in parametric expression for the Waterloo train shed are the minor and major trusses that form an arch. More specifically, their horizontal spanning distances B and C respectively, as shown in **figure 22.5**.

The size of the reduced truss is dictated by the parametric truss scaling factor (hx/H). The position of reduced trusses is determined by a parametric relationship which maintains the vertical east pin dimension of 2915mm, as shown in **figure 22.6**. H and hx can then both be derived from a simple pythagorean equation (the square on the hypotenuse is equal to the sum of the squares on the other two sides). In a conventional CAD approach (in which all key dimensions are *explicitly* modelled), any of the key arch dimensions (hx (or H), B, C) could of course be changed, but only by means of a long and laborious series of delete operations followed by new CAD drawing operations. A parametric CAD model (in which some dimensions are derived from others), on the other hand, can quickly and more easily be changed by choosing a particular dimension and changing its value. Just one of the graphical arch objects in **figure 22.6**, together with the associated parametric expressions, constitutes a parametric CAD model. Any other arch can be derived by supplying new values to the parametric expressions.

The size of the reduced truss is dictated by the parametric truss scaling factor (hx/H). The position of reduced trusses is determined by a parametric relationship which maintains the vertical east pin dimension of 2915mm.

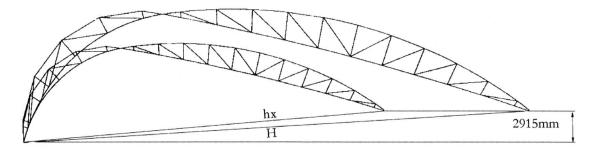

Figure 22.6: parametric expression of truss scaling factors.

The truss scaling factor is based upon the ratio of the pin hypoteneuse (hx) to the other sides of the triangle, i.e.

$$hx = \sqrt{(2915^2 + (B + C)^2)}, \text{ where B = minor truss span; C = major truss span.}$$

The parametric model can be extended from just the description of arches, through to the description the connections between pairs of arches, as shown in **figures 22.7** and **22.8**. This model can then in turn be extended to the whole shed form, so that when any dimensional change is made, it is then propagated through the whole model. Parametric expressions, therefore, allow users to change the values of key parameters, and to observe the propagation of changes on dependent expressions, and hence upon the dependent geometry. This is often referred to as *strategic manipulation*.

With advances in graphical user interfaces (GUIs) at the time of the Waterloo project, it was possible for the structural engineers at YRM Anthony Hunt Associates to *interactively* explore parametric changes in a graphically dynamic way. The engineers could graphically move the handles corresponding to parameters on the computer screen, and observe in real time the propagation of these modifications through the parameterised CAD model. This has been referred to as *intuitive manipulation* (Aish, 1992).

Figure 22.7: connections between major trusses.

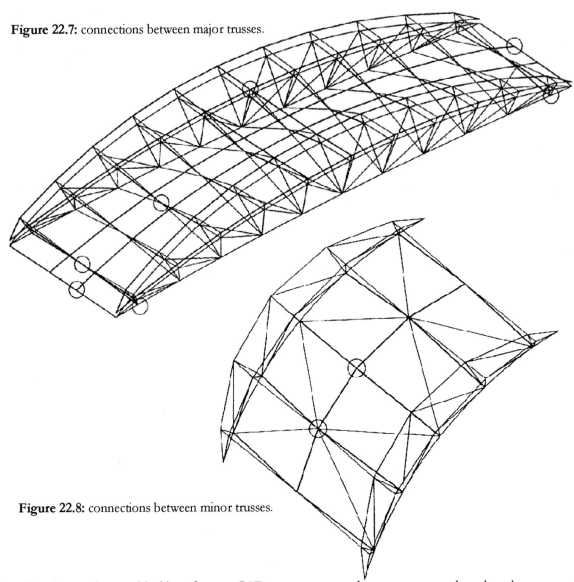

Figure 22.8: connections between minor trusses.

Nowadays, interactive graphical interfaces to CAD systems are much more commonplace than they were at the time of the Waterloo project. This is also true of the use of object-oriented environments in the implementation of CAD systems. Putting these two factors together, CAD environments are now being developed that are ideally suited to the expression of parametric relationships. Design changes in such environments can be made by exploiting the object-oriented technique of *message passing*, with each graphical object sending messages to its dependent objects.

The use of conventional CAD objects and operations generates graphical expressions that represent only one design solution. Alternative outcomes are then derived through a laborious process of editing this solution. Parametric design, on the other hand, provides an environment in which whole families of design solutions are possible. Parametric modelling techniques are particularly useful in the case of complex building forms such as the train shed at Waterloo, in which individual components have well-defined relationships to other elements.

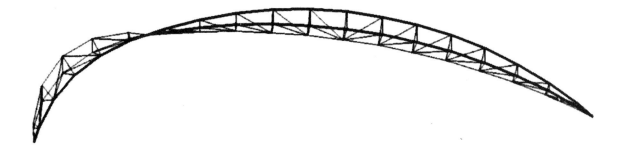

Figure 22.9: an instance of the parametric arch form.

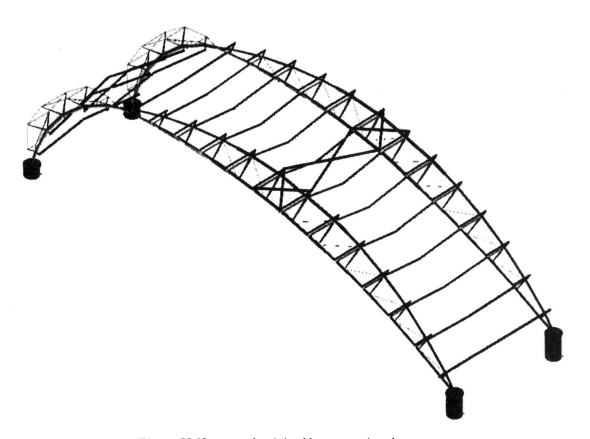

Figure 22.10: two arches joined by connecting elements.

The complex structural form of the whole train shed resulted in particular problems in relation to the skin or cladding on the structure. Although **figure 22.11** is a CAD generated 3-D model that shows the cladding fitting tightly in between the arches and connecting elements, things turned out differently on site. Since the train shed twists and expands as it approaches the station platforms, a standard glazing system for such a structure would have been extremely expensive, since it would have involved potentially thousands of different sized components. The construction of such a glazing system would have been very complex and difficult to achieve within the time scale of the project. To overcome this, a loose fit approach was adopted, in which a limited number of different sized glass sheets were used, each held in its own frame, and overlapping at top and bottom like roof tiles. They were joined at their sides by a concertina-shaped neoprene gasket, which can flex and expand to accommodate turns and varying widths.

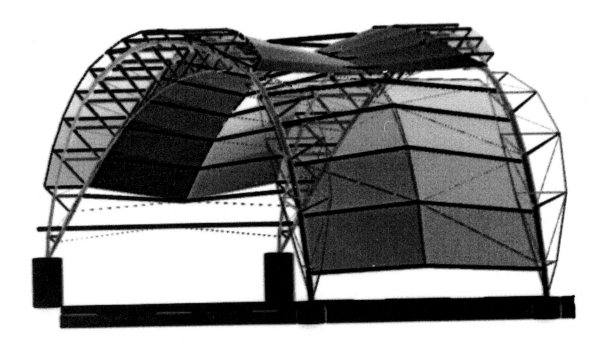

Figure 22.11: two arches with connections and cladding.

It should become apparent at this stage that the form of the train shed, although complex, emerges from the application of parametric expressions to the regular geometry illustrated in **figure 22.4**. The cladding system is in turn related to the structural system. This is a *compositional* approach to design, in which the whole design scheme is broken down into component parts, which can then be distributed amongst various manufacturers. This approach to design thinking is more commonly found in industrial and mechanical design and manufacture. There is a strong connection between compositional design and the use of parametric modelling techniques, which are well established in the aforementioned design disciplines.

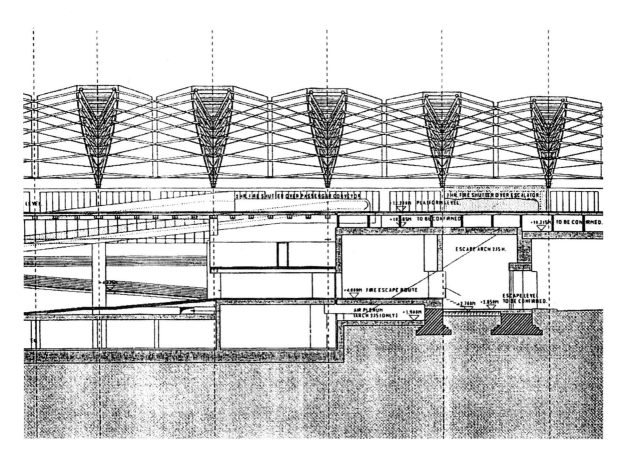

Figure 22.12: a long section through platform 22.

Although the train shed roof was the impressive part of the project, it was only 10% of the cost. Perhaps this figure in itself is a justification for the use of structural analysis software in the early design stages. The rest of the project was divided into three major components: a basement car park spanning over the shallow underground lines immediately below, and forming the foundation for the terminal; a two-storey viaduct sitting on this base and supporting the platforms, forming the enclosure for two floors of passenger accommodation arrivals and departures facilities. The final component was works to the brick vaults under the existing station, much of which is unseen by the public.

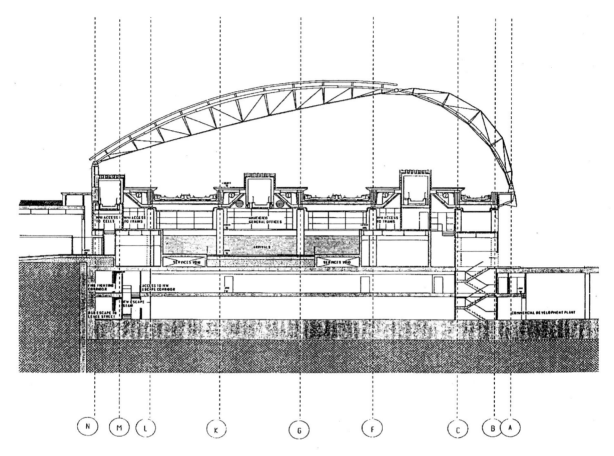

Figure 22.13: a cross-section from the station end.

Parametric Expression

Although fully parametric CAD software is not yet being exploited by small to medium architectural practices, the basic idea of parameterised objects now exists in some form or another even on desktop platforms. This manifests itself in simple ways such as in the use of control points (or handles) for certain kinds of curves (e.g. Bezier). The ability to define, determine and reconfigure geometrical relationships is the essence of parametric expression. Parametric expressions have the effect of *constraining* CAD models. To adopt a parametric design strategy, CAD users first need to identify constants and variables. The initial construction of parametric CAD models may sometimes be complex, but once made, the manipulation of the resultant CAD models is straightforward. Several changes to parametric CAD models can often be made in one operation, since the changes have a *knock-on effect* as they *propagate* through to other elements in the model.

Figure 22.14: train shed composed of parametric arches.

Figure 22.15: train shed interior.

A design strategy is essential for parametric design to be able to make an effective impact on a design scheme. Returning to the theme of chapter 2, parametric design has a potentially important role to play in the overall transition from design idea through to its construction. The ability of parametric design to support iterative design refinement can be regarded as contributing significantly to the second of the three stages of design, namely, the preparatory study stage. If architectural designers can identify the degree of flexibility that they need for important geometrically related design decisions within this stage, they can then explicitly incorporate ranges of design outcomes in a parametric CAD model. Geometries, therefore, need to be described in ways that define *approximate forms*. The design strategy, therefore, is one in which designers keep their options open by planning ahead and making these plans explicit in the form of parametric expressions.

At present, it is still the case that parametric design software is expensive and runs on powerful computing environments. Parametric design software has to date primarily been developed for mechanical engineers, civil engineers and industrial designers. The design strategies adopted in these fields tend to be compositional in nature, thus lending themselves to parametric representation. The extent to which this approach is appropriate for architectural design is an issue for further debate.

In summary, parametric expressions can represent a set of geometrical forms instead of just one. The parametric expression of design relationships allows for the exploration of variation. The downside of parametric expression is that designers invariably have to think a little differently from conventional CAD system users. CAD based on parametric expression, however, is at the leading edge of CAD technology. Parametric design is a relatively new form of expression in architectural design, with the potential to support design creativity. It is also a further argument in support of the case for modelling vs drafting approaches to CAD.

Chapter 23: The User-Definition of CAD Functionality

The previous chapter looked at a case study in which forms of expression beyond conventional CAD modelling techniques formed an important part of the project. GUIs have been developed in which it becomes feasible to use parametric design techniques within CAD modelling environments. The case study in this chapter, however, involves an even further radical departure from conventional CAD modelling, in that all the CAD images shown were produced by working directly within a programming environment. For designers to be able to express their ideas in terms of computer programming languages implies an even greater level of computer literacy than is required for using conventional CAD modelling systems.

Case Study: St. Polten Festival Hall, Austria, Klaus Kada

Figure 23.1: wire-frame of hall interior.

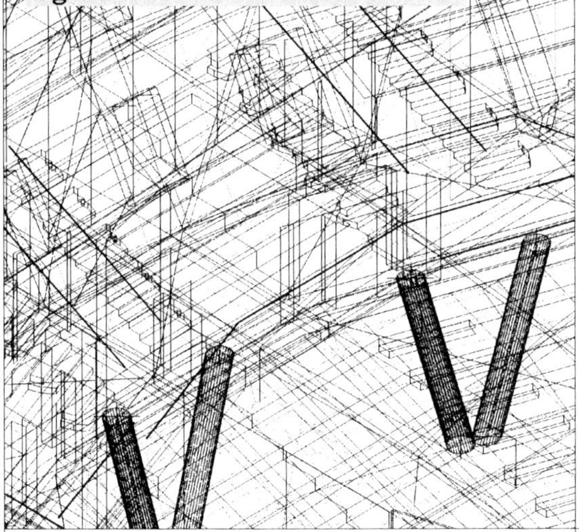

Figure 23.2: model of hall.

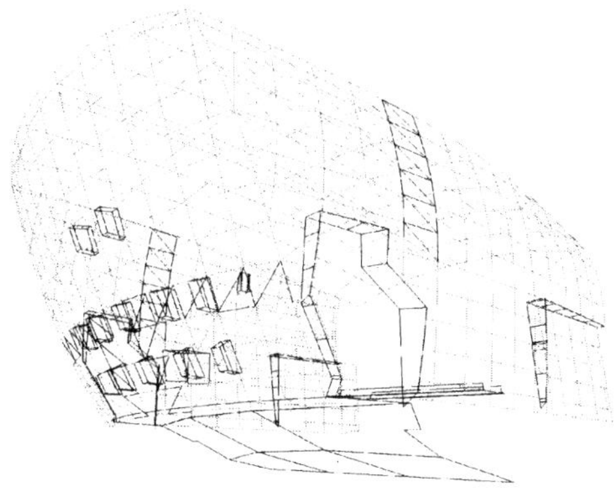

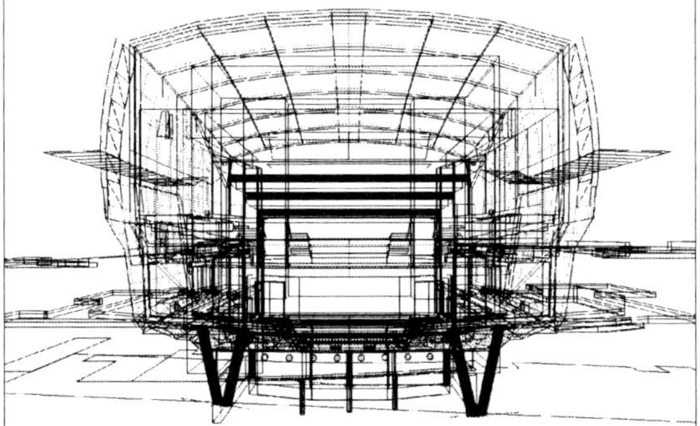

Figure 23.3: interior perspective of hall.

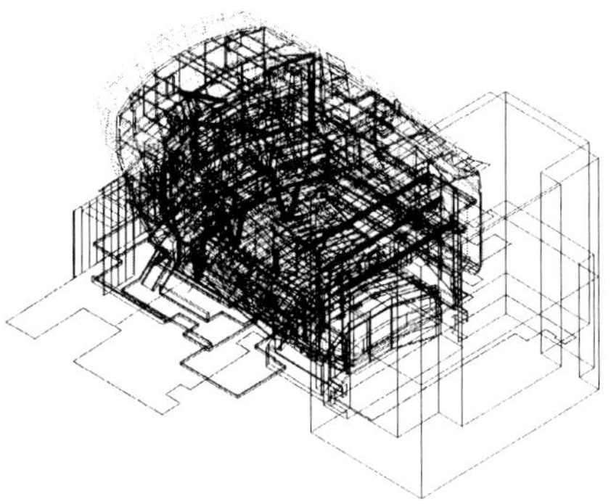

Figure 23.4: context of hall.

The new Festival Hall in St. Polten, Austria, was designed by Klaus Kada. It is a large concert hall with two side stages, a backstage and flies. It also has a rehearsal stage, ballet room and a small Kammersaal (a practice/recording room). In the initial plans, the main hall was an amorphous blob placed amongst an outer framework of circulation zones and secondary areas. During design development, increasingly precise CAD models were produced and computational analysis of the curved geometry of the concert hall was carried out. The end result of this process was a volume standing freely on three sides, unencumbered by emergency staircases, corridors and ancillary rooms. The main formal element is a huge concrete shell that is curved in two directions. The shell appears light by being clad in a backlit skin of translucent glass. Because of the complex geometry and the minimal tolerances required for the glass shell, laser technology, directly controlled by CAD software, was used to survey the substructure and the cutting of the glass panels, which are flat throughout. The glass panels hang on a network of cables anchored into the edges of the eaves, and at key points are braced against the concrete wall with compression rods. There is space between the concrete and the glass for narrow, service walkways and batteries of floodlights. Their light is reflected off the white painted concrete and filtered through the translucent glass panels to the outside to produce a uniform lighting of the surfaces.

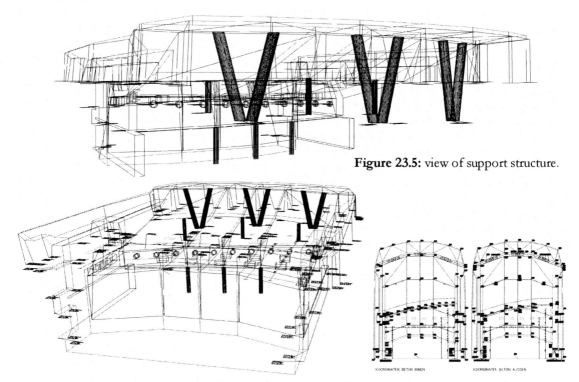

Figure 23.5: view of support structure.

Figure 23.6: support structure
with associated co-ordinate values.

Figure 23.7: co-ordinates for inner
and outer concrete elements.

Because of the millimetric accuracy required for the project, every identifiable point in the CAD model was associated with a precise co-ordinate value, and **figures 23.5 – 23.7** were a typical form of output. The only way in which such precise output could be produced was to bypass the CAD operations provided by the CAD system altogether because of the rounding errors they introduced, and generate alternative positionings of CAD objects provided by the CAD system through user-defined computer program functions.

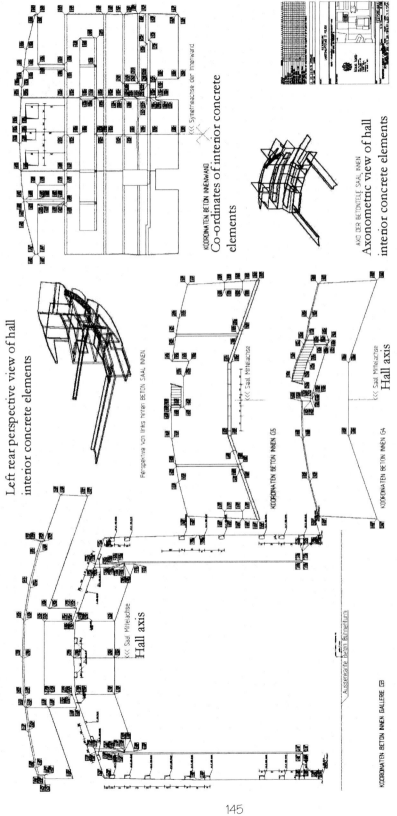

Figure 23.8: co-ordinates associated with the interior concrete elements of the concert hall.

145

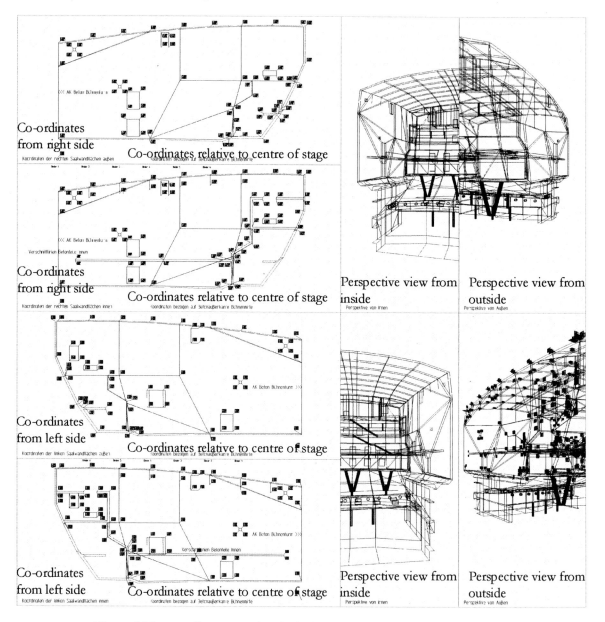

Figure 23.9: co-ordinates associated with key points of the concert hall in section.

As can be seen from **figures 23.8** and **23.9**, the type of data that emerged from the central CAD component of this project was extremely accurate 2-D plan and section information obtained from 3-D models. Because of the complexity and size of the project, in conjunction with the fact that drawing directly in any CAD environment invariably introduces rounding errors, precise user-defined functions were written in the A-Lisp and Visual Basic programming languages. Program routines were developed, particularly 2-D functions, which supported quick, precise, and simple changes to small datasets. The generation of mixed 2-D and 3-D data output, or purely 3-D data output, was avoided, since it was decided that the amount of such data required for a project of this size would be too large, complex, and difficult to edit in 3-D form.

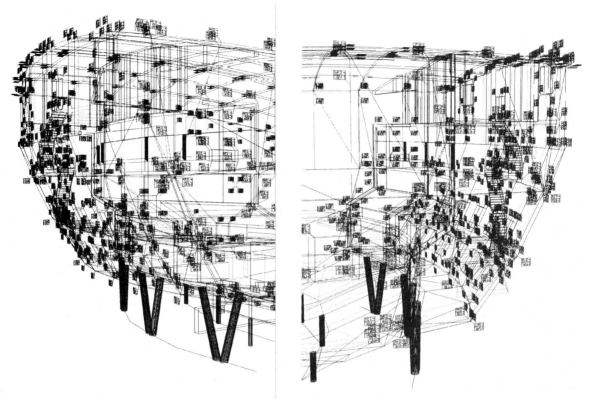

Figure 23.10: 3-D co-ordinate information generated for the concert hall.

Only the following necessary and complex parts of pure 3-D model data were processed:

- solid modelling of the whole hall with all installations
- the sloping foyer level with installations
- all ramps and bridges around and on the solid-modelled hall
- the glazing around the whole foyer and hall area
- the stage installations for the orchestra
- the chamber hall ceiling
- the main stair and handrail
- a whole site model with administration buildings, i.e. festival hall, library and museum (the latter was required for the competition submission)

The key aspect of the design process focused on the relationship between the form and the choice of material, namely, glass. The multiply curved outside shell of the main hall resulted directly from the data evaluation possibilities in Kada's office, in conjunction with the need for on-site laser measurement and positioning of the glass panels. As a direct consequence of the intention to adhere to precise measurement, thus effectively supporting CAD-based planning on the building site, a free-form modelling of the hall solid became eminently possible.

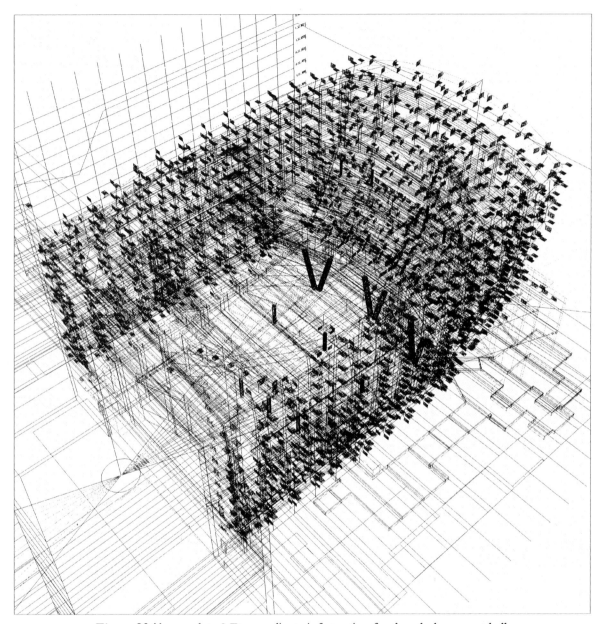

Figure 23.11: complete 3-D co-ordinate information for the whole concert hall.

To support the tasks associated with free-form CAD modelling of this project, it was necessary to program routines which extended the normal range of inbuilt CAD operations, and which supported useful, accurate, and fast geometric work within the spaces of the CAD model. These user-defined functions included functions for accurately finding key points such as intersections, endpoints, and midpoints, for example. In order for designers to be able to develop and exploit such routines, however, two essential prerequisites are knowledge of analytical geometry, and a good three-dimensional imagination.

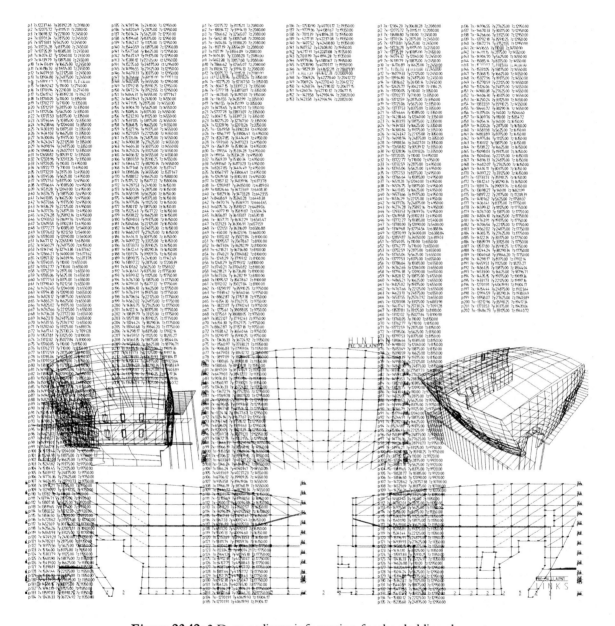

Figure 23.12: 3-D co-ordinate information for the cladding elements.

From **figure 23.5**, it can be seen that the concrete support structure of the main hall is such that the hall rests its primary mass on V-formed concrete supports. The solid concrete elements were therefore divided into suitable polygonal surfaces (**figures 23.8** and **23.9**) and constructed according to different geometrical principles from the cladding elements, which from **figure 23.12** can be seen to be predominantly regular panels.

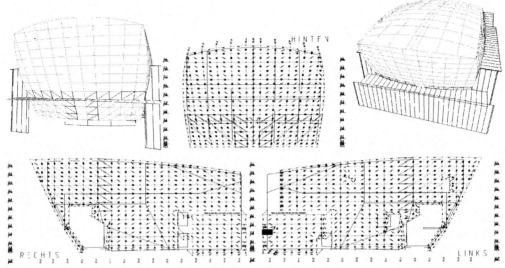

Figure 23.13: interconnections between cladding elements.

The major advantage of working directly within a programming environment is that the written pieces of program code are independent of domain knowledge, where the domain in question includes the typical range of tolerance values anticipated within CAD environments. By using a functional programming language as in this case study, designers are effectively exercising responsibility in ensuring that the expressions of the program code correspond with their intentions. Incidentally, logic or object-oriented languages would have been just as good, since these are all high-level languages that allow the programmer not to have to worry too much about how high-level expressions are mapped into low-level machine operations. Each of these programming frameworks has a particular philosophy and ontology that is beyond the scope of this book, except to say that they make it feasible for users to focus on problem descriptions rather than on computational procedures.

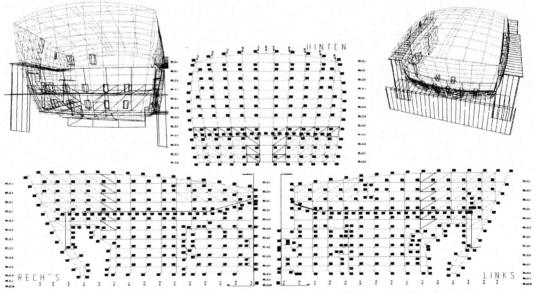

Figure 23.14: sectional co-ordinate information for the cladding elements.

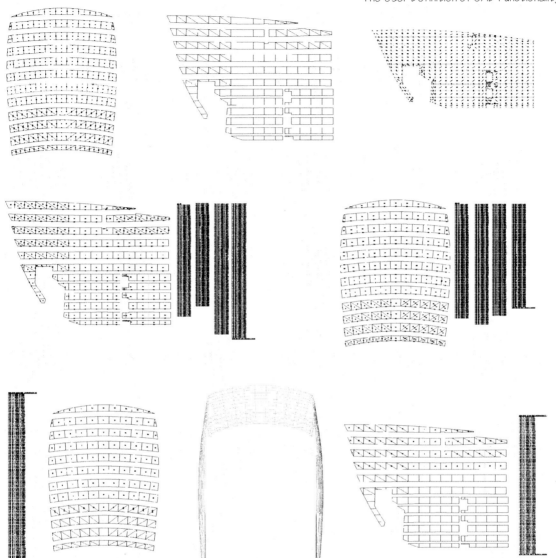

Figure 23.15: cladding data arranged in linear sequence for construction.

Until this case study, we have explored issues and principles relating to the possibilities of using CAD system functionalities in architectural design applications. This particular case study illustrates a potential further direction for the development of CAD environments, which allows designers to become less dependent upon CAD system functions, and instead develop their own ways of describing functionalities which are driven by the design domain. In the case of the St. Polten concert hall, a particular need was for the millimetric accuracy of the co-ordinate locations of the glass cladding panels to be positioned on site with laser-guided positioning tools. It had been determined at an early stage in the project that successive applications of CAD system functions that deal with geometric functions such as finding intersections and midpoints, for example, invariably lead to rounding errors. This was unacceptable on a project of this nature. By working directly within the programming environment, therefore, the designers, and Peter Szammer in particular, were in complete control of the accuracies and tolerances required for this scheme.

Figure 23.16: formwork co-ordinate data for concrete hall floor.

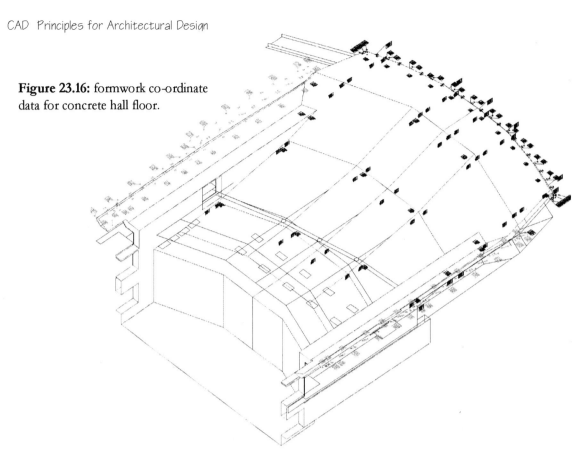

The positions of 3-D solid objects were calculated using 3-D co-ordinates with reference to the central axis of the stage tower. This kind of calculation ensures clear and unequivocal measurement, and reduces errors through chains of relative measurements. By having a clear zero reference point, and a space axis on the ground slab, it is then relatively easy to determine formwork points on the building site. Additionally, the supporting hall solid (concrete shell) was already marked off by free-form polygonal surfaces, so programmed routines were necessary to calculate the following:

- intersection points defined by three planes
- intersection lines between two planes
- intersection points between a vector and a plane
- three dimensional offset values from planes
- automatic layer intersection routines

To model the formwork, the individual corner points of each of the polygonal formwork elements needed to be specified. These were calculated by using the developed routines dealing with planar intersections. Laser measurement of the complex surface hall volume was not necessary, because inaccuracies in the concrete elements had been pre-calculated. After modelling the concrete elements, they were recalculated, because precise data was needed in order to control tolerance limits. For the installation of the exterior glass facade, a steel frame was used. The frame supported a glass cover at a variable distance to the supporting concrete shell. The installation points for the glass panels were located on adjustable struts, which were held in place (stayed) by means of steel ropes. The contractor kept within the tolerance limits with respect to all the concrete parts. Therefore no change between the glass outside shell and supporting concrete shell was necessary. The glazing of the hall volume was made from single security glass. The glass panels were prefabricated and drilled and fastened to point holding devices. The position of the holding devices was adjusted by using two 3-D lasers and space co-ordinates.

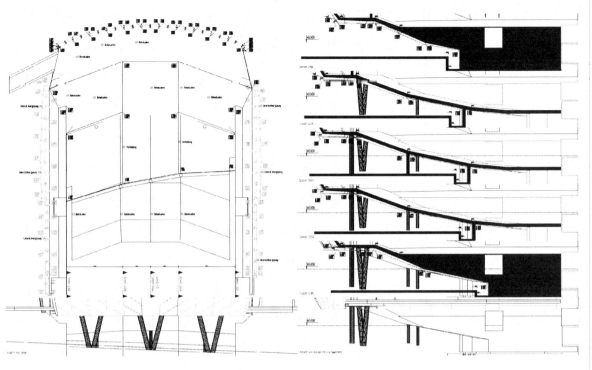

Figure 23.17: sections taken through the concrete hall floor.

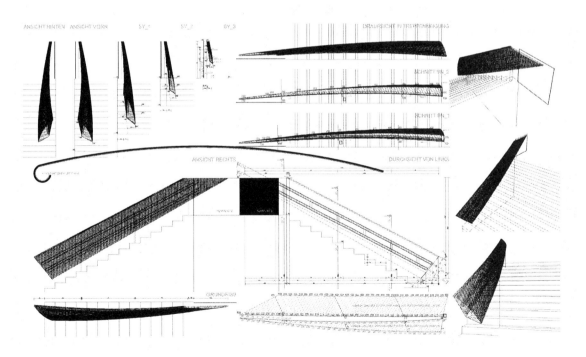

Figure 23.18: main stair and handrail details.

Figure 23.19: 3-D model of foyer with superimposed co-ordinate values.

Figure 23.20: 3-D model of stair and handrail.

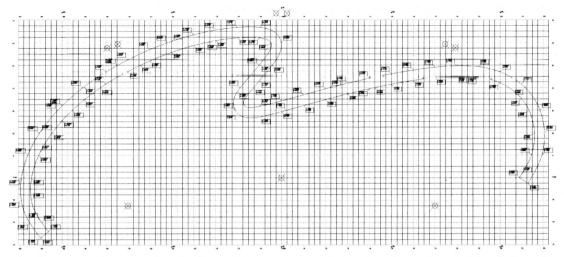

Figure 23.21: test output of offset and intersection routines, generating 2-D co-ordinate information from a 3-D model on a tartan grid.

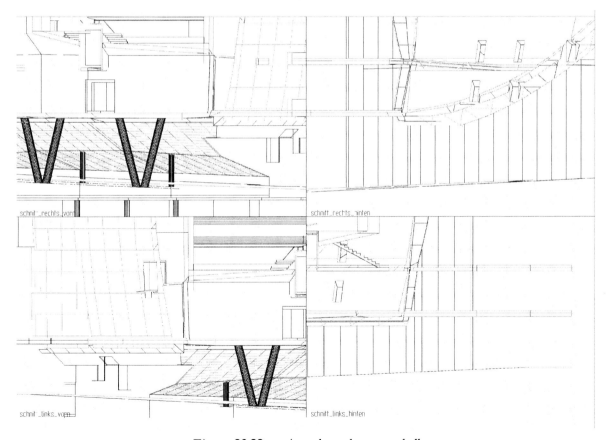

Figure 23.22: sections through concert hall.

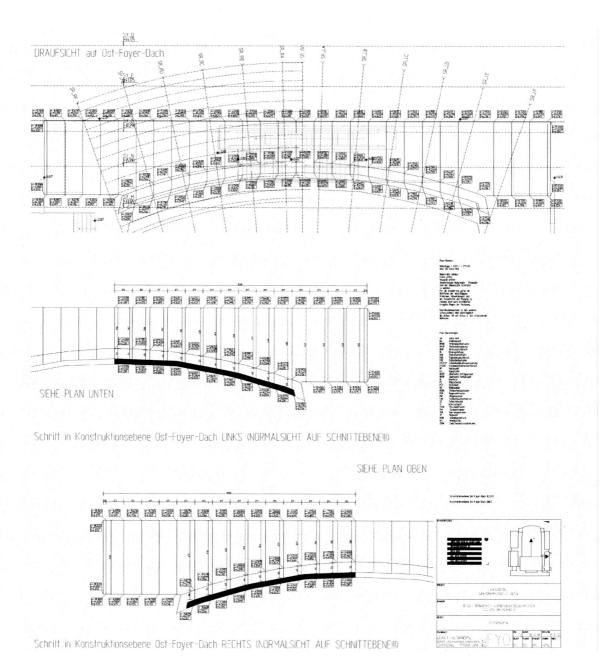

Figure 23.23: plans of the east foyer roof with sumperimposed co-ordinate values.

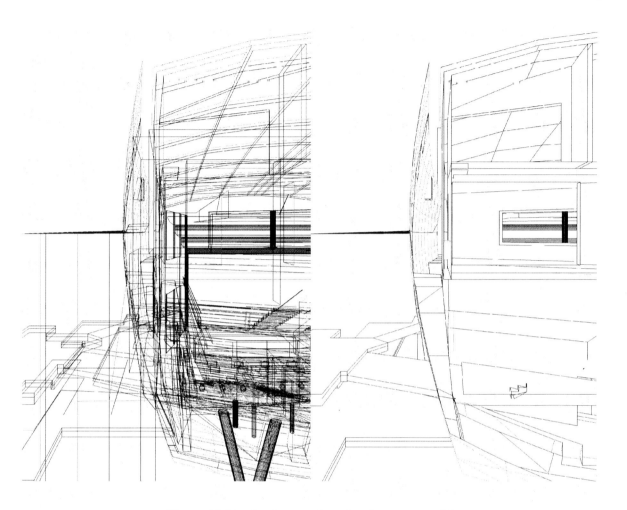

Figure 23.24: wire-frame and rendered cutaway models.

In the St. Polten Festival Hall project, user-defined CAD functions needed to be implemented in order to handle the constraint tolerances that were essential to the construction process. These CAD functions were concerned with maintaining the spatial consistency of the project, and therefore constituted extremely strong design rules for this particular scheme. They effectively replaced the more conventional CAD approaches, which rely upon using the built-in modelling functions of CAD systems in order to determine where various salient three-dimensional co-ordinate intersections will occur. This reliance is fine up to the point where the built-in CAD function tolerance limits become inadequate in meeting the detail needed for particular schemes. It is invariably the case that most CAD systems have predefined (by the CAD system programmer) tolerance values that lead to rounding errors. In a project of the complexity of St. Polten, these errors can quickly multiply around the model and thus lead to unresolvable inconsistencies. The reason that the design office resorted to this particular method of generating co-ordinate information is a direct consequence of the *prescriptiveness* built into most CAD systems.

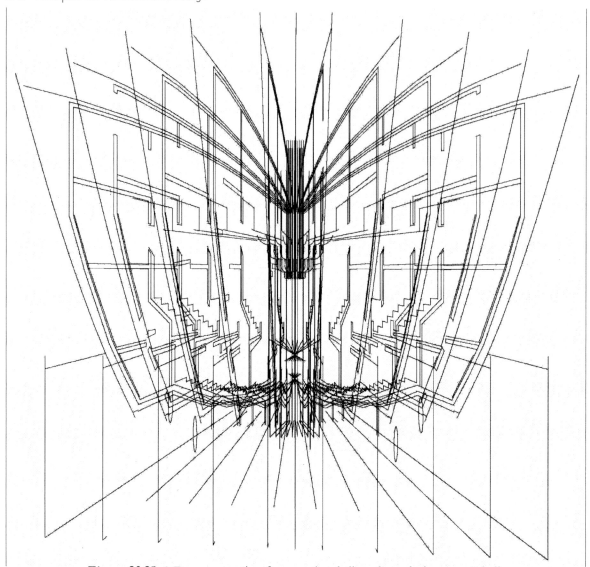

Figure 23.25: 3-D reconstruction from sectional slices through the concert hall.

Prescriptiveness refers to the manner in which information, and in this case functional information, is embedded within the software such that it is not subsequently modifiable by users. In this case, the non-modifiable information was related to the accuracy and tolerance information needed to position elements on site, including formwork and actual construction elements such as the glass panels. The built-in drawing functions that allow users to place elements at various types of intersection points were found to be insufficiently accurate for this scheme. Prescriptiveness, therefore, can be seen to set boundaries to the things that designers as users of CAD systems can do. The problem of prescriptiveness in CAD systems is likely to become worse the more that CAD systems are designed to perform domain-specific tasks. A central ambition of new-generation CAD software should be to allow designers to construct their own models within systems, resulting in CAD expressions that can then be exchanged with other design specialists. Responsibility for formulating and interpreting expressions should rest with the designers using the CAD system. In other words, new developments should focus on developing systems that support the maximum freedom of expression with minimum interpretative responsibility.

Part 7: Design Interoperability

Chapter 24: Referencing Common Project Models

In this and the following chapters, the focus of the case studies will shift onto the relationships between the different design disciplines involved in the projects, and the ways in which information is communicated between specialists for analytical purposes.

Case Study: The Snowdome, Milton Keynes, FaulknerBrowns Architects

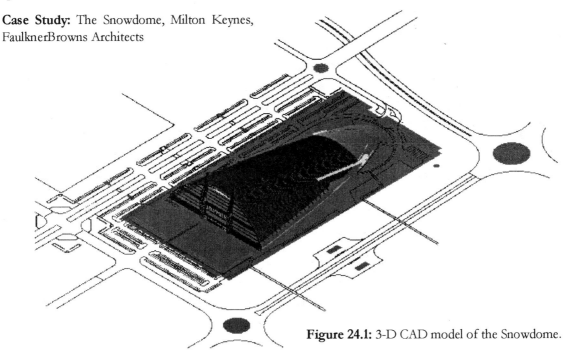

Figure 24.1: 3-D CAD model of the Snowdome.

The Snowdome occupies an important central site in Milton Keynes. The building form was influenced by the geometry of the ski slope contained within it. It is expressed as a simple cylinder angled to the ground. Thus, the constant curvature of the roof results in a very dramatic solution. The indoor ski slope is enclosed in a building complex which is a very simple shape – an angled slice taken from a cylinder.

The architectural theme for the building is to use a very simple and distinctive geometrical shape which provides an envelope around the various facilities incorporated within. The size of the envelope on this project was 240m long by 145m wide and 44m to the highest point of the gable elevation. The building takes the form of a slice cut off a cylinder at an angle of 9.6 degrees to the horizontal, creating a building which reduces in height and width at each cross-section. The main feature inside the building is an indoor, real snow ski slope, which starts at a high level above cinema areas, and slopes down through the building at angles between 15 and 8 degrees towards ground level at the opposite end. The ski slope is contained within an insulated box inside which snow is kept at a temperature of $-6.5°C$ to provide the surface for skiing. The width of the slope is from 40m to 60m. The surface snow can be brushed down into a pit at the bottom of the slope, and replaced with new snow. The other facilities provided inside the building include a shopping centre on the ground floor with pubs, food outlets, leisure areas and retail facilities. Above this, level 2 provides further retail and leisure areas together with a sixteen screen multiplex cinema. At the opposite end of the building, further leisure and social areas are provided which incorporate fitness rooms, aerobic studios, swimming pool, cafes, bars and changing facilities.

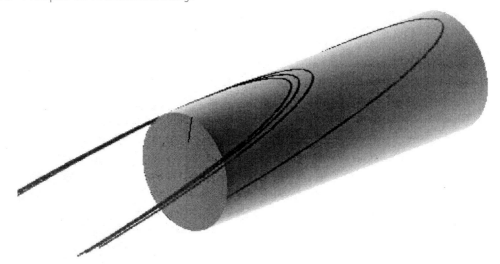

Figure 24.2: basic form generated by Boolean subtraction from a cylinder.

This and subsequent chapters will begin to look at the ways in which 3-D CAD models were used during early design stages. On the Snowdome project, two specific models were used. During the outline design, RIBA Stage C, a basic 3-D CAD model was created to set the overall principle of the building geometry. This model was also used to check the geometry of the envelope relative to the ski slope, cinema and retail spaces within. The 3-D model, therefore, provided a useful benchmark against which the maximum available floor space and volume could be checked. Towards the end of RIBA Stage C, and the commencement of RIBA Stage D (Scheme Design) the initial model was found not to be accurate enough, and a new simplified 3-D CAD model was created. This was used to define the exact geometrical setting-out information for the ellipse and, from this, the structural engineers created their own 3-D CAD model to further develop the structure.

From mid-RIBA Stage D, the engineers independently developed their own computer model with no real exchange of 3-D CAD data with the architects. Also, the conversion of 3-D CAD model information into 2-D cross-sections and floor plans was found not to be accurate enough at this stage. Precise 2-D geometrical descriptions of the floor plans and sections were, therefore, developed to assist with further design work and area/volume checks.

A standardisation of sections was made by comparing the results of a number of costed structural analyses of different frame types. Economic sections were chosen which satisfied the design parameters required in a number of areas. This also allowed some similarities to be maintained between the choice of sections. Due to the individual nature of the structure and the desire to achieve an economic solution, almost every beam, rafter and column on the structure was individually designed. Detailed fabrication drawings were prepared in a similar way. The preparation of the 3-D model of the structure at the design stage also gave a considerable advantage to the preparation of the detailed fabrication drawings, as the 3-D model was set up in advance, thus allowing the detailing to commence earlier than would have been possible had traditional CAD drawings been used. Huge and complex buildings often result in elaborate architectural solutions. The impressive aspect of the Milton Keynes Snowdome is its simplicity of form. The inclined cylinder form has allowed complete freedom internally to respond to the spatial demands of the extremely varied needs of different tenants, without compromising the integrity of the enclosing shell. The relationship between early stage CAD modelling, further analysis of these models in terms of structure, for example, and the consequent output of construction/fabrication data from the CAD models in order to facilitate the design process and to reduce costs will become a recurrent feature of the later case studies.

Chapter 25: The Relationship between Physical and Computational Modelmaking

Case Study: The Harbourside Centre for Performing Arts, Bristol, Behnisch, Behnisch & Partner

The significance of this particular project from a CAD perspective is as much in the process of design used by Behnisch's office as in the form itself. Prior to this project, the office had no real history of using CAD systems to develop their designs, and instead had a tradition of generating many physical sketch models, each responding to the brief in some way, and none of which was thrown away. For their invitation to participate in a selection process for a concert hall in Bristol, the Behnisch office submitted little detailed material, but talked about their approach, their attitude to collaboration, the qualities of the site, and their way of doing buildings. A few tentative physical sketch models were given to the prospective client as a way of involving them in a participative design process. To their surprise, the office won this selection process in March 1996. After this, work continued on the design development in preparation for an application to the Arts Council for lottery funding. In September 1997, the Arts Council awarded £4.3m of lottery money for detailed design work to continue and construction to begin.

Through a succession of drawings, physical and CAD models, the Harbourside concert hall evolved into a dramatic form. Because of the detailed acoustic and sight-line analysis of the main hall, it was also an eminently realisable project. Although the parties involved were all satisfied with the scheme, it could not proceed without the £58m of lottery funding towards the £89m needed for construction. In July 1998, after two years of work by the architects, the final year of which involved the client, Buro Happold structural engineers, Max Fordham environmental engineers, BBM Muller acoustical engineers, Theatre Project Consultants who carried out sight-line analysis, and other specialists, the Arts Council panel turned down the £58m lottery application.

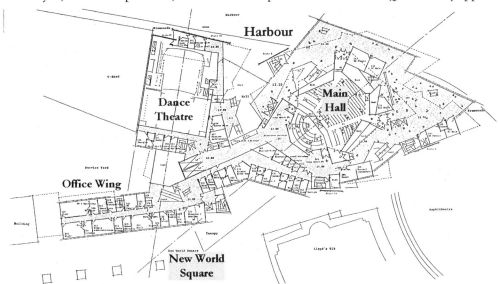

Figure 25.1: stage level floor plan scheme design drawing of Harbourside proposal (April 1998).

The site is on the south-east facing corner of the old Bristol harbour. One of the later drawings produced is shown in **figure 25.1**, and gives a sense of the final proposal. The plan of the scheme was organised around three main axes. The two axial lines in **figure 25.1** locate the two public auditoria: the dance theatre and the main hall. The dance theatre is at the north end of the site, abutting onto a neighbouring dock building. The third axis, not shown, is that of the office wing at the north-west end of the site.

Figure 25.2 shows two plan sections taken at higher elevations and therefore show some of the roof detail. An interesting observation at this point is that the plans in **figures 25.1** and **25.2** were all CAD generated, but have the *appearance* of being hand drawn. Many lines were intentionally generated to pass *through* intersection points instead of simply ending at intersection points. The latter option is the most convenient from a CAD point of view, since snapping to points such as the ends of lines is common practice. However, the motivation for intentionally creating overlapping lines was a presentational one. The plans were intended to be read by some of the less computer literate senior partners in the office, for whom the repetitive precision of conventional CAD drawings was anathema. Drawings that looked as if they were hand drawn were more readable to them.

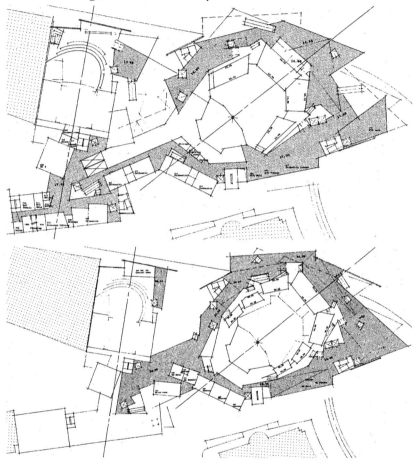

Figure 25.2: higher level CAD-generated, pseudo-hand-drawn plans.

The Behnisch office is driven by the philosophy of situation architecture, in which architectural design proposals are derived from and inspired by a particular place and need. They develop their understanding of the situation by allowing a design to evolve, reflecting in its complexity the conditions to which it responds. Working initially with physical models, they produced an external form that was distinct from the interior form, composed of folded roof and wall plates. Some of these models are shown on the following pages. Once the project received Arts Council backing in September 1997, it became essential to generate 3-D CAD models, initially to develop the scheme represented in the physical models, and to show the scheme in greater detail in relation to the site. Subsequently, CAD models were used as vehicles for two particularly important analytical functions critical to the resolution of the main auditorium space, namely, sight-line analysis and acoustic analysis. These analytical models are also shown.

Physical Models

Figure 25.3: early physical sketch model without roof form.

Figure 25.4: early physical sketch model showing roof form.

Figure 25.5: early physical sketch model showing facade form.

Figure 25.6: outline proposal model of main auditorium (November 1997).

Figure 25.7: physical model of stage, choir gallery, and orchestra risers.

Figure 25.8: physical model of auditorium.

Behnisch's office typically develop a whole series of rough physical models (e.g. **figures 25.3-25.5**) that are analysed as they evolve into more detailed models (e.g. **figures 25.6-25.8**). The main spaces that needed to be modelled were a large concert hall seating 2,300, a smaller dance hall seating around 500, a rehearsal hall, public foyers and restaurants, and offices and changing rooms. Although the main hall defined the overall form, the circulation space through the building to the harbour front was also a dominant feature. The foyer space between the two halls was to be as transparent as possible, with light entering through a massive sloping glass roof. It was even proposed that parts of the auditorium should be glazed, contrary to the recommended practice of many acousticians.

Figure 25.9: early presentation model (July 1996) showing foyers projecting over the floating harbour, and a folded plate roof form distinct from the internal acoustic roof.

Figure 25.10: late presentation model (June 1998) with a flatter roof form
compressed down onto the form of the internal acoustic roof.

As the detail design work progressed, the Arts Council started to squeeze the project both financially (initially from £58m down to £38m) and literally. They queried whether a city such as Bristol needed a concert hall for as many as 2,300 seats, even though they had themselves approved this in September 1997. The seating was subsequently reduced to 1,850, along with the flattening of the roof, and removal of the fly-tower. The flattening of the roof is noticeable between the physical models shown in **figures 25.9** and **25.10**.

Figure 25.11: late physical model (May 1998) showing the spatial complexity of the concert hall.

The model in **figure 25.11** was used by the architects to investigate the extent to which the heights and lengths of reflecting walls in the stalls could be minimised in order to better integrate the seating area, i.e. that certain parts of the audience didn't feel as if they were somehow segregated from other parts by intrusive reflecting walls.

CAD Models

The major use of CAD in Behnisch's office kicked in at the RIBA Stage C phase of the project, just after it got the backing of the Arts Council around September 1997. Behnisch's office freely acknowledge that prior to the introduction of various CAD techniques, the proposal simply did not work: the scheme was far too big and generous, and both the structural and the acoustic systems hadn't been worked out. In addition, new analytical functions needed to be investigated at this point in the design development. These included sight-line analysis within the concert hall, and the positioning of ductwork for the ventilation services, as carried out by Max Fordham and partners. The importance of the latter was that the cross-sectional area of the ductwork was as great as 15m in some places, since it was necessary to keep ventilation noise levels down to an absolute minimum, whilst at the same time minimising energy input. This was really the first time that Behnisch's office had seriously used CAD techniques on one of their schemes, and they appreciated the way in which it became possible to investigate alternative geometric arrangements by making simple and rapid changes to complex CAD models. It was this aspect of CAD use that made it particularly useful for both the sight-line analyses, and for the acoustic analyses, both of which required the assessment of many alternative geometric arrangements.

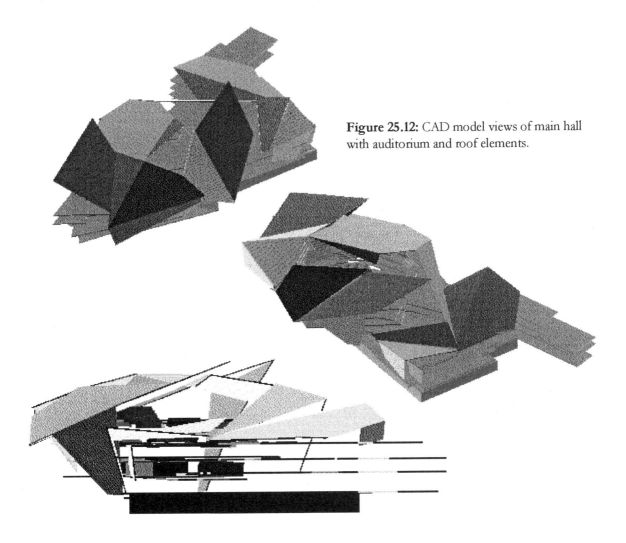

Figure 25.12: CAD model views of main hall with auditorium and roof elements.

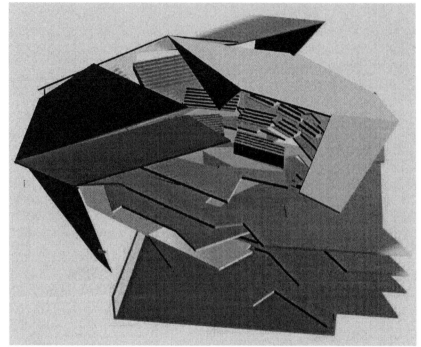

Figure 25.13: CAD model showing the folded-plate nature of the roof.

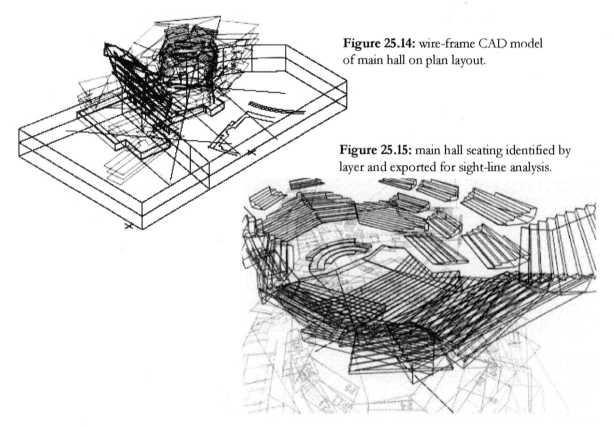

Figure 25.14: wire-frame CAD model of main hall on plan layout.

Figure 25.15: main hall seating identified by layer and exported for sight-line analysis.

Sight-line Analysis

Figure 25.16: sight-line analysis CAD model produced by Theatre Project consultants (April 1998).

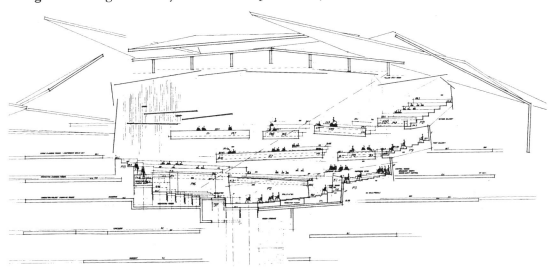

Figure 25.17: longitudinal section (February 1998).

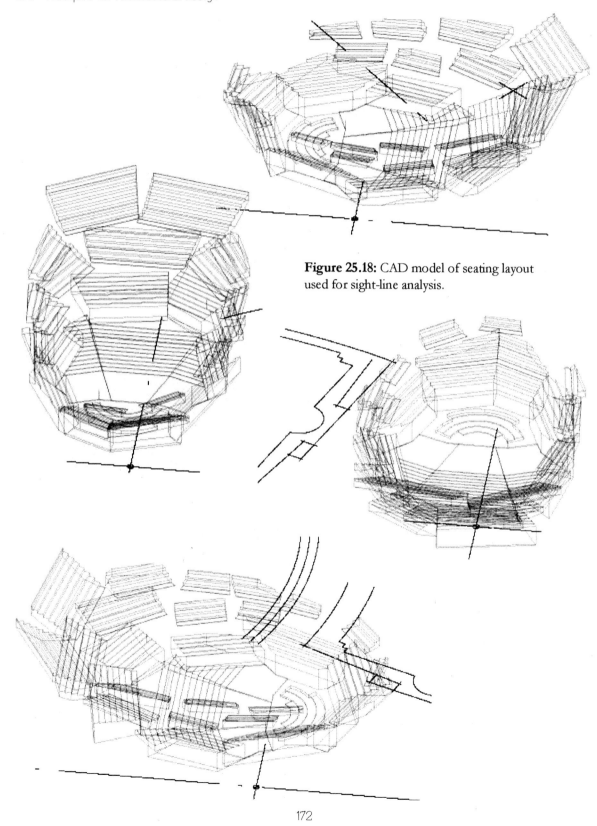

Figure 25.18: CAD model of seating layout used for sight-line analysis.

Acoustic Analysis

The design concept of the concert hall, based as it was upon the Berlin Philharmonie, required that the audience in the hall should be divided into a series of irregular seating terraces, using the fronts as acoustic reflectors. The acoustic analysis of the concert hall was carried out by acousticians at BBM Muller, some of whom had also been involved with the acoustic work on Scharoun's Berlin Philharmonie. Time permitting, it was intended to carry out acoustic analysis of both sound reflections and sound intensities for every single seat in the concert hall. The main focus was on the stage, and the immediate reflections from its walls, and from the side walls at the front of the stalls which were the most problematic. In addition to analysing the lengths and heights of these walls, their inward angle of tilt was analysed for angle values between $5°$ and $25°$. Similar analyses were later to be applied to each of the balconies, as well as considering whether the seating should be in line with the balconies, or rotated towards the stage. An important property of CAD models in such cases, therefore, is the fact that they can be broken down into parts in relatively straightforward ways (e.g. through the use of layering). These parts in turn become the focus of attention for subsequent analyses.

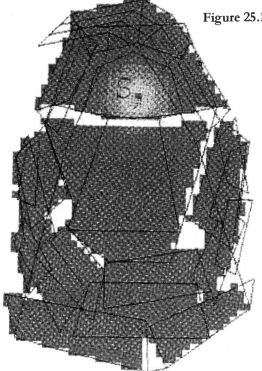

Figure 25.19: acoustic map showing direct sound.

Figure 25.20: acoustic map of sound reflections between 5 and 50ms.

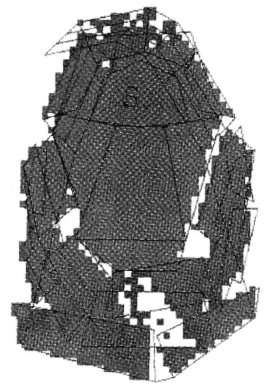

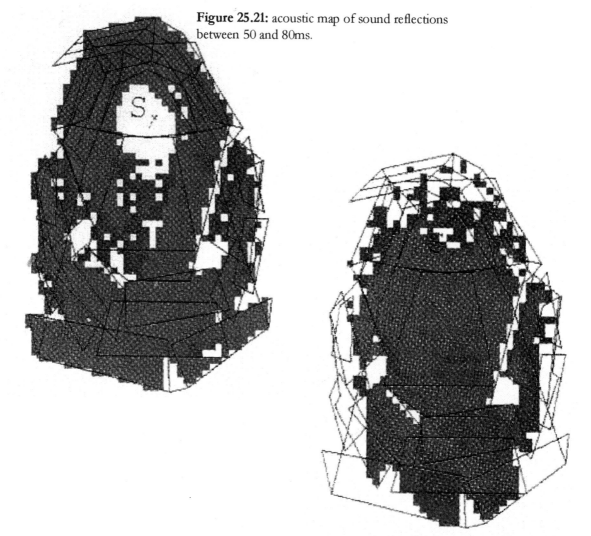

Figure 25.21: acoustic map of sound reflections between 50 and 80ms.

Figure 25.22: acoustic map of sound reflections between 80 and 200ms.

A central aim of the acoustic analysis was to identify acoustic measures that would allow members of the orchestra to hear their own playing optimally, and to perceive that of the other musicians much more clearly. A special height-adjustable reflector above the orchestra was developed to provide the best listening conditions for any orchestra configuration. To support modern musical performance requiring electro-acoustical amplification, measures were developed that substantially reduced the naturally long reverberation time in the hall. Special movable wall and ceiling elements were designed which reduced reverberation times not only in the medium and high frequency ranges, but also in the low frequency range.

The tragedy of this beautifully worked out and thoroughly analysed scheme was that it never came to fruition. The opportunity to build a world-class concert hall and to regenerate a semiderelict dockland area was sadly missed.

Chapter 26: The Interdisciplinary Nature of CAD Project Development

The use of CAD models in the context of design projects is such that the models produced reflect and advance the interests of the different participants and contributors to these projects. CAD models evolve from the experiences of different members of a design team, and the need to present these models to other people. As a consequence, different design practices have developed their own particular kinds of models and modelling techniques. Several of the previous case studies have shown that a major influence upon the types of CAD models produced was the central analytical strategy. Other influences, as in the following case study, stem from the need to present CAD information to particular end-users, such as clients and potential occupants, for example.

Case Study 1: Reichstag, Berlin, Germany, Sir Norman Foster & Partners

Foster and Partners' Reichstag scheme focused analytical attention particularly on a wide range of energy conservation measures. These included mechanical shading devices, automatically controlled windows, a power plant fuelled by renewable oils, solar panels, and an amazing use of underground lakes as thermal storage devices. All of these analytical features have been well documented, but an equally important aspect of the scheme concerned the style of presentation of CAD-generated images for the client. Style is often perceived as being an idiosyncratic way of approaching design problems, often associated with particular design practices. It is a method of constraining design solutions to fit within a particular range of outcomes. This constraining mechanism can then be used to resolve conflicts that occur between different participants in the design process.

Figure 26.1 shows a CAD-generated image of Fosters' proposal for the main debating chamber in the Reichstag building, Berlin, and is typical of the kind of computer-generated output produced for clients by the office of Foster & Partners on an increasingly wide range of projects. In it, there is no rendering other than the depiction of elements using hidden-line removal rendering. The intention in such presentations is to convey the essential form without causing distractions through the application of colours, textures, and lighting effects. It is this very basic form of CAD presentation that Fosters believe is the most appropriate medium for illustrating the essence of the spatial form. The Fosters' style of presentation, therefore, attempts to avoid the conflicts that could potentially occur between architect and client if more contentious forms of rendering had been applied to the CAD models. By keeping the rendering down to the bare minimum, the dialogue between architect and client is kept open and interactive, and any further CAD modelling can respond to the concerns and demands of clients and users in a participative process.

Architectural practices that possess high levels of technical competencies, such as Foster and Partners, for example, are at the same time extending the scope of new computing technologies within the design process. The acoustic analysis of the GLA building described in chapter 5, and the CFD wind flow analysis of the Swiss Re building described in chapter 7, are two examples of the practical realisation of what were until comparatively recently very specialised analytical techniques, with output that was often unintelligible to non-specialists. By presenting building performance information associated with specific analytical criteria in visually accessible ways, this information then becomes more relevant and accessible to an interactive design process in which the views of all parties are better reflected.

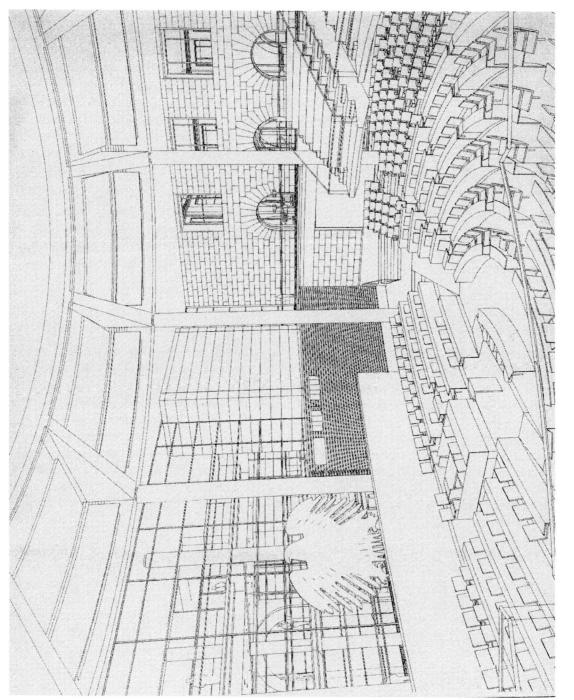

Figure 26.1: a CAD-generated interior view of the Reichstag debating chamber with minimal rendering.

Figure 26.2: a CAD modelled interior of the Reichstag.

Figure 26.3: a CAD modelled interior of the Reichstag.

Case Study 2: Middleton Botanic Garden, Sir Norman Foster & Partners

The Middleton National Botanic Garden in Dyfed, Wales, was constructed between 1997 and 1999. The 5000m² scheme is an example of interdisciplinary participation which determined the future of this particular site through a co-ordinated understanding of its history and potential. The extensive team of consultants on the project included Anthony Hunt Associates as structural engineers, Max Fordham and Partners as service engineers, and Colvin and Moggridge as landscape designers. Many of the original landscape features of the former 18th century Middleton Hall were restored, including five lakes.

Figure 26.4: an early design development CAD model of the Great Glass House examining the visual impact of the roof design.

The architectural centrepiece of Middleton is the Great Glass House, a 95m x 55m *elliptical dome* with different temperature and humidity zones, set into the landscape. This encloses one major volume which creates an ideal climate for the display of Mediterranean species across the world. The domed roof is a simple, continuous arched form with a minimal structure, which maximises the transmission of light whilst minimising maintenance. The glass house is solid on the north face, responding to the cold in winter, with generous ventilation to avoid overheating in summer. Surrounding the Glass House are a series of intensively managed botanic gardens. The northern part of the site is dedicated to science and education, the intellectual heart of the garden, while South Park Hill will become an arboretum, focusing views on to the various buildings and landmarks. The landscape design was carried out by Colvin and Moggridge, and responds to the natural features of hills and valleys and, above all, to water. The underlying framework of Sir William Paxton's fine late 18th century parkland with its woodland, lakes, dams, cascades and unique double-walled garden was also restored.

Interdisciplinary CAD

The interaction between architectural and landscape design is one of many interdisciplinary issues that are now becoming increasingly supported within CAD environments. At present, it is still generally the case that the use of CAD for landscape design at the level of single buildings is similar to its use in architecture. In this case, the concern for landscape designers is with the hard landscaping of roads, footpaths, and other paved areas, with some areas of planting. This type of detail generally follows site and building grids defined by architects. Where landscape CAD begins to differ from architectural CAD is at wider scales, when it is often necessary to create digital terrain models from site survey or ordnance survey data. CAD operations relevant to landscaping such as cut and fill can then be applied to evaluate and explore alternative landscaping possibilities. Although free-form sketching is as important in landscape design as it is in architectural design, accurate setting-out details are particularly important types of CAD drawings. Virtual environments of existing sites and cities have also been constructed from CAD models, and these then form the starting point for the contextualisation of both landscape and architectural design projects. The key issue here in the interaction between architects and landscape designers is the ability for each of them to demonstrate design concepts and principles to each other during the design process in responsive ways which give the designers control and rapid feedback.

An increasingly important aspect of CAD in landscape design is the use of Geographic Information Systems (GIS) for the construction of regional databases that can be accessed at the start of design projects. This information includes social, economic, and environmental/physical aspects. GIS systems enable designers to achieve a more comprehensive understanding of a site and its context. GIS, in conjunction with census data, allows designers to obtain strong visual understandings of land use, as well as of building types and scale. Subsequent design development can then be situated within this *virtual* context which is accessible for the duration of the project. GIS and census data are becoming increasingly available and accessible across the internet to users in remote locations. An increasing amount of information, therefore, is becoming available in digitised form.

Another expanding area that can potentially support interdisciplinary CAD is the use of *object-oriented technology*, which encourages the continuous development of design schemes within integrated environments. In object-oriented environments, it is feasible to represent similar objects in different design disciplines (e.g. 'pavement' may be an architectural object with minimal detailing, but a landscape object with associated details such as manhole locations and material properties). An architectural object can be derived from a landscape object or vice versa by means of *inheritance* (i.e. one object inherits properties from another). This is useful for reusing object descriptions instead of starting from scratch. Objects can also send *messages* to each other to communicate information (e.g. an architect could ask a landscape designer to produce a detailed rendering of his pavement object).

In architectural design, therefore, object-oriented CAD environments now make it feasible to integrate conventional modelling techniques with analytical evaluations such as energy calculations and lighting simulations. These were all ambitions of architects and landscape designers in the 1970s when computer power restricted the successful implementation of these ideas. Instead, the commercial trend at that time moved towards isolated specialist design tools in particular areas. Prior to recent innovations in computing, the closely related disciplines of architecture and landscape, for example, were separated through the unnecessary development of their own symbolic representations, and subsequent computer applications. This has led to an unnatural separation between what were once closely related disciplines.

Object-Orientation and the Internet

Present-day designers using computer-based technology are more demanding, better educated in CAD, and have generally higher expectation levels. These include ambitions to integrate CAD with the internet and web-based technologies.

Object-oriented technologies also facilitate the support of collaborative design work in which divergent models can be separately modified by different users, potentially using different applications. CAD systems are now becoming increasingly object based. Web-based software development also seems to be moving in a similar direction with developments such as JAVA, which offers the capability of demonstrating concepts and principles, and the provision of immediate feedback and user control (Pang and Edmonds, 1997; Macgill and Openshaw, 1997). Object-oriented graphics applications are highly suited to the support complex, multiple-user design projects. The representation of descriptions of *how* to regenerate design drawings is a central idea which leads to more efficient ways of working on team projects. Device independence enhances the transportability and exchange of files and data.

Recent trends in CAD system development have included attempts to integrate GIS with facilities management software. This type of development involves making connections between graphical and non-graphical (i.e. textual and numerical) information, and object-oriented environments for supporting such integration are increasingly being used.

Until the arrival of object-oriented applications in the CAD sector, the graphical and non-graphical aspects of designs were treated as separate and incompatible components, each represented with their own software environments. Computer systems that assist in building design should provide support for the visualisation of design proposals which are viewable and accessible by all participants in the design process.

The development of new CAD software will lead architectural practices to change their working practices in redefining the boundaries of CAD systems in the course of their application to real projects. The knock-on effects of such projects will inevitably have benefits in the following areas:

- the same CAD-generated information can be used to support the design processes associated with different disciplines, thus improving information exchange between design specialists.

- design projects can develop through the *incremental refinement* of information by successive project groups, thus leading to improved collaboration between different members of a design team.

- design information can be created once, and then made available to anyone who needs it over the lifetime of a project, thus resulting in more integrated design environments without duplication of information.

- the same information can be used in the different phases of a design project such as briefing, design and documentation, contracting, procurement, commissioning, scheduling and facilities management. This will improve co-operation between different partners, such as manufacturers and developers.

- applying object-orientation techniques to graphical environments will lead to improvements in the formulation and visualisation of design proposals from multiple design viewpoints.

International Standards

Conventional data transfer between CAD systems is typically accomplished using ASCII text data exchange formats. Data exchange formats are necessary because different CAD systems store information in different ways. The three most commonly found data exchange standards are the initial graphics exchange specification (IGES), drawing interchange format (DXF) and standard for the exchange of product data (STEP). DXF is used mainly for the exchange of graphical data, and therefore common in most CAD systems. STEP is a standard data format used to store all the data relevant to the entire life cycle of a product, including design, analysis, manufacturing, quality assurance, testing and maintenance, as well as product definition data. The use of standard data exchange formats in CAD systems has a number of associated problems:

- Data transferred is usually a lowest common subset. This often means just the geometry. In the worst case it may just be points or polylines. More sophisticated formats may offer some graphical attributes such as colour, linestyle and layer.

- Associated attributes (e.g. that a window belongs to a wall), or associated methods (e.g. how the construction of a window in a wall is costed), are lost.

- Drivers (programs) supporting exchange formats must be written many times over for a wide diversity of systems and formats.

- Drivers are costly to write and maintain because entities within the file and within the CAD system must be mapped onto each other. The structure of these entities is subject to change with time to accommodate additional modelling features. A DXF file created in a newer version of a CAD system often cannot be read by older versions which have older DXF formats.

Data exchange formats such as IGES, and more recently STEP, address some of these issues by overcoming the necessity for proprietary formats and promoting a standard, supposedly comprehensive format supporting a wide range of modelling structures. IGES has been driven by the requirements of mechanical engineering systems, whose models (solids and analytic curved surfaces) have been under-used in architectural design. Furthermore, CAD system developers have found it difficult or expensive to support the complete specifications of formats such as IGES and DXF. Typically, however, only a subset is implemented, which makes these formats less useful. Complex entities such as dimension lines and text tend to get corrupted or lost during the transfer process.

What is needed is that information, both graphical and non-graphical, should be shared by several applications. In several systems, the information concerning design objects includes *behaviours*, such as the ways in which the element can be drawn, manipulated or measured, as well as the more static properties of location, construction and style. This behavioural data is lost on transfer to other systems using standard exchange formats.

Object orientation may offer a solution to these problems, since objects can define interface behaviours to data, i.e. they can define how this data can be used. This will lead to the definition of new exchange formats that are potentially more powerful as they will be customisable rather than fixed. Objects can be shared not only between applications but across distributed computing environments, such as across the internet.

From Interdisciplinary Design to Integrated CAD

An emerging phenomenon in contemporary architectural practice is a more interdisciplinary design process in which computing technology is playing a major part. The outcome of such a development is that it is bringing together architectural practices, construction companies, building owners, building end users (occupants) and CAD software developers, to work together in a more integrated fashion.

Architectural Practices

Architectural practitioners are becoming more involved in the use and development of leading-edge CAD software. The successful development of this software will in the long term lead to a greater efficiency in working practices between architects and engineers, for example.

Service and Structural Engineers

Initial decisions on servicing in Britain are typically made with reference to the RIBA guidelines on the servicing of buildings. A more integrated computer-based approach to this procedure would potentially integrate this part of the design process with other computer-based parts. In early design stages, structural engineers need to make comparative assessments of different constructions for the same spans, and this in turn has severe cost implications.

Construction Companies

An advantage of more integrated CAD environments to construction companies is that site layout and organisation as well as construction methods, become important parts of the representation of the overall design scheme itself. Construction companies need to be able to make evaluations of planning and fitting-out arrangements based upon the nature of the ground and cut and fill operations required. The outcome of these calculations can have major cost implications.

Building Owners

Building owners need to be able to make assessments of their buildings in terms of comparisons of demolition costs as opposed to new build. Another form of comparison is between restyling and reordering of existing space vs new build. Rapid comparative analyses are needed, and assessments of available options have strong financial implications.

Occupants

Occupants can potentially be provided with online manuals concerning the maintenance of buildings, which include information about the longevity of building elements as well as decisions to be taken concerning repairs. An excellent reference work on this subject is *How Buildings Learn: what happens after they're built* by Stewart Brand (Brand, 1994).

Software Developers

Of benefit to CAD software developers is the valuable feedback they obtain from the end-users of their software, namely architects and engineers already using a range of computer-based design systems, and who are consequently best placed to make assessments about new developments.

The case studies in the following two chapters should illustrate how integrated CAD is being adopted on large-scale design projects by leading-edge architectural and engineering practices.

Chapter 27: The Integration of CAD with Construction

Case Study: Kansai International Airport Terminal, Renzo Piano

The spectacular Kansai International Airport terminal building in Japan is a massive steel and glass structure with a distinctive skeletal frame that was completed in 1994. It was designed by the renowned Italian architect, Renzo Piano, in consultation with the late Peter Rice of Arup Associates. Piano was closely concerned with all the structural details and with all changes made to them later in the design process. Arup did the steelwork drawings up to tender stage for the entire building. After tender, Nikken Sekkei controlled the work. The client for the new airport, located on an artificial island in Osaka Bay with severe subsidence problems, was the Kansai Airport Authority. Contracted to it was a joint venture design company with four members: Renzo Piano Building Workshop, Japan Airport Consultants, Aeroports de Paris and Nikken Sekkei, the Japanese executive architect/engineer. Arup was a sub-contractor to Piano. Watson Engineering of Bolton won the tender for the job of manufacturing the structure consisting of 3,900 tons of steel, as Japan's major fabricators initially considered this project to be unbuildable.

The T-shaped plan consists of a large rectangular main terminal building from which passengers move into a 1.6km side building, called 'the wings', from which planes are boarded. The wave-like roof is made almost entirely of steel tubes, and connects to the *semi-elliptical* section of the wings. The wings are framed by curved ribs and diagonal braces, and slope gradually down towards their ends. The critical geometrical form from a CAD point of view is a *toroid*, like the top section of a giant inner tube, with a radius of 16.8km centred on a point not directly below the building.

Figure 27.1: the geometry of Kansai airport.

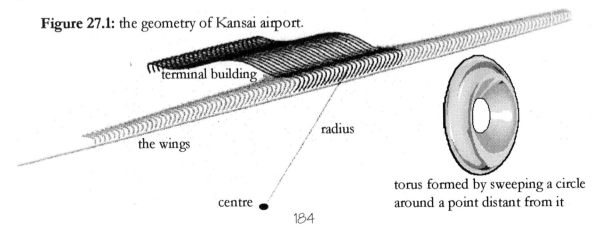

the wings

terminal building

radius

centre

torus formed by sweeping a circle around a point distant from it

The ribs of the building each contain five different circular radii in their semi-elliptic shape. These ribs are themselves radii of the 16.8km circle, so the central ones are vertical but each of the rest slopes successively 0.02 degrees more per bay towards the ends of the building. However, all the construction above ground level is strictly standardised. Only the bottom joints and panels of the building are special elements; the standard rib shape is simply increasingly cut off at the bottom towards the end of the building.

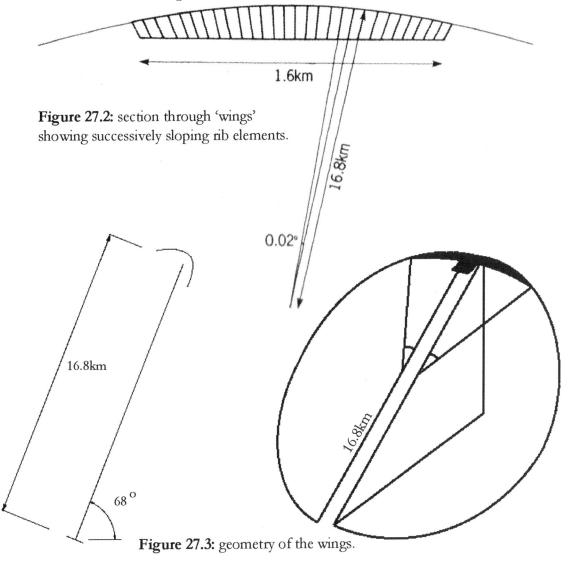

Figure 27.2: section through 'wings' showing successively sloping rib elements.

Figure 27.3: geometry of the wings.

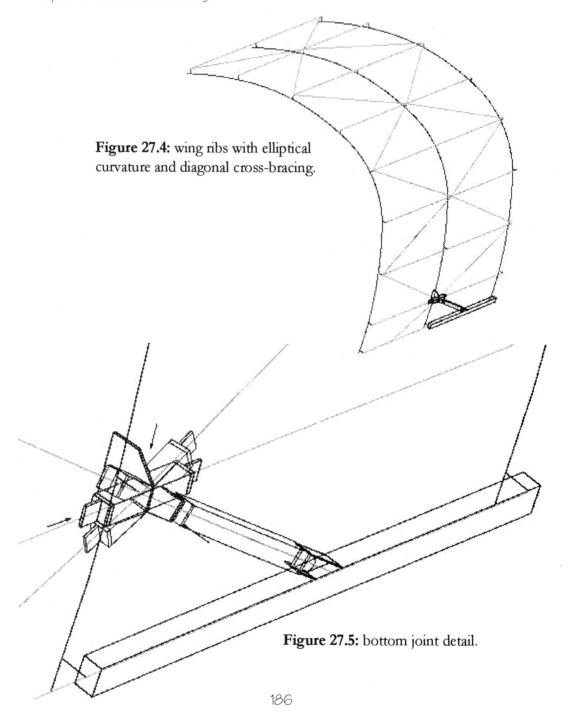

Figure 27.4: wing ribs with elliptical curvature and diagonal cross-bracing.

Figure 27.5: bottom joint detail.

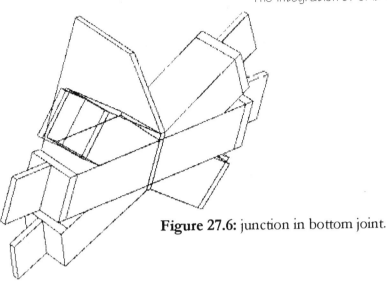

Figure 27.6: junction in bottom joint.

In addition to the geometry of the form, this case study is of interest in terms of the use of CAD at the construction stage, and the integration of CAD with the construction, particularly the CAD/CAM (Computer Aided Manufacturing) aspect. Of the three contractors involved, Nippon Steel and Kawasaki Heavy Industries each built half of the main terminal building, while Watson Engineering was responsible for the wings, a complicated part of the structure. Arup did 90 tender drawings in Japanese. A common currency for transferring information was through the use of common data exchange formats on computer disks. Watson made refinements to the detailed geometry, and prepared CAD shop drawings which were checked by Nikken Sekkei. Then information was transferred to the shop-floor machines either on tapes or by direct downloading from the CAD system. Of the shop floor machines, most were for ordinary operations such as sawing sections to length, drilling holes or cropping plate. An end mill, for cutting sections accurately, handled faces up to 4.8m X 1.8m. Welding was carried out on a Bode track-mounted boom welding machine which makes large, neat welds on workpieces up to 36 X 4 X 5m. Two multi-head CNC (Computer Numerically Controlled) profile burners cut plates up to 31m X 3m to any shape. A Welca Vari-piper tube profiler, an analogue controlled thermal cutter, was used to produce accurately shaped ends on any tube up to 1.2m diameter, allowing tubes to be mitred. The Japanese client insisted that curved tubes were exactly circular, even though bending normally causes slight flattening of the section. This job was done by a subcontractor with an induction bending machine, which electrically heats a very short length, around 40mm to 50mm say, so that adjacent cold parts maintain their circular form. Many tiny bends produce a smooth curve. Each curved rib was made in several parts and assembled in a large jig.

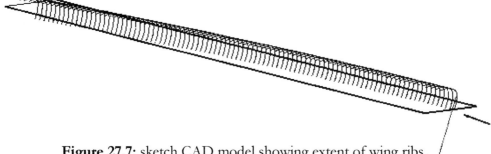

Figure 27.7: sketch CAD model showing extent of wing ribs.

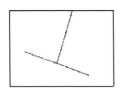

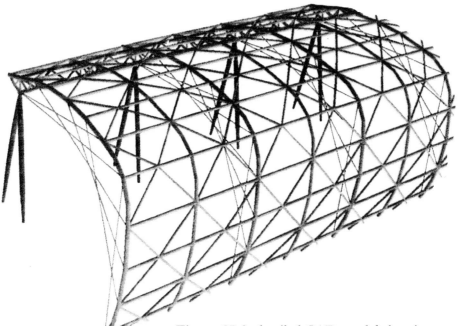

Figure 27.8: detailed CAD model showing connected ribs.

At the time of the Kansai project, Watson Engineering employed about 400 people at Bolton, 250 in the works, 50 site staff and the remaining 100 in the office, including many design engineers. An important feature of their office is that they have a large planning staff, as they specialise in complicated fabrications and difficult construction problems. Though they can handle 40,000 tonnes of steel a year, the focus is not on high throughput. Instead, they concentrate on complex engineering, quality, technology and high added value. It was the first UK fabricator to achieve BS 5750 certification.

The integration of design and manufacturing is now progressing through the development of computerised process planning techniques. The aim is to be able to select the machines needed to produce a part, to determine the sequence of operations on those machines, to estimate the time needed for setting up and production, the scheduling of production, and the identification of tooling and raw material requirements. CNC machining tools are being developed with increasing degrees of freedom in order to better direct the motions of both cutting tools and parts, and even to change tools during the cutting process.

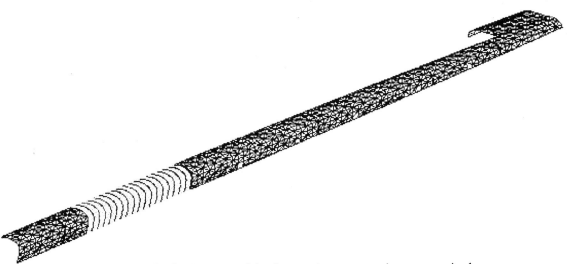

Figure 27.9: CAD model of one wing connecting to terminal.

Chapter 28: Integrated CAD

The creative use of state-of-the-art CAD technology on structures such as the Guggenheim Museum in Bilbao has realised ambitions in CAD that have lain dormant since the 1970s, the central principle of which was that of the *integrated CAD system*. This radical and ambitious concept first arose in the early days of CAD when computing power was comparatively weak, but architectural aspirations high. The aim was to be able to describe a design from inception to production entirely within the CAD environment. The emphasis was less on *particular* design functions and more on the expression and manipulation of design information to serve *all* possible functions. Although serious attempts were made to develop integrated CAD software to support the design of particular building types such as hospitals (OXSYS, used by the Oxford Regional Health Authority), and houses (SSHA, the Scottish Special Housing Association), they suffered from the effects of having to fit the users to the available software, rather than the other way round (Bijl, Stone, Rosenthal, 1979). Invariably, users had to conform to using systems that anticipated precisely how buildings would be perceived, down to a level of fine detail. Such systems were characterised as *prescriptive* (Bijl, 1989).

Case Study: The Guggenheim Museum, Bilbao, Frank Gehry Associates
On the Guggenheim Museum project, a CAD environment was used which not only supported the modelling of surfaces and volumes, but which also interfaced with a 3-D digitising device (a Faro arm) allowing Gehry's office to integrate physical models with CAD models. Furthermore, since the CAD software was originally developed for aircraft design, the analysis of the curvatures and stresses on the complex curved surfaces was also possible. Finally, another of the inbuilt functions enabled the definition of paths that milling machines could use. This allowed the computer cutting of physical models in order to verify the accuracy of certain forms, as well as the cutting of actual elements to be placed on site.

Gehry's use of CNC systems in conjunction with new construction techniques has meant that his office has effectively redefined what is buildable, rather than having relied upon known methods anticipated within CAD environments.

Figure 28.1: CAD model of Guggenheim Museum.

Figure 28.2: parameterised CAD model of Guggenheim Museum generated from digitised physical models and generating CNC output.

As far as the geometry of the Guggenheim is concerned, the straight lines and rectangular blocks traditionally associated with CAD presentations have been replaced by complex curves and fluid, organic forms. It seems as if Gehry's own sketches have been transferred directly into the CAD environment.

Since surfaces were represented in terms of *parameterised polynomial equations*, it was relatively easy to represent a variety of cladding panels with a single set of equations. As the shape of the external form of the Guggenheim was of central importance, the CAD model was developed from the outside in.

Initially, Gehry was resistant to using the computer in his design process (Van Bruggen, 1999). He subscribed to the still common perception of CAD as somehow restricting the modelling of architectural form to symmetries, mirror imagery, and simple Euclidean geometries. Gehry's office wanted to be able to visualise gestural moves, resulting in sculptural 3-D forms that retained the immediacy of sketches, which could then be scaled up to large objects. The office developed a process of digitising physical models, followed by the manipulation of computer models, and then back to the physical models in the form of milled objects.

Regarding the construction of these sculptural forms, the layout process was accelerated and, as sculptural shapes could be computed, a more time-saving, economic way of building was devised, affecting, for instance, the structuring of a steel frame, or figuring out what it takes to fit panels together on a wall. The new process could work for both high technology in terms of construction, such as numerically controlled machines, and traditional craft equally well, as demonstrated in the Nationale Nederlanden office building in Prague, where many full-scale templates were used to design shapes.

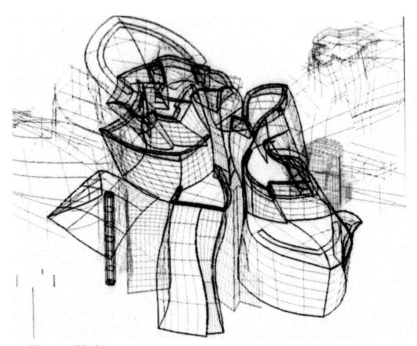

Figure 28.3: CAD model used to generate structural frame.

After making a large-scale physical model, and digitising points over the surface of the model, surfaces were regenerated inside the CAD environment, and control surfaces and setting out points identified. The structural zone was identified by marking offsets from the control surfaces. Within the structural zone, the structural engineers (SOM) were able to develop a structural concept based on a braced frame using modular sections and minimal shoring (LeCuyer, 1997). This frame was made up of wide flange sections on a 3m grid. All of the members used except those in the boat gallery and tower, were straight sections. The structural members were positioned within a tolerance of 300mm by the structural engineers, then left it to Gehry's office to finalise the positions. Between the steel frame and the control surface, two layers of secondary structure were used, horizontal ladders at 3m vertical intervals established the horizontal curvature, and were connected to the primary structure with a universal joint enabling fine adjustment in all directions. The innermost and outermost layers of the secondary structure create the vertical curvature, made from vertical steel studs curved in one or more directions. The complex geometries, nodes of intersections, clearances and interferences for all of the layers of construction were calculated by the system, so that every member could be sized and located accurately within what was essentially a wire-frame model.

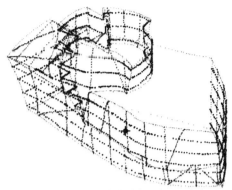

Figure 28.4: an initial digitised model.

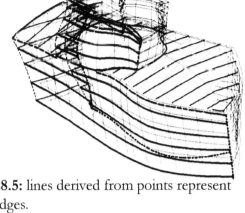

Figure 28.5: lines derived from points represent surface edges.

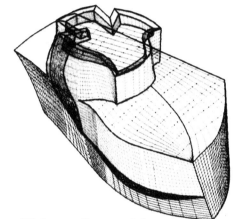

Figure 28.6: a surface model.

Figure 28.7: a CNC model for verification.

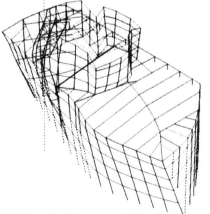

Figure 28.8: wire-frame model refinement.

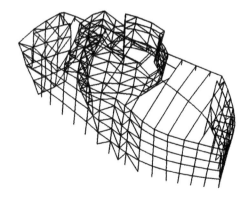

Figure 28.9: primary structural elements.

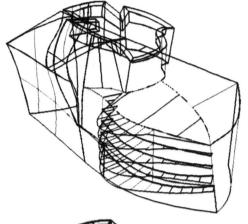

Figure 28.10: model indicating horizontal curvature elements.

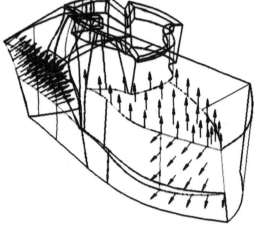

Figure 28.11: model showing magnitudes and directions of internal forces.

Figure 28.12: a curvature analysis model.

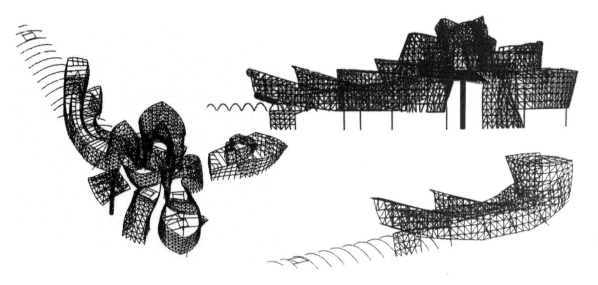

Figure 28.13: wire-frame models of structural frame.

In earlier projects, Gehry had wanted to create full 3-D computer models of the structure, but had not been able to find software to make it feasible. Urssa, the Spanish steel fabricators, used software originally developed for bridge and highway construction. Using this, they could import wire-frame models from Gehry's office, and convert them into comprehensive models of the structural steelwork. From this structural model, it was possible to convert it into either 2-D fabrication drawings, or computer numerically controlled (CNC) data for the complex end configurations of the steel. The structural analysis software ensured that the primary structure could be built with hardly any site cutting or welding. One of the main problems in the construction process was to position the individual pieces of steel. Sometimes cranes had to be doubled up to push and pull the steel into place. After the experience of Bilbao, both Urssa and Gehry realised that the positioning of the steel could be rehearsed within the CAD environment, thus improving the sequencing and reducing the costs for cranes.

During the construction, every structural component was bar-coded and marked with the nodes of intersection with the adjacent layers of structure. The bar-codes were scanned on site revealing the co-ordinates of each piece of structure. The CAD model was also linked to laser surveying equipment, enabling each piece to be positioned relative to the model. This form of construction is in contrast to traditional methods in which the secondary structure is typically measured relative to the primary structure. Using the computer model as a base for every piece of structure, whether primary or secondary, minimises the accumulation of tolerances and the need for site measuring and cutting.

Figure 28.14: wire-frame models of structural frame.

Several full-scale physical models were created in order to test the extent to which the galvanised steel sheets could be subjected to the complex curvature without buckling, as well as testing the tolerances in the standing seams. From these physical models, the information gained was added to a database associated with the CAD system, enabling rationalisation of the metal surfaces. Despite the complex shape of the building, the cladding for 80% of it was supplied in four standard panels. The same principle was applied to the glazing; the complex curved geometry was realised by means of triangulation. Since glass cannot warp, however, and minimal tolerances were permitted in the connections, almost 70% of the glazing is unique. The stone cladding was milled using CNC machining techniques based directly upon the CAD data. This involved bringing a three-axis CNC milling machine onto the site, where the fabrication took place.

Whilst Gehry himself focused on the design of the sculptural forms, his team analysed alternatives in terms of volumes, surfaces, structures, and ultimately of cost. Revised physical models were then reassessed by Gehry in this cyclical process. In comparing this process with conventional methods, Jim Glymph of Gehry's office stated, '*Bilbao could have been drawn with a pencil and straight-edge, but it would take us decades*' (Van Bruggen, 1999).

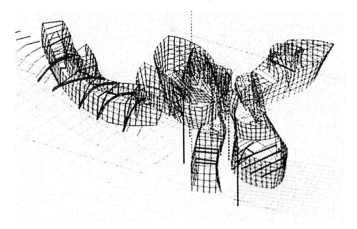

Figure 28.15: structural frame model.

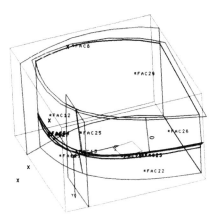

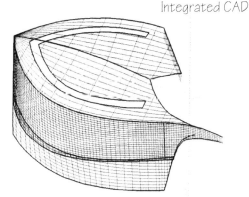

Figure 28.17: surface model with cladding.

Figure 28.16: surface model with distinct faces.

According to Randy Jefferson and Jim Glymph, computer managers in Gehry's office:

'Our idea was to create a process for controlling geometries and dimensions and for documenting the projects, which is an entirely different realm from the concept of using computers for presentation. We do not use the computer for that at all. The first job we did with the computer was the fish in Barcelona. We used it in order to facilitate what was an extremely fast construction period and a very tight budget. It had nothing to do with presenting it to the client. It had nothing to do either with the design process, because the design was already finished. Unlike many other architects who use the computer rendering and animation programs to convey ideas to the client, we began past that stage, so the only applications that we were interested in were those that would assist manufacturers and contractors in producing the job cheaper and more efficiently. It was a pure exercise in how to execute the design that already existed and that led us to a sort of narrow space approach in what was in reality a non-building project. We discovered that the manufacturers could really use the information we produced much more effectively than any form of traditional documentation.'

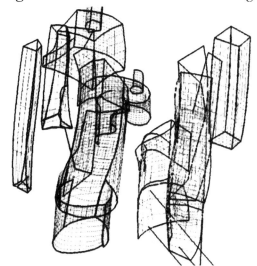

Figure 28.18: vertical elements.

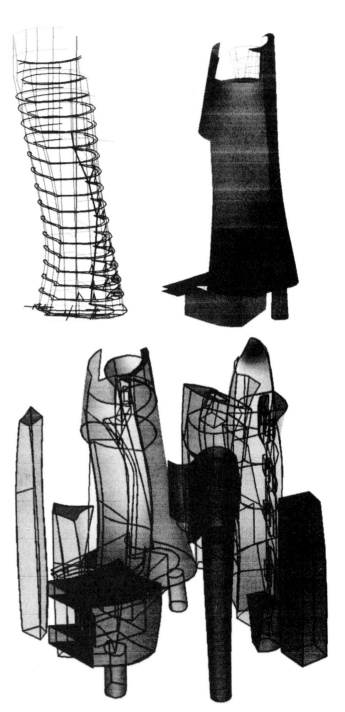

Figure 28.19: detailed models of tower and other vertical elements.

There is a whole cultural change that I believe will take place with the young kids who are growing up computer literate.

Two-dimensional drawings are actually much more of an abstraction than if we did everything in a three-dimensional space. But construction industry specifications are generally in 2-D, out of habit. As the workforce at all levels becomes more computer literate, the need to go through the two-dimensional intermediate step could be eliminated, together with a lot of waste, a lot of errors, a lot of redundant operations. It is surprising how fast, particularly in Europe, manufacturers and contractors are picking up on this idea: many steel producers are now starting to work in three-dimensions; the same is occurring in the stone industry.' (Zaera, 1995)

Figure 28.20: rendered models of tower forms situated within the central atrium space.

In less than two years, Gehry developed his improvisational method of designing with physical models, into a process in which powerful CAD environments supporting the expression of fluid forms played a central role. Physical modelling was integrated into this process through 3-D digitisation and CNC machining.

199

Figure 28.21: model showing metal cladding pattern.

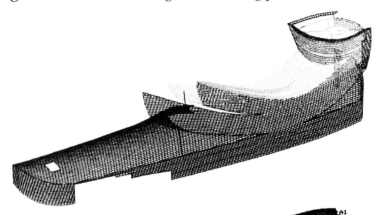

Figure 28.22: model showing surface elements.

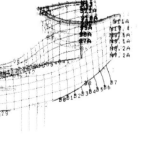

Figure 28.23: elevation showing structural frame.

Figure 28.24: isometric showing structural frame.

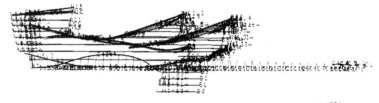

The modelled curvilinear forms were transformed directly into the data needed for construction, transforming fluid forms into economically viable technical specifications. The end result was the construction of forms previously thought to be impractical and unbuildable, particularly within the added complications provided by the site. The illustrations show CAD-generated models used for a wide variety of purposes, e.g. structural layout, cladding specifications, surface models, and models for CNC machining which in turn generate new physical models for further design and analysis. The multiplicity of models were generated within an integrated CAD environment which allowed the superimposition of alternative descriptions within the same three-dimensional reference space. Modelling directly in three dimensions was absolutely central to modelling forms of this complexity. Any plans and sections necessary for construction could be generated routinely from the 3-D models.

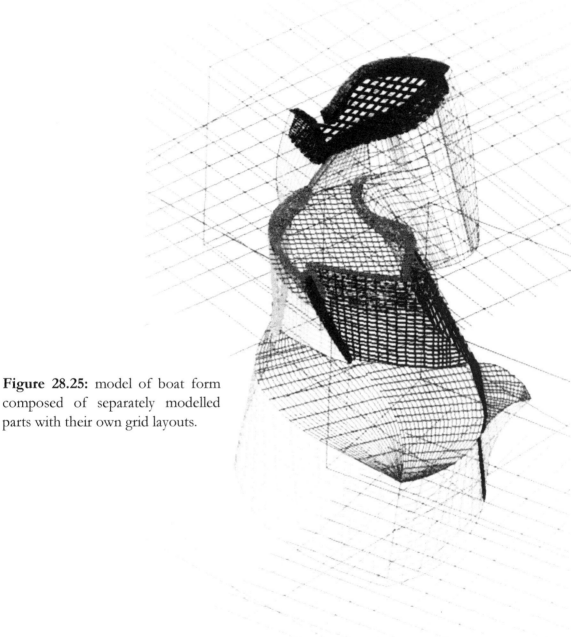

Figure 28.25: model of boat form composed of separately modelled parts with their own grid layouts.

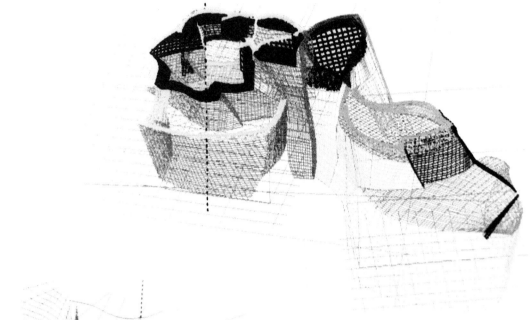

Figure 28.26: addition of a further object on its own grid system.

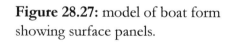

Figure 28.27: model of boat form showing surface panels.

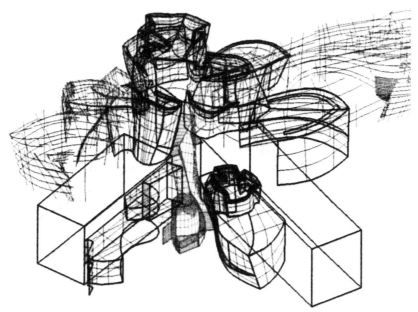

Figure 28.28: composite CAD model with linked components indicated by bounding boxes.

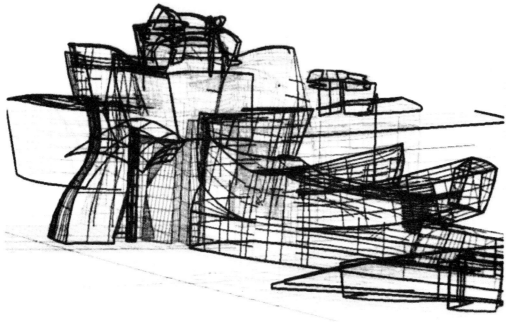

Figure 28.29: composite CAD model with similarities to Gehry's original sketches.

In the Guggenheim Museum, Gehry fully exploited the possibilities of *structural optimisation* CAD techniques (see chapter 3). In addition to modelling each element, the link with construction was made by analysing and evaluating optimal component shapes within the constraints of Gehry's designed topology. An important by-product of this *shape optimisation* process was the *sizing optimisation*, which in turn affected the *costs* of the project. With these analytical techniques, therefore, the separate phases and techniques of conceiving and executing the building were totally integrated: from the initial surface and volumetric 3-D CAD models, through to assembly models of the steel frame and cladding, and culminating in fabrication from CAD-generated construction information. The Guggenheim could not have arisen out of the application of disparate analytical software. A building of this geometrical complexity could only have been constructed without costly trial and error by the use of integrated CAD.

The CAD modelling work for the Guggenheim was inextricably linked to the analytical design intentions behind it, responding crucially to the pragmatic aspects of the design context. This case study has shown the creative possibilities of CAD when used within integrated design frameworks. This approach to CAD has moved on greatly from the prescriptive systems approaches which anticipate the properties and structures of objects separate from, and prior to, a designer's own description of them.

New computing developments in CAD are becoming more responsive to the methodologies of design associated with design practices that are pushing this technology, several of which have been referred to in the context of the case studies. In being guided by the design domain itself, rather than by fashionable computing techniques, it is possible to envisage the direction of new CAD developments, as well as anticipating the limitations of existing CAD environments.

The case studies, culminating with the Guggenheim, have pointed towards an integrated approach to the use of CAD systems, in order to support the full extent and scope of architectural design. Each of the case studies has been presented in terms of content at a fairly high and general level. However, it was also possible to see the manifestations of these high-level features in relatively specific and precise ways when the CAD software was actually being used. The next and concluding section will revisit and investigate the general issues that are of concern in this integrated approach towards CAD.

Part 8: Summary

Integrated CAD

From the previous case study, it can be seen that integrated CAD environments can be characterised by a number of features:

- Appropriate representation

Whenever a designer chooses to use a particular CAD environment, he consequently commits himself to a particular underlying computational *representation*. This will inevitably affect the suitability of this environment for particular design tasks. A system having points as primitive elements (as is common in most desktop CAD environments), therefore, will not behave in the same way as a system in which points are defined in terms of pairs of intersecting lines (a line-based CAD environment allows for the description of lines in equational form, and can therefore potentially be *parameterised*), for example. The latter in turn is not the same as a system in which points are defined in terms of triples of intersecting planes (a surface-based system). Gehry's choice of a *surface-based CAD environment* was capable of supporting the kinds of 3-D distortions needed to develop the Guggenheim form. Once a commitment has been made to a particular choice of CAD system, an appropriate representation is one which can effectively support the expression of design tasks and sub-tasks in the mind of the designer.

- Comprehensive design description

As design information is expressed and described at various stages of the design process, an integrated CAD environment is capable of supporting both the expansion of this design information, and the application of analytical tasks upon it, as required by the designer.

- Analytically driven

Different design practices develop their own particular types of CAD models that vary over time and in response to changing demands. They therefore need to be able to mould analytical applications to their own requirements. Analytical CAD functions need to meet temporal, designer-specified demands, to a degree which makes software expendable.

- Support cyclical design development

As discussed in chapter 2 of this book, design does not progress in a linear fashion, but instead tends to be cyclical in character. This cyclical nature is determined by various factors. Conflicts and inconsistencies can arise between any of the many possible analytical criteria, e.g. between the positioning of a structural frame and a required spatial organisation. An early stage design response to a given brief can lead to a redefinition of constraints upon a scheme, together with a redefinition of the parameters associated with these constraints. Although cyclical design development needs to be supported, pragmatic factors invariably come into play, particularly in relation to the costs of making changes to detailed CAD models.

The Integration of CAD with Construction

The integration of CAD with construction through the exchange of computer-based information in common data-exchange formats is becoming an increasingly common aspect of contemporary architectural practice that allows the efficient transfer of design information to fabricators and construction companies. The CAD work on the Guggenheim Museum, for example, demonstrated the interaction between designers and contractors through the detailed production co-ordination of the museum design.

Many of the key issues relating to the integration of CAD with construction revolve around being able to decompose a design scheme into component parts, each of which can then be constructed by specialist contractors, e.g. foundations, steelwork, stairs and lifts, cladding, services, etc. In addition to communicating information concerning the geometries of the component parts, the issues of integration revolve around the orientations of these components, their locations, and relationships and adjacencies to other components. Some of these relationships are constrained by building regulations that need to be anticipated by architects, but sometimes are not. Contractors often have to complete the detailed descriptions of component parts, such as the connecting rods and brackets that were needed for different truss types in the Waterloo Terminal project. The relationships between components are particularly significant for efficient scheduling and planning of the construction process.

CAD modelling in terms of predefined components and structures revolves mainly around the spatial layout of these components. Knowledge of CAD system *constraints* that restrict the placement of objects is crucial for this kind of work. Improvements in co-operation between manufacturers and designers now makes it feasible for manufacturers to provide designers with databases of components together with the constraint rules upon them.

There are two kinds of constraint, often referred to as geometric constraints and engineering constraints. Parallelism, perpendicularity, tangency, dimensionality are geometric constraints. The constraint of construction elements, on the other hand, will affect their degrees of freedom and tolerance values, and hence their positioning on site.

Integration has a greater chance of success if designers use 3-D design environments directly, rather than working with discrete abstractions (e.g. plans and sections) which then need to be assembled together to generate on overall view of the scheme. Plan and sectional information can always be generated as by-products from 3-D CAD models as and when needed.

The Interdisciplinary Nature of CAD Project Development

Co-operative design activity is an increasingly important aspect of architectural practice. Large, top-down design practices are structured so that designers of different levels of experience and skills can work together. The computational aspect of such practices consists of many components which include modelling and analysis amongst other things, such as databases and document processing. Since major design decisions are typically made in the early stages of design, this is when the analysis of various alternatives relating to different technical disciplines needs to be carried out. Comparative costs of these alternatives also need to be estimated at this time. Through the standardisation of CAD input/output formats, it is now possible to integrate several software applications; for example, those that deal with modelling, energy analysis, and cost.

Design practices are also beginning to achieve greater integration between CAD modelling environments and database systems, such as those that deal with bills of quantities, for example. CAD in architectural practice is now more than the production of drawings and 3-D views. CAD modelled building elements have very complex cross-references to other kinds of information. Most commercial CAD environments now provide simultaneous concurrent access to data in a central master project from an unlimited number of sites.

Designers should be encouraged to know that it is now possible to describe a wide range of design schemes, *without* needing to rely upon computational visualisation and presentation techniques, such as conventional object creation and transformation, rendering and texture mapping. Although these presentation techniques are necessary at certain stages of design development, it is still more important to be able to support the *reflection-in-action* that takes place in design practice, particularly on interdisciplinary design projects. A typical interdisciplinary project requires support for multiple representations of design forms, including rapid hand-drawn sketches made either by individual designers, or by several members of a design team. The communication of these kinds of presentations between design team members becomes more important than how they were produced, particularly in the early stages of a project. The use of Computer Supported Co-operative Work (CSCW) technology is now increasingly being used in design offices, though its use in architecture has yet to be fully exploited.

There are currently many students in schools of architecture, however, who are seriously undertaking collaborative projects using internet and web technologies (ETH in Zurich, with the PhaseX project, for example), and many practices who work together exchanging files and interacting on shared digital models.

The Relationship Between Physical and Computational Modelmaking

Several of the case studies have shown how initial sketch design ideas need to be tested against 3-D models, whether physical or computational. Physical modelling is still an intuitively easier medium to work with, as was illustrated in the case of the Harbourside project. Behnisch's office has a reputation for taking a part of the building and examining it in great detail through drawings and models. They believe that each part of a building proposal has to be explored three dimensionally, and to this end scale models and full-size models are used very early in the design process. However, as was shown in the Guggenheim case study, physical models themselves provide a convenient interface to CAD models through a process of digitisation, after which the CAD models can either be used for analytical purposes, or for further modelling and design development. Modelling, whether physical or computational, allows three-dimensional assessment of sketch ideas to take place. Formal, design theoretic aspects, as described in chapter 9, can be investigated. CAD models as developed in the Guggenheim case study have shown the advantages over physical modelling when building geometries are particularly complex.

In the relationship between physical and computational modelmaking, some researchers have observed a progressive acceleration in the so-called *craft – design – CAD progression* (Aish, 1992). In the traditional craft process, users *directly manipulate* the form of an object, allowing design intent and the object form to interact. The development of improved manipulation techniques for 3-D CAD models means that it is now possible to establish closer relationships between design intent and object form than has previously been possible. The manipulation techniques themselves could not have been developed without corresponding improvements in the underlying computational representations of CAD objects.

CAD systems are beginning to provide design environments that support the co-ordination of multiple representations of a design scheme. Evaluations of schemes through the use of analytical software allows designers to focus on the *form-giving* process. Direct interaction between the designer and the object form, achieved by the dynamic manipulation of form, was a valuable feature of the craft process that was lost during the progression to conventional design, but which may now be potentially recovered by the new generation of integrated CAD systems.

A central CAD principle, therefore, associated with the ability to manipulate models, is an *awareness of the underlying representation*. In other words, understanding how units and structures in computational representations are linked together, and how these in turn correspond to a designer's understanding of design objects. The representation of information that a CAD system uses will always affect the abilities of users to access and use required parts.

Referencing Common Project Models

The single user method of using CAD systems often doesn't reflect the structure of a design practice, which by its very nature requires closer collaboration between different teams working on various aspects of the same project. The need for co-operation between architects, structural engineers, service engineers, quantity surveyors, etc. means that it should be possible to see copies of each other's drawings, not only for reference purposes, but also in order to carry out explicit geometrical constructions on their own layers in relation to underlying ones, e.g. snapping, intersections, etc.

Design practices are now beginning to realise the importance of the issue of multi-user multi-tasking systems. This fits in with the idea of integrated systems, since it would become possible for users with different specialisations (structural engineers, quantity surveyors, etc.) to use the same system simultaneously. Moving from single user to multiple user environments, however, brings with it problems of sharing information between users; whereas moving from single machine to multiple machine environments brings with it problems of distribution of information across a network of machines. There follows therefore all the associated computational problems of multiple access, security, priorities, and permissions. The development of multi-user multi-access systems seems therefore to demand of designers a conceptual leap in their thinking process, from thinking merely in terms of graphical objects that depict design objects, to thinking also in terms of other representational concepts.

Design intentions should be considered as projections/reflections of design ideas, often requiring the representation of design objects in multiple ways simultaneously. Multiple representations of alternative design concept models have to date been difficult to develop. All such models are abstractions of the real world that omit details in order to focus on the aspects of reality important to a given design task. Models developed for different design tasks therefore omit different kinds of details. Building a model that is adequate for more than one task requires a clear articulation of the demands that each task places upon the model. I hope that this book has at least given the reader some insights into what such tasks might be in the context of various analytical areas of architectural design.

The User-Definition of CAD Functionality

In order that designers can fully exploit CAD systems, they need firstly to be able to customise them to suit their own needs and working practices, and secondly, to become more involved in developing their own computer programs. Computer programming for CAD applications is no longer an esoteric technical specialisation now that programming environments with visual interfaces are commonplace. This means that users can minimise the amount of programming language syntax they have to learn, making it easier to create programs. However, certain basic programming constructs, such as conditionals, loops, and parameter passing mechanisms, do need to be understood by end users. Although there are still many possible programming languages to choose from, there is an increasingly important trend in the use of object-oriented techniques in CAD applications. There are big advantages in using object-oriented programming environments for CAD systems:

- the graphical objects within CAD systems can be naturally represented as objects receiving and responding to messages.
- the powerful inheritance mechanism of object-oriented languages supports program development since object descriptions can be reused, and makes it easier for users to customise applications for particular design tasks.
- the interactive instantiation of objects and subsequent refinement of object instances allow diverse design proposals to co-exist within the same CAD model. Apart from obviating the need for storage-intensive file copying of alternate CAD solutions, the instancing mechanism also has a strong pedagogical role in allowing design students and practitioners to record their design explorations.

User-defined descriptions of tasks, such as those used to identify intersections and offsets in the St. Polten concert hall project were defined to be as general as possible, and relatively independent from one another. Although the program functions in this particular case were implemented in a list processing language, this is still compatible with the programming strategy used in object-oriented programming in which *methods* specific to particular views of *objects* are defined.

User-defined object types need to be created by designers rather than programmers, who naturally have a better understanding of design projects. The user-declaration of abstract data types, however, may not be a straightforward task for designers with little experience of programming. The user-definition of types, inevitably places the onus on the user to know how to employ types and operators for purposes of constructing task descriptions. From an educational perspective, there is evidence (e.g. Streich, 1992) that incorporating programming into an architectural curriculum develops students' critical attitudes towards CAD application software, such that they become better able to evaluate the effectiveness and limitations of available CAD systems.

The Propagation of Form Through Parametric Expression

One of the issues that has been of central concern in this book has been the expressive power of CAD environments. One manifestation of the improvements in expressiveness has been the ability to be able to express *parametric relationships*. This occurred in several of the case studies, including the Guggenheim Museum and the Sagrada Familia in particular. A major benefit of parameterisation is that in the description of curved surfaces, relatively few control points can effectively describe a wide range of surface profiles. It then is up to the designer to modify the locations of control points to achieve the desired forms. It is interesting to note here that some of the large-scale CAD projects described in the case studies have exploited developments in parametric design software that originated in the field of mechanical engineering.

The Waterloo terminal case study demonstrated the need to be able to maintain important relationships *between* complex CAD elements, whilst continuing to work on the modification of the descriptions of their parts. Through parametric expression, users can express relationships determining dimensions between parts of CAD models. Parametric design allows key building elements to be grouped according to *families of* parameterised objects. Parameterised descriptions can save time and expedite further modifications to related CAD objects. A parameterised object defines a set of objects, each of which has differently dimensioned parts. In order to describe a whole family of objects, all that is required is a topological description of object parts, together with a description of the relationships between these parts.

Another potential application area relating to the construction industry in particular, is that of *configuration design*. This usually consists of either the development of an assembly from a standard set of components, or of the development of a non-standard form by redesign or directly from the functional requirements. Again, one of the crucial issues in configuring assemblies is the representation of geometry and spatial relations among parts. The ability to design in the presence of abstract or incomplete geometry, however, is still an important issue. This is also a recognised problem in architectural design (Szalapaj, 1988), and representation formalisms to support partial geometrical descriptions are beginning to be developed (e.g. Szalapaj, 1988).

The Development of Architectural Form from CAD Objects

Users of CAD systems need to be aware of the techniques used for representing architectural form, since the method of representation chosen will inevitably affect the subsequent behaviour of a CAD model, including the ways in which changes can be made to it. An illustration of this point is the study of a compositional representation of Terragni's Casa Giuliani Frigerio (the subject of Peter Eisenman's Ph.D. Thesis (Eisenman, 1971)), generated by means of shape grammar (Flemming, 1981), as contrasted with Eisenman's awareness that the facades on this building alternate between compositional (composed of an aggregation of planar elements) and volumetric (composed from additions and subtractions of volumetric elements) (Kane and Szalapaj, 1992). Typically shape is defined in terms of a geometry (a location and a dimension), and a topology (a set of connectivity relations). In modelling architectural design objects and spatial organisations, a number of options are open to the CAD system user:

- which shape properties is it necessary to represent?
- whether the model should occupy 2½-D (see CAD Objects section) or 3-D space?
- what constraints on geometry need to be represented?
- what shape approximations are possible?
- how spatial information can be mapped onto non-graphical design information and vice-versa?

The ways in which CAD systems are used should always reflect the intentions of the designer using the system. For example, one might want to preserve the connectivity relations between lines meeting at a point during subsequent changes to a drawing (Szalapaj, 1988). The expression of relationships between CAD objects will inevitably impose particular syntactic structures upon stored information (Szalapaj, 1984). That is to say, at a logical level, relationships provide *particular views of information*, and, in implementation at a physical level, support particular patterns of access. The choice and expression of CAD objects and CAD operations then is central to designers' understanding of the design scheme being modelled.

CAD Operations

Boolean operations are especially useful when the modelling process can be thought of in terms of sculpting solid objects by means of addition, subtraction, and intersection. Groups of CAD objects can be composed of elements from different layers, and layers can in turn include blocks taken from different layers. The phenomenon of layering has a precursor in traditional drawing practice, but the use of grouping does not. Concepts such as grouping are computational ideas that affect the way designers design.

With operations such as extrude, sweep and loft, users need to anticipate the dominant cross-sections of objects, together with the axes along which the cross-sections will move to generate 3-D objects. In the case of extrusion, the axis is always orthogonal to the cross-section. Sweeping can be controlled by relating cross-sectional profiles with locus points, about which the sweep operation takes place. In the case of lofting, the cross-section itself can vary in shape as it moves. It is often the case that the intervals between cross-sections are also significant when the path of the cross-section is curved.

Some architectural design practices have invested a great deal of time and energy into the standardisation of layers in CAD systems. Layering evolved from the fact that as drawings build up and get more complex, they become harder to manipulate. It becomes harder to read the drawing, and harder to snap to the right part (Richens, 1989). With layered drawings, each graphical primitive is assigned to a layer; layers can be given different colours, and they can be switched on and off individually. For example, annotation, dimensioning and hatching can be assigned to separate layers, and turned off except when they are needed. Layering, therefore, can reduce the complexity of drawings, and increase the speed of panning and zooming.

The discreteness or continuity of a CAD environment will determine the effects that CAD operations will have. For example, when working on a grid, and needing to move a CAD object to a new location off grid, it is necessary to prepare the transformation by first refining the grid prior to the transformation. A further common issue relating to working on grids is that of non-orthogonal grids. A typical solution is to construct separate objects on separate, orthogonal grids, and then to rotate one object (with its corresponding grid) onto another. Such a procedure frequently leads to errors, however. Small errors in general plans can become magnified in details.

Without parameterisation, there are still difficulties in propagating changes throughout CAD models. There is frequently a need for further editing of adjacent objects to those that have just been modified using conventional CAD system operations.

CAD Objects

In most computer-based architectural practices, 3-D CAD models are defined in terms of *polygon meshes*, sometimes referred to as *boundary representations* (*B-Reps*), since the points that define the polygons describe the boundaries or surfaces of objects. The characteristics of many if not most architectural models is that they are often composed of planar surfaces. Many architects still work with what are referred to as *2½-D models*, in which the plan is central, and in which 3-D objects are formed by extruding 2-D polygons.

In certain areas of engineering design in which the emphasis is on modelling individual objects, CAD representations based upon constructive solid geometry (CSG) are used. Modelling is carried out by applying successive *global* Boolean operations to geometric primitives such as spheres, cones, cubes, etc. In CSG modelling, the history of successive operations constitutes an object's representation. CSG modelling is computationally expensive and generally not used in architecture. The more commonly encountered Boolean operations in the B-rep-based systems used in architectural design do not record histories of operations as part of object representations. They are applied *locally* to parts of objects, rather than globally to the whole model.

The methods for modelling free-form or sculptured surfaces were originally developed as long ago as the 1970s. The most advanced method currently used, is *NURBS* (Non-Uniform Rational B-Splines). At the present time, most systems combine two systems, B-Reps and CSG, or use B-Reps as a shell that allows multiple representations. Although the techniques are not new, the interesting development is the application of these to large-scale architectural projects, as exemplified by the Guggenheim Museum. The use of parametric surface modelling representations such as *NURBS* are ideally suited to the representation of free-form surfaces.

This book has attempted to describe the understandings of design that are necessary to work with and within CAD environments. In traditional views of CAD, 2-D and 3-D understandings of design schemes were always separated out. Designers were then advised to manipulate relationships via 2-D layouts/descriptions, because otherwise those layouts would somehow be hidden, or buried within 3-D models. Designers came to associate 2-D understandings with externalised 3-D snapshots, such as with perspective views, for example. The development of contemporary CAD environments, however, has made it possible to understand complex relationships within 3-D forms in much more direct ways. The commonly understood 2-D views are still available should they be needed.

CAD Modelling and Analysis

The introduction of CAD work at increasingly earlier stages of the design process means that CAD models have to be generated for analysis prior to production models. Analytical models are abstractions of design models, in that they contain the information needed to carry out the analyses. For example, in energy analysis, the composition of materials in the building fabric is of more importance than the precise geometrical shape of the building itself, which can be approximated by closed polyhedral forms. In a design theoretic analysis such as circulation, on the other hand, wall thicknesses become irrelevant, and the topological relationships between spaces take precedence. In the sight-line analysis of the Harbourside project, all elements other than seating and reflecting surfaces are unnecessary. Users of CAD systems need to be able to distinguish between CAD models which are abstractions to be used for analytical purposes, and those which are used for further design development. In mainstream CAD, these distinctions are made by copying files, by referencing files from other files, and by layering. The use of named files and layers can become unwieldy in the case of complex models, and introduce an undesirable level of *prescriptiveness* if the naming process has been carried out by someone else. What is needed is the ability to represent CAD objects at multiple levels, each corresponding to a different analytical or design aspect. Again, object-orientation offers a way of achieving this, since each of the different *views* of an object form part of the object's own representation.

The short case studies in chapters 2 to 9 demonstrated the use of analytical processes across a wide range of specialist disciplines. A common analytical technique, for example, is the finite-element method (FEM), in which the analytical models consist of small but interconnected mesh elements upon which the analytical calculations are carried out. This method can be used for energy analysis, structural analysis, and the analysis of fluids (liquids or gases), for ventilation in buildings, for example. Although formal methods such as FEM have been around for a long time, computing power is now considerably faster, allowing quicker evaluations of different design proposals. The importance of quantitative assessments of specific design proposals had often been exaggerated and overemphasised in the past, partly because of the effort that had been invested in their production. These are now being replaced by a multiplicity of analytical evaluations, often more qualitative in nature because of improvements in graphical output and visualisation techniques, and juxtaposed with the results of evaluations from different specialisations, thus allowing intuitive assessment of these results by designers, and in turn resulting in better design solutions.

Postscript

The traditional view of CAD in architectural design is changing. This view rested on a fundamental premise which was that demarcations between different kinds of design task could be *modularised*. Once design tasks were identified, the characteristics of each task would be analysed by particular resources provided by different pieces of software. In the past history of CAD, once differentiation between tasks took place, the problem was always one of linking them together again, so that a totality of tasks could be applied to particular projects. This segregation and then reintegration led to the development of large and cumbersome CAD environments with a wide range of *modular components*.

The point that was missed in this approach was that in drawing demarcations between tasks, CAD software developers were drawing demarcations *between activities carried out by people*. It was subsequently found that designers did not have to recognise these demarcations, nor to accept their validity in practice. A frequent consequence of modularisation was the rationalisation and standardisation of use of CAD systems in the context of precious centralised computing resources.

Contemporary CAD strategies, on the other hand, are capable of supporting a diversity of design practices in which building models vary over time and in response to changing demands. Contemporary CAD functions have to meet temporal, designer-specified demands, to a degree which makes software expendable. The view of CAD which has now emerged is one in which low-cost computing facilities allow design practices to mould analytical applications to their own requirements. In effect, integrated CAD systems are now being established within individual design practices.

The concern of this book has been with the expression of design possibilities in CAD environments. A general set of techniques and a collection of case studies illustrating how designers from many backgrounds and different design disciplines use CAD have been presented. It should be apparent that it is now the case that current CAD systems free users from the tedium and detail typically required in the 'CAD as drafting' model, allowing them to sketch new ideas and to make modifications to existing designs in intuitive ways. We want to encourage designers to work within a medium that is radically moving away from following conventional prescriptive CAD procedures with precise dimensioning. The ability to move swiftly between design models supports designers' creativity, and allows fast exploration of many design solutions. Contemporary CAD, therefore, rather than simply being a drafting accessory which is used after designs have been developed is instead a comprehensive working environment for the creation of designs from the early stages through to the final form.

A central objective of this book has been to show various ways in which CAD systems are currently being used by designers to model and analyse design information. I have endeavoured to illustrate the ways in which some major design practices appear to be exploiting CAD technology. Hopefully, by showing how CAD is being used in contemporary architectural practice, this will positively affect the perceptions of designers and design students intending to develop the role that CAD has in their offices. I have tried to present the general functions that are necessary to support design interventions within a design scheme, together with the language of CAD environments that controls and guides design progression from initial design proposal, through to the analysis of particular parts and features.

In architectural CAD, abstract technical questions cannot be divorced from the genuine issues that occur in design practice. There are important connections to be made between technical developments and actual design projects. As a CAD researcher and teacher in a School of Architecture, I feel that it is important for students to understand the ways in which techniques and representation schemes from other fields continue to impinge upon design practice. I hope that this will enable design students to become more than mere users of techniques handed down from other fields. This book has focused on the kinds of user interaction that can take place between designers, and processes that can be executed by computers. It is always designers, however, that are the arbiters of acceptable machine behaviour.

Glossary of CAD Terminology

Addition a Boolean operation in which, when combining two objects, intersecting parts are merged leaving a single object.

Analysis the evaluation of a formal aspect of a design scheme requiring a simplified model representation for a specific part of design.

Attribute a property or characteristic of a graphical object, e.g. its colour. Attributes can also be non-graphical, e.g. cost.

Bezier a curve with control points located off the curve itself, pulling the curve tangentially towards the control points.

Bitmap a grid of dots containing the information needed to display a two-dimensional image on a computer screen.

Block a 2-D or 3-D region, usually rectangular or cuboid, containing a group of objects, often referred to as a symbol in other CAD systems.

Boolean operation an operation between two objects, either 2-D or 3-D, such as addition, subtraction, or intersection, resulting in a new object.

B-Spline a curve with control points located off the curve, but with a greater degree of local control than a Bezier.

Clipping a way of deleting unwanted objects, in which a selected graphical object is clipped relative to a clipping object.

CNC abbreviation for computer numerically controlled.

Curve in CAD systems, typical forms of curves including circles, arcs, ellipses, Beziers, splines, B-splines.

Cut removal of part of a CAD model, either temporarily before pasting it elsewhere, or permanently by cutting with Boolean operations.

Class a generic way of categorising objects in a CAD model according to their type, thus organising CAD models, e.g. in object-oriented systems.

Cone a solid or surface generated by sweeping a right-angled triangle 360° about an axis through the right-angled corner.

Conic section a generic name for circles, ellipses, parabolas and hyperbolas, since they are all derived from planes cutting cones.

Conoid a solid or surface generated by sweeping an ellipse, parabola or hyperbola, about a central axis.

Copy to duplicate a graphical object

before pasting it elsewhere, leaving the original object where it was.

Constraint a limitation imposed on a

CAD operation, e.g. drawing a line parallel to an existing line, or snapping to grid points or vertices of objects.

Control Point a point associated with curves

such as Beziers or B-splines, not on the curve itself, that can be manipulated to control the shape of the curve.

Cuboid a 3-D solid with six

rectangular faces, typically formed by extruding a rectangle.

Database a collection of data in a file

made up of records (rows) and fields (columns) with operations for searching and sorting.

Dimension a property of CAD objects

indicating their lengths, heights, and thicknesses, for example.

Ellipse a conic section formed when

a plane slices through a cone without cutting its base.

Ellipsoid a surface or solid formed

when an ellipse is swept about one of its two axes.

Expression a manifestation of an aspect

of a design idea in the form of objects with structure and function, within a medium such as a CAD environment.

Extrusion a common way of generating

a 3-D object by moving a 2-D cross-section through 3-D space.

File a basic unit of storage with

a name and information of a certain type. Files can be modified, saved, deleted, or sent to users or devices.

Fractal an irregular shape with parts

having the same properties as the whole object, often used to model natural objects such as landscapes.

Geometry the properties of CAD objects

that determine their shape, such as their construction in terms of points, lines, and angle values.

Grid a set of intersecting lines,

often, but not necessarily, at right angles.

Grouping making a set of objects

behave as one object, so the group then moves as a whole.

GUI Graphical user interface

— an environment in which users issue commands by clicking on icons and selecting from menus.

Hidden line a line in a CAD model that would be hidden if objects were rendered as solids rather than as wire-frame models.

Hyperbolic paraboloid a quadric surface formed by sweeping a parabola along another parabola, and whose cross-sections are hyperbolas. Constructed as a ruled surface.

Hyperboloid a quadric surface formed by sweeping a hyperbola, or by sweeping an angled straight line about an offset axis. Constructed as a ruled surface.

Icon a small graphical image representing a command.

Image a 2-D picture usually stored in a standard format such as PICT, TIFF, GIF, and JPEG.

Integrated CAD a strategy for modelling a design project in which all modelling and analytical functions exist within the same environment.

Intersect a Boolean operation between two objects resulting in an area or volume common to both objects.

Intersection a point where two lines meet, or the outcome of the Boolean intersect operation.

Knowledge Base a database used in specialist areas of design, based upon the premise that knowledge can be extracted from people and put into computers.

Layer a way of organising CAD information, typically by associating objects with building levels or function in architectural design.

Lofting the generation of a 3-D solid or surface by means of sweeping cross-sectional curves along user-defined paths.

Line a basic CAD object with length, thickness, colour, line style, and endpoint co-ordinate properties.

Mesh a representation of a 3-D object in terms of lines and points. By temporarily converting solids to meshes, objects can be reshaped.

Model a 3-D representation of an object consisting of solids, surfaces, and lines, each with properties, and relationships to parts that can be changed.

Modify to add or delete parts of objects, or to change their properties.

Move to transfer a CAD object from one location to another removing it from its original location.

NURBS Non-uniform rational
B-splines — a representation for surface modelling with weighted control points.

Object-oriented systems in which descriptions of objects encapsulate their properties and functions; can instantiate new objects, and inherit properties from others.

Operation a basic CAD system function.

Orthogonal at right angles,
perpendicular.

Orthogonal projection a 2-D view of a 3-D model formed by the endpoints of perpendicular lines from points in a 3-D model, e.g. plans and elevations.

Paste to place a graphical object that has been cut or copied from one place into another.

Paraboloid a quadric surface formed by sweeping a parabola about its central axis.

Parallel a constraint for drawing lines or edges of objects in the same direction as a selected line without crossing it. Can be a property of parametric objects.

Parallelopiped a six-sided prism, all of whose faces are parallelograms.

Parametric a CAD object is parametric if its geometric properties are related to each other or to the properties of other objects.

Perspective Projection a view of a 3-D model where heights of objects are smaller the further away they are from the viewpoint.

Pixel Short for picture element. A dot in a grid of dots forming an image on a computer screen. The total number of screen pixels is the resolution.

Plane a flat surface such that straight lines can be drawn on it in any direction.

Polyhedron a solid with plane faces, often formed by extruding a polygon.

Polygon a 2-D closed shape whose sides are straight lines.

Prescriptive a characteristic of CAD systems programmed to anticipate how models of design objects will behave, often in undesired ways.

Programming the creation of computer programs using languages to define algorithms — sets of instructions to carry out particular tasks.

Projection a mapping of points from a 3-D model onto a plane, e.g. orthogonal, perspective, isometric, parallel, oblique.

Raster a rectangular array made up of horizontal lines of pixels.

Relative Co-ordinates co-ordinates defined in terms of their distance from a given starting point. Absolute co-ordinates are measured from the origin.

Rendering the way in which CAD models are presented, often involving the use of colours, textures, and lights to give models a realistic appearance.

Rotate to turn an object about a point by a specified angle.

Scale to enlarge or reduce the size of a graphical object.

Section the result of cutting a 3-D model with a plane, which can either be a new 3-D model, or a 2-D image.

Snapping a way of constraining drawing operations, either by locking onto predefined grid points, or onto the vertices of existing CAD objects.

Sphere a 3-D object formed by sweeping a semicircle about its diameter.

Spline a smooth curve through a set of points based upon a polynomial equation.

Spreadsheet a table consisting of rows and columns of data, numeric or textual, taken from CAD object properties, or calculated from formulae.

Subtraction a Boolean operation in which one object is cut out of of another object.

Surface a 3-D object generated by sweeping a line or curve about an axis; often the boundary of a solid object.

Sweep the generation of a 3-D object from a 2-D object by rotating the 2-D object about an axis.

Symbol a group of CAD objects used repeatedly in a CAD model can be stored as a symbol, edited, and inserted into the model when needed.

224

Tangent a line which touches a curve at a point.

Typology the study of types.

Tolerance the degree of accuracy required to position, measure, or dimension CAD objects.

User definition a way in which users can describe the properties, functions, and behaviours of CAD objects as distinct from built-in system definitions.

Topology the properties of CAD objects that are preserved when the objects are transformed, particularly connectivity relationships between parts.

Vector a line drawn in a certain direction from a start point to an end point. 2-D images can be represented as vectors instead of rasters.

Torus a solid or surface shaped like a ring, formed when a circle is swept along a circular path.

View an image of a 3-D model taken from a particular viewpoint.

Toroid a solid or surface generated when a closed curve is swept along a path.

Visualisation a graphical presentation of a design idea.

Translate the same as the move operation.

Virtual reality an illusion of realism created by computer modelling, rendering, and simulation of natural phenomena, with peripheral user-input devices.

Transform to modify a CAD object in some way, usually by changing its geometry or its topology.

Volume a 3-D CAD object.

Type a category or class of objects sharing similar characteristics.

Wire-frame the presentation of a 3-D CAD model in terms of lines in 3-D space.

Bibliography

Aish, R.; *CAD Software Design to Augment the Creation of Form*,
Penz, F. (ed.), International Symposium on Computers in Architecture: Tools for Design, 1990, published as *Computers in Architecture* by Longman, 1992.

Angerer, F.; *Surface Structures in Buildings*,
Alec Tiranti, London, 1961.

Baker, G.H.; *Design Strategies in Architecture.*
An Approach to the Analysis of Form, Van Nostrand Reinhold, 1989 and 1993.

Behnisch, Behnisch & Partner, *Das Bristol Projekt.*
The Harbourside Centre for Performing Arts, B, B & P, 1999.

Bijl, A.; *Computer Discipline and Design Practice: Shaping our Future*,
Edinburgh University Press, 1989.
The wall junction descriptions on pages 199–205 were the end-product of extensive revisions arising out of Bijl's research on user-defined attachment operations at EdCAAD, Edinburgh University, during 1988.

Bijl, A.; *The Way of IT Research: Review of Research Assumptions and Directions*,
in Advanced Technologies (Beheshti & Zreik eds), proc. 4th EuropIA conf. on the application of AI, Robotics and Image Processing to Architecture, Building/Civil Engineering, Urban Design and Urban Planning, Elsevier, Delft, the Netherlands, 1993.

Bijl, A.; *Ourselves and Computers: Difference in Mind and Machines*,
Macmillan Press Ltd, 1995.

Blundell Jones, P.; *Harbour Master*,
Architectural Review 204, no. 1222, pp. 41–45, December 1998.

226

Brand, S.; *How Buildings Learn: What happens after they're built,*

Viking, 1994.

Ching, F.D.K.; *Architecture: Form, Space, and Order,*

Van Nostrand Reinhold, New York, 1996.

Burry, M., Dunlop, G., Wood, P., Gomez, J. and Coll, J.;

Boolean Operations and Architectural Form Finding,
proc. 2nd International Conference on Mathematics & Design,
San Sebastian, Spain, 1998.

Burry, M.; *The Expiatory Church of the Sagrada Familia,*

Phaidon Press Limited, London, 1993.

Clark, R.H. and Pause, M.; *Precedents in Architecture,*

Van Nostrand Reinhold, New York, 1985.

Coons, S.A.; *An Outline of the Requirements for a Computer Aided Design*

System, proc. AFIPS Spring Joint Computer Conference,
Pp. 299−304, (1963).

Curtis, N. C.; *Architectural Composition,*

J.H. Jansen, Cleveland, Ohio, USA, 1926.

Darke, J.; *The Primary Generator and the Design Process,*

in Developments in Design Methodology, Cross, N. (ed.), 1979.

227

Eisenman, P.D.; *From Object to Relationship II*:
Giuseppe Terragni - Casa Giuliani Frigerio,
Perspecta, pp.38-61, nos.13-14, 1971.

Faux, I.D. and Pratt, M.J.; *Computational Geometry for Design and Manufacture*,
Ellis Horwood Ltd, Chichester, 1981.

Glenn, J.A. and Littler, G.H.; *A Dictionary of Mathematics*,
Harper and Row, London, 1984.

Graves, M.; *The Necessity for Drawing: Tangible Speculation*,
Architectural Design, Vol. 47, 1977.

Guhl, E. and Koner, W.; *The Greeks and Romans*:
Their Life and Customs,
Studio Editions Ltd., London, 1989.

Henn, W.; *Buildings For Industry*,
Volume One: Plans, Structures and Details,
Iliffe Books Ltd, London, 1965.
Originally published in Munich, Germany, in 1961.

Hewitt, M.; *Representational Forms and Modes of Conception*
(An Approach to the History of Architectural Drawing),
Journal of Architectural Education, Winter 1985.

Hoskins, E.M.; *The OXSYS System*,
Computer Applications in Architecture,
Gero, J.S. (ed.), Applied Science, pp. 343–391, 1985.

Kapfinger, O.; *Klaus Kada: Concert Hall, St. Polten,*
in Domus 793, May 1997.

Ketchum, M.S. and Ketchum, M.A.; *An Ideabook for Designers,*
a web-based publication, 1997.

Klee, P.; *Pedagogical Sketchbook,* Faber, London, 1953.
This was first published as *Padagogisches Skizzenbuch,*
the 2nd of 14 Bauhaus Books edited by
Walter Gropius and L. Moholy-Nagy in 1925.

Knight, T.W.; *The generation of Hepplewhite-style chair-back designs,*
Planning and Design: Environment and Planning B,
Volume 7, pp. 227–238, 1980.

Koning, H. and Eizenburg, J.; *The Language of the Prairie.*
Frank Lloyd Wright's prairie houses,
Planning and Design: Environment and Planning B,
Volume 8, pp. 295–323, 1981.

Krier, R.; *Architectural Composition,* Academy Editions, London, 1988.

Krishnamurti, R.; *The Construction of Shapes,*
Planning and Design: Environment and Planning B,
Volume 8, pp. 5–40, 1981.

Lee, K.; *Principles of CAD/CAM/CAE Systems,* Addison-Wesley, 1999.

LeCuyer, A.; *Building Bilbao,*
Architectural Review, Vol. 202, December 1997, pp. 43–45.

Macgill, J. and Openshaw, S.; *Using JAVA to animate an exploratory spatial analysis tool,*
workshop on Graphics, Visualisation, and the Social Sciences, Loughborough University, May 1997.

Pang, K.W. and Edmonds, E.A.; *Designing Learning Environments Using Java: New Functionality,*
Design and the Net,
Proceedings of the 6th International EuropIA Conference, Edinburgh, April 1997.

Pollalis, S.P.; *A Visual Database for Online Access to Bridge Precedences,*
in Advanced Technologies (Beheshti & Zreik, eds), proc. 4th EuropIA conf. on the application of AI, Robotics and Image Processing to Architecture, Engineering, Urban Design and Planning, Elsevier, Delft, the Netherlands, 1993.

Powell, R.; *Ken Yeang: Rethinking the Environmental Filter,*
Landmark Books PTE Ltd, 1989.

Rawson, J.; *Cutting Steel for Kansai,*
Architects' Journal, Vol. 197, No. 1, 6 January 1993, pp. 37–40.

Richards, I.; *Tropic Tower,*
Architectural Review 192, no. 1152, pp. 26–31, February 1993.

Richens, P.; *MicroCAD Software Evaluated,*
A Critical Evaluation of Microcomputer Based CAD Systems for the Construction Industry, CICA, Cambridge, 1989.

Rooney, J. and Steadman, P.; *Principles of Computer Aided Design*,
The Open University, 1987.

Rowe, C.; *The Mathematics of the Ideal Villa*,
Architectural Review, 1947.

Salvadori, M.; *Why Buildings Stand Up: The Strength of Architecture*,
W.W. Norton & Co., London, 1990.

Gomez Serrano, J., Coll, J., Melero, J.C. and Burry, M.;
The Need to Step Beyond Conventional Architectural Software,
proc. 11th Conference on Education in Computer Aided Architectural
Design (ECAADE) in Europe, Eindhoven, the Netherlands, 1993.

Gomez Serrano, J., Coll, J., Melero, J.C. and Burry, M.;
La Sagrada Familia. De Gaudi Al CAD,
Universitat Politecnica de Catalunya, Barcelona, 1996.

Schon, D.A.; *The Reflective Practicioner: How Designers Think in Action*,
Temple Smith, London, 1983.

Slessor, C.; *Atlantic Star*,
Architectural Review, Vol. 202, p. 30−42, December 1997.

Stein, K.D.; *Project Diary: Guggenheim Museum Bilbao*,
Architectural Record, Vol. 185, No.10, p. 74−87, 1997.

Stiny, G.; *Pictorial and Formal Aspects of Shape Grammars and Aesthetic Systems,*
Ph.D. Thesis, System Science, UCLA, 1975.

Stiny, G. and Mitchell, W.J.; *The Palladian Grammar,*
Planning and Design: Environment and Planning B,
Volume 5, pp. 5 – 18, 1978.

Streich, B.; *Should We Integrate Programming Knowledge into the Architect's CAAD Education?,*
proc. ECAADE ' 92, International Conference on Computer Aided
Architectural Design in Europe, pp. 399 – 406, Barcelona, Spain, 1992.

Sutherland, I.E.; *Sketchpad: a man-machine communication system,*
proc. AFIPS Spring Joint Computer Conference, pp. 329 – 346, 1963.

Szalapaj, P.J.; *Logical Graphics.*
Logical Representation of Drawings to Effect Graphical Transformation,
Ph.D. Thesis, EdCAAD, Department of Architecture,
University of Edinburgh, 1988.

Szalapaj, P.J.; *Design Out Of All Proportion,*
proc. 2nd International Conference on Mathematics & Design,
San Sebastian, Spain, 1998.

Szalapaj, P.J. and Bijl, A.; *Knowing Where to Draw the Line,*
IFIP Working Conference on Knowledge Engineering in CAD,
Budapest, Hungary, 1984.

Szalapaj, P.J., and Kane, A.; *Teaching Design by Analysis of Precedents,*
proc. ECAADE ' 92, International Conference on Computer Aided
Architectural Design in Europe, pp. 478 – 495, Barcelona, Spain, 1992.

Szalapaj, P.J. and Kane, A.; *Computationally Assisted Design Formulation*, in Advanced Technologies (Beheshti & Zreik eds), proc. 4th EuropIA conf. on the application of AI, Robotics and Image Processing to Architecture, Building/Civil Engineering, Urban Design and Urban Planning, Elsevier, Delft, the Netherlands, 1993.

Van Bruggen, C.; *Frank O. Gehry: Guggenheim Museum Bilbao*, Guggenheim Museum Publications, New York, 1999.

Van der Laan, H.; *Architectonic Space*, Brill, Leiden, 1983.

Watt, A.; *3D Computer Graphics*, Addison-Wesley, 1993.

Wilson, C.B.; *Airflow Around Buildings*, Edinburgh Architecture Research, Volume 9, 1982.

Wojtowicz, J. and Fawcett, W.; *Architecture: Formal Approach*, Hong Kong, Privately Printed, 1985.

Yeang, K.; *Designing With Nature: The Ecological Basis for Architectural Design*, McGraw-Hill Inc., 1995.

Zaera, A.; *Information Technology at Frank O. Gehry & Associates*, El Croquis 74/75, pp. 152–155, Madrid, Spain, 1995.

Index of Case Studies

Harbourside Centre for Performing Arts, Bristol

Behnisch, Behnisch & Partner
pages 163–174

Reichstag, Berlin, Germany

Foster & Partners
pages 175–178

Middleton Botanic Gardens, Wales

Foster & Partners
page 179

Kansai International Airport Terminal, Japan

Renzo Piano
pages 184–189

The Guggenheim Museum, Bilbao, Spain

Frank O. Gehry Associates
pages 190–204

INDEX